Bristol Studies in Law and S

Series Editors: **Alan Bogg**, University of ~~Bristol, UK and~~
Virginia Mantouvalou, University College London, UK

This series explores the role of law in securing social justice in society and the economy. The focus is on 'social justice' as a normative ideal, and the law as a critical tool in influencing (for good or for ill) the social structures that shape people's lives.

Out now in the series:

Beyond the Virus: Multidisciplinary and International Perspectives on Inequalities Raised by COVID-19
Edited by **Sabrina Germain** and **Adrienne Yong**

Class and Social Background Discrimination in the Modern Workplace: Mapping Inequality in the Digital Age
By **Angelo Capuano**

Climate Litigation and Justice in Africa
Edited by **Kim Bouwer, Uzuazo Etemire, Tracy-Lynn Field** and **Ademola Oluborode Jegede**

Forthcoming in the series:

Labour Law and the Person: An Agenda for Social Justice
By **Lisa Rodgers**

Access to Social Justice: Social Rights and the UK's Access to Justice Gap
By **Katie Boyle, Diana Camps, Kirstie English, Jo Ferrie, Aidan Flegg** and **Gaurav Mukherjee**

Find out more at
**bristoluniversitypress.co.uk/
bristol-studies-in-law-and-social-justice**

International advisory board

Find out more at
bristoluniversitypress.co.uk/
bristol-studies-in-law-and-social-justice

LOW-PAID EU MIGRANT WORKERS

The House, the Street, the Town

Catherine Barnard, Fiona Costello and
Sarah Fraser Butlin

BRISTOL
UNIVERSITY
PRESS

First published in Great Britain in 2024 by

Bristol University Press
University of Bristol
1–9 Old Park Hill
Bristol
BS2 8BB
UK
t: +44 (0)117 374 6645
e: bup-info@bristol.ac.uk

Details of international sales and distribution partners are available at bristoluniversitypress.co.uk

British Library Cataloguing in Publication Data
A catalogue record for this book is available from the British Library

ISBN 978-1-5292-2957-8 paperback
ISBN 978-1-5292-2958-5 ePub
ISBN 978-1-5292-2959-2 OA PDF

Cover design: Blu Inc
Front cover image: Zoja Petrosiute

Contents

Series Editors' Preface

Bristol Studies in Law and Social Justice explores the role of law in securing social justice in society and the economy. The focus is on 'social justice' as a normative ideal, and the law as a critical tool in influencing (for good or for ill) the social structures that shape people's lives. This international series is designed to be inclusive of a wide range of methodologies and disciplinary approaches. Contributions examine these issues from multiple legal perspectives, including constitutional law, discrimination law, human rights, contract law, criminal law, migration law, labour law, social welfare law, property law, international and supranational law. The Series has broad jurisdictional coverage, including single-country, comparative, international and regional legal orders, and encourages a critical and interdisciplinary approach to legal analysis.

List of Figures, Tables and Boxes

Figures

Tables

Boxes

Notes on the Authors

Catherine Barnard is Professor of European Union Law and Employment Law, Fellow of Trinity College, Cambridge, and Senior Fellow, UK in a Changing Europe.

Fiona Costello is Research Associate, University of Cambridge, and Fellow of St Edmund's College, Cambridge.

Sarah Fraser Butlin is Fellow of Selwyn College, Cambridge, and a barrister at Cloisters Chambers, London.

Abbreviations

ACAS	Advisory, Conciliation and Arbitration Service
ADR	alternative dispute resolution
AR	administrative review
CJEU	Court of Justice of the European Union
CRD	Citizens' Rights Directive
CV	curriculum vitae
EEA	European Economic Area
EU	European Union
EU (PS)	EU pre-settled status
EU (SS)	EU settled status
EUSS	European Union Settlement Scheme
EU2	countries that joined the EU in January 2007: Bulgaria and Romania
EU8	eight (of ten) countries that joined the EU during enlargement in 2004: Czech Republic, Estonia, Hungary, Latvia, Lithuania, Poland, Slovakia, Slovenia (Cyprus and Malta also joined at this time)
EU14	countries that were members of the EU prior to 2004 (excluding the United Kingdom): Austria, Belgium, Denmark, Finland, France, Germany, Greece, Italy, Luxembourg, the Netherlands, Portugal, the Republic of Ireland, Spain and Sweden
FGM	female genital mutilation
GP	general practitioner
GYROS	Great Yarmouth Refugee and Outreach Support
HMO	house of multiple occupation
HMRC	His Majesty's Revenue & Customs
HRT	habitual residence test
IMA	Independent Monitoring Authority (established under the Withdrawal Agreement)
LASPO	Legal Aid, Sentencing and Punishment of Offenders Act 2012
NEFM	non-EU family member (of EU national)

NHS	National Health Service
NRPF	no recourse to public funds
OISC	Office of the Immigration Services Commissioner
PPE	personal protective equipment
R2R	Right to reside
TB	tuberculosis
TFEU	Treaty on the Functioning of the European Union
UC	Universal Credit
WA	Agreement on the Withdrawal of the United Kingdom of Great Britain and Northern Ireland from the European Union and the European Atomic Energy Community 2020

Preface

Throughout the campaign for the 2016 referendum on the United Kingdom's (UK's) membership of the European Union (EU), migrant workers from the EU were variously portrayed as a burden on the British economy and a drain on public services. Although Brexit was about more than immigration, 'free movement' was one of the most contested and emotive issues.[1] The refrain that migrants are 'coming over here and taking our jobs'[2] was familiar, albeit contested. Employers and recruitment agencies in areas such as the East of England (including the town of Great Yarmouth, the setting for the research discussed in this book) did rely on EU nationals to meet worker shortages in labour-intensive sectors such as agriculture and food processing[3] – work seen as less desirable to locals[4] and where the pay is low and conditions are poor.

What we know now is that many more EU nationals had exercised their free movement rights under EU law than the government had previously thought.[5] There have been over seven million applications to the European Union Settlement Scheme (EUSS),[6] the scheme set up by the UK government requiring EU nationals and some others to register to continue

---

[1]   G. Wemyss and K. Cassidy, '"People think that Romanians and Roma are the same": everyday bordering and the lifting of transitional controls' (2017) 40 *Ethnic and Racial Studies* 1132.

[2]   A. Travis, 'Are EU migrants really taking British jobs and pushing down wages?' *The Guardian* (20 May 2016), available at: www.theguardian.com/politics/2016/may/20/reality-check-are-eu-migrants-really-taking-british-jobs, accessed 18 March 2023.

[3]   J.C.P. Almeida and D. Corkill, 'Portuguese migrant workers in the UK: a case study of Thetford, Norfolk' (2010) 26 *Portuguese Studies* 27, 30–31.

[4]   S. McKay and E. Markova, 'The operation and management of agency workers in conditions of vulnerability' (2010) 41 *Industrial Relations Journal* 446, 458.

[5]   'Population of the UK by country of birth and nationality: 2020' *Office for National Statistics*, available at: www.ons.gov.uk/peoplepopulationandcommunity/populationandmigration/internationalmigration/bulletins/ukpopulationbycountryofbirthandnationality/2020, accessed 21 November 2021.

[6]   Home Office, 'EU Settlement Scheme statistics', available at: www.gov.uk/government/collections/eu-settlement-scheme-statistics, accessed 20 November 2023.

to exercise their post-Brexit rights to live and work in the UK – this is double the government's estimates at the time of the EU referendum.

A lot of research has been done on EU migration to the UK, usually looking at its effects on cities such as London[7] or Manchester.[8] This work also predominantly features (Western) EU nationals[9] who speak English and so can participate more easily in UK-based academic research. For example, Favell, in *Eurostars and Eurocities*,[10] considers EU free movement through the prism of (largely) West Europeans, who are mostly skilled, mobile and multilingual and tend to move to EU capital cities. For this group, EU free movement law represents opportunity, benefits, excitement.[11]

Our focus is on a different group: EU migrants, mostly from Portugal and post-2004 EU member states, with poor, if any, English language skills and coming to work in a very different location, which is semirural and coastal – namely the fields and food production factories in and around Great Yarmouth (the 'Town' of our title).[12] These people make up some of the most marginalized and invisible communities in the UK, living in areas that are significantly deprived. The aims of our research are: first, to understand the lives of these EU migrant workers – their experiences of coming to the UK, their living and working conditions and how they navigated their new immigration status in the period leading up to Brexit and now in the post-Brexit world; second, to understand what they do when things go wrong; and, third, when they seek help to resolve their problems from Great Yarmouth Refugee and Outreach Support (GYROS – a migrant support charity in the Town), we wanted to understand how GYROS' advisers respond to the problems presented.

GYROS shared their data with us, amounting to 6,856 case notes on interactions with almost 1,400 EU nationals from 2015 to 2020. This has been complemented by the stories of eight EU migrant workers living in a house of multiple occupation (HMO – the 'House' of our title) just off

---

[7] A. Lulle, R. King, V. Dvorakova and A. Szkudlarek, 'Between disruptions and connections: "new" European Union migrants in the United Kingdom before and after the Brexit' (2019) 25 *Population, Space and Place* e2200.

[8] A. Rzepnikowska, 'Racism and xenophobia experienced by Polish migrants in the UK before and after Brexit vote' (2019) 45 *Journal of Ethnic and Migration Studies* 61.

[9] B. Brahic and M. Lallement, 'From "expats" to "migrants": strategies of resilience among French movers in post-Brexit Manchester' (2020) 9 *Migration and Development* 8.

[10] A. Favell, *Eurostars and Eurocities: Free Movement and Mobility in an Integrating Europe* (Oxford: Blackwell Publishing, 2008).

[11] Ibid, 3.

[12] Some other research has been done with similar groups of EU migrants, but it is quite limited. See, for example, T. Guma and R.D. Jones, ' "Where are we going to go now?" European Union migrants' experiences of hostility, anxiety, and (non-)belonging during Brexit' (2019) 25 *Population, Space and Place* 1.

St Peter's Road, one of the main streets in Great Yarmouth (the 'Street' of our title), situated in one of the most deprived parts of a deprived town. One of the authors lived in this house (see Chapter 1). Our research has also been enriched by the accounts of community leaders from the Town who participated in focus groups and interviews.

This data and our interviews show high levels of precarity among this population[13] exacerbated by the COVID-19 lockdowns, which occurred during our research period. For example, many EU migrant workers are agency workers on zero-hours contracts, uncertain as to when and how much work is available. Low pay, combined with variable hours under zero-hours contracts, can lead to 'problem clustering'[14] – for instance, if bills cannot be paid, workers get into debt, putting them at risk of losing their housing. In addition, the health of these EU migrant workers is often poor, meaning there are periods when they cannot work. While all of this may also describe the experience of low-skilled, low-paid British nationals, for EU nationals, these problems are exacerbated by poor language skills and issues with immigration status, difficulties applying for status under the EUSS, confusion among administrators over the operation of the EUSS and the constant need for migrant workers to prove their status. This is particularly the case when applying for benefits, especially for those with only pre-settled status (that is, those with less than five years' residence in the UK).

So, what happens to EU migrants when things go wrong? In Great Yarmouth, as mentioned, many turn to GYROS. The advisers in this organization mostly arrived in the UK via the same migration routes as their clients, and they speak the languages of their clients. The response by GYROS advisers is pragmatic and holistic. They might phone a recalcitrant employer who is refusing to give holiday pay or a landlord threatening to evict; they might accompany a client to the GP and translate the doctor's words; they might provide foodbank vouchers; they might help a client with CV (curriculum vitae) writing and looking for a new job.

This is rather different to what we, as lawyers, were expecting. The traditional narrative for lawyers (simply defined) is that when faced with a legal problem, a client goes to a solicitor, who advises them; when there are grounds for a claim, proceedings may be started which could end up in a court or tribunal, or the client may take the case to court themselves. This trajectory was not what we saw among GYROS' clients. The existing literature, particularly on legal consciousness and access to justice, was

---

[13] H. Zhang, L. Nardon and G.J. Sears, 'Migrant workers in precarious employment' (2022) 41 *Equality, Diversity and Inclusion: An International Journal* 254, 260.

[14] H. Genn, *Paths to Justice: What People Do and Think about Going to Law* (Oxford: Hart Publishing, 1999), 31.

useful but focused predominantly on the law and the courts. For example, legal consciousness, as defined by Sally Engle Merry,[15] is the way people understand and *use* the law. But what we saw was the opposite of what the literature described. It was quite clear that EU migrant workers approaching GYROS were conscious of problems they had, but were not aware that these problems were necessarily *legal* problems; they were not understanding or using the law. In respect of access to justice, many of the clients wanted their problems resolved quickly and holistically, without any delay; they did not want access to the legal system, let alone the courts. GYROS' advisers took a similar view to their clients. They recognized their clients' various intersecting problems, and they delivered problem resolution that involved early intervention but not formal dispute resolution.

The approach adopted by GYROS (and, we anticipate, countless other frontline advice organizations up and down the country) is what we describe as 'pragmatic law' – 'pragmatic' because that is how GYROS advisers work with their clients and 'law' to recognize that the issues facing GYROS' clients (relating to housing, welfare and employment) are all legal, albeit the advisers and clients do not necessarily think of them as such. Rather, outside of GYROS' support on immigration (from advisers with specific Office of the Immigration Services Commissioner (OISC) qualifications and thus some training in the law), advisers and clients see not law but rules or hurdles that must be navigated in order to resolve problems.

We know that GYROS' clients appreciate the service they receive, because their feedback is overwhelmingly positive (Chapter 8). Yet, is it necessarily in the clients' best interest not to have recourse to the courts to resolve a justiciable issue? In our work on pragmatic law, we evaluate the benefits of (legal) advice in encouraging early resolution of problems, thus preventing problems from developing further and causing additional stress, hardship and often yet more (legal) problems. We examine this particularly in the context of vulnerable EU migrants who lack the English language skills to navigate British (legal) systems.

Parts of this book build on research papers, reports and blogs published elsewhere. All have been revised and substantially edited for the purposes of this book and now form part of what we hope is a coherent narrative that pulls themes together. Chapter 2 draws on our article 'When (EU) migration came to Great Yarmouth' (2023) 18 *Contemporary Social Science* 150. Chapter 3 develops an earlier article – 'The changing status of European Union nationals in the United Kingdom following Brexit: the

---

[15] S. Engle Merry, *Getting Justice and Getting Even: Legal Consciousness among Working Class Americans* (Chicago: University of Chicago Press, 1990), 5.

lived experience of the European Union Settlement Scheme' (2021) 31 *Social & Legal Studies* 365 – as well as a report on the EUSS and numerous blogs published by UK in a Changing Europe. These blog posts have proved a useful catalogue of issues arising on the frontline during our fieldwork. Chapter 4 builds on '(Legal) assistance in employment matters to low-paid EU migrant workers in the East of England' (2022) 42 *Legal Studies* 491. Chapter 5 develops 'The darker side of the EU internal market ideal: free movement of workers living in a coastal town' (J. Adams Prassl et al, eds, *The Internal Market Ideal: Essays in Honour of Stephen Weatherill*, Oxford: Oxford University Press, 2024). Where material is drawn on, this is noted. We are very grateful for the rigorous academic review process that our work has been through. The acceptances have obviously encouraged us; the rejections have required us to go back to the drawing board.

We have benefited too from many discussions over the years with interested colleagues in the various seminars and conferences where we have presented our work. We are particularly grateful to Simon Deakin, Dennis Galligan and Nicky Padfield for being critical friends and sounding boards. We would also like to thank those who participated in conversations, responded to questions and provided advice: among others, Nigel Balmer, Nigel Bowles, Margaret Doyle, Jon Franklin, Mia Gray, Jaroslaw Grochowski, Monique Hawkins, Chris Hodges, Kuba Jablonowski, Peter Jones, Nabil Khabirpour, Sarah Kyambi, Amy Ludlow, Audrey Ludwig, Alex McDonald, Louise Merrett, Clare Moriarty, Charlotte O'Brien, Jonathan Pearson-Stuttard, Luke Piper, Pascoe Pleasence, Jonathan Portes, Sir Ernest Ryder, Katie Saunders, Nicola Shaw, Madeliene Sumption, Joe Tomlinson, Barend van Leeuwen, Charles Wynn-Evans, Alison Young and representatives from the Independent Monitoring Authority. There are numerous others we have talked to who do not wish to be formally acknowledged. We are very grateful to them all.

Equally, we owe a huge debt of thanks to the people who directly participated in our research – first and foremost, the residents and landlord of the HMO, the interviewees and focus group participants, and the staff at GYROS. Most wish to remain anonymous, so we cannot thank them by name. We can, however, thank: the GYROS board of trustees and senior staff members Louise Humphries and Armine Nikoghosyan. We would also like to thank the team at the Bristol Studies in Law and Social Justice series for their encouragement and support throughout, together with the dedicated work of the staff at Bristol University Press.

Finally, this work could not have been done without the financial support provided by the Economic and Social Research Council via the UK in a Changing Europe programme, the enthusiastic engagement of Anand Menon, the director, and Dan Wincott, research director at Governance after Brexit, and the emotional support of our long-suffering families, who have learned to know and love Great Yarmouth.

1

Themes, Issues and Methods

A. Introduction

We have been working in Great Yarmouth to understand the lives of European Union (EU) migrant workers, the (legal) problems[1] they experience and what they do to resolve these issues. Great Yarmouth is a particularly deprived seaside town in the East of England which has seen a significant increase in its migrant community, particularly those from Central and Eastern Europe who were exercising their rights to free movement under EU law. These migrants work predominantly in what are called the 'three Ps' ('picking, packing and plucking'),[2] doing low-paid, labour-intensive, often precarious work. Their accommodation, financial position and health are equally precarious. We lived in the community and interviewed its people to better understand the lives of low-paid EU migrant workers at the time of Brexit and the COVID-19 pandemic. We worked with a local charity, Great Yarmouth Refugee and Outreach Support (GYROS), which offers EU migrant workers and their families a free advice service that is holistic, multidisciplinary and multilingual. GYROS gave us access to its dataset, which records all the cases they are involved with, for the period between 2015 and 2020. They also helped with access to their clients and advisers so that we could gain a deeper understanding of the issues facing this community and how GYROS responds to their clients' needs.

The aim of this chapter is to explain what we have been doing, why we have been doing it and how. Specifically, it describes the aims and purpose

---

[1]   We use the phrase '(legal) problems', with 'legal' in brackets to highlight the fact that the problems are rooted in the law (for example, employment law, housing law, immigration law), albeit the advisers and clients at GYROS do not always perceive it that way.
[2]   J.C.P. Almeida and D. Corkill, 'Portuguese migrant workers in the UK: a case study of Thetford, Norfolk' (2010) 26 *Portuguese Studies* 27, 33.

of this research (Section B), the justification for basing the research in Great Yarmouth, a brief outline of our methods and the themes arising from the research (Section C), and the theoretical framing of the book (Section D). We begin by considering the questions we set out to examine.

B. Purpose of the research

We are interested in three sets of questions:

(1) What is life like for low-paid EU migrant workers in Great Yarmouth, and what problems has this group experienced since 2015 (when our data started), particularly against the backcloth of Brexit, the changing legal status for EU migrant workers and COVID-19?

(2) What are the responses of EU nationals in Great Yarmouth to the (legal) problems they are experiencing?

Some sort out their problems themselves with help from friends or family. Many, in fact, go to GYROS for help. This prompts a further set of questions:

(3) How does GYROS help EU migrants navigate and resolve their (legal) problems? What do these responses tell us about how (legal) problems are addressed and resolved on the frontline? Is this a different way of approaching law and lawyering? And if so, how might it be described and what are the risks and the benefits of this approach?

To answer our first question, we looked at each case note in the GYROS database and considered the themes that arose. We undertook ethnographic research in Great Yarmouth. One author spent time living in a house of multiple occupation (HMO) with eight other EU nationals. We also interviewed key stakeholders and others working with the migrant communities in the Town, such as representatives from the local police, the library and the Salvation Army. More details about our methodology are provided in Appendix I. What we witnessed was considerable precarity: of employment, finances, housing and health. These issues are considered further in Section C.

In respect of the second question – considering the responses of EU nationals to the (legal) problems they experience – we drew on the same data as outlined earlier. We saw that those with precarious lives are more likely to rub up against the rough edges of the law (in relation to eviction, debt, benefit overpayments). They know they have a problem and may go to advice agencies, such as GYROS, to get help. Darius' story (Box 1.1) provides an example of both the problems EU migrant workers experience and what they do about their problems.

Box 1.1: Darius' story

Darius[3] is Lithuanian and the primary carer of two boys. He moved to the United Kingdom (UK) in 2015, and since then he has engaged frequently with GYROS' services. Back in Lithuania, he had seen an online advertisement for a company offering help with finding accommodation and work to individuals wanting to come to the UK. He had been told by friends there would be better opportunities for him and his children in the UK. He contacted the company and bought a ticket. The company met Darius and his family at London Stansted Airport and brought them to Great Yarmouth. Darius initially lived in an HMO, a seven-bedroom house, with other families. He did not receive a tenancy agreement and paid rent in cash. The job promised by the company never materialized and he had to look for work himself. Initially, he found employment in a local food processing factory. According to a GYROS case note:

> When client found job at a chicken factory, he arranged with another family to work ... different shifts so that someone could look after children at all times. After about six months at this house ... [the] other family moved out and client had to find somewhere else to live too, as otherwise house was too big and unaffordable. Client found advertisement on Facebook and moved to new flat.

He subsequently moved between jobs in various food processing factories, struggling to manage on zero-hours contracts:

> Client wanted to know if employment agency is obligated to provide the client with minimum work hours per week. I explained to client that agency normally is zero-hours contract, [and] as client hasn't got a contract, I was unable to confirm this for him. Client said that he hasn't been called in for work for last 2 weeks and when he calls his manager on site, he doesn't answer his phone. I helped client to register with another agency.

The insufficient hours under zero-hours contracts left Darius unable to pay his bills. He ran into financial arrears and then faced court fines, adding to the debts he could not pay.

> Client moved into his current address in Oct[ober] 2015, he is renting flat through a letting agency. Client didn't take electricity meter readings when he moved in, but he is sure those were taken by engineer from Southern Electric. Client has a bill to pay of £926.20, this is for six months as he hasn't made any payments since he moved in. Client's electricity meter readings are estimated – on the bill.

---

[3]   Client ID 18.

As client believes he hasn't used this much, I advised him to get meter readings and come back to [us] if he needs help with calling company.

On more than one occasion, GYROS accompanied Darius to the Housing Options office at Great Yarmouth Borough Council to negotiate a repayment plan for unpaid Council Tax and to try to explain his financial situation.

Client has received unpaid C[ouncil] T[ax] Liability Order for £848, dated ... July 2016. I will accompany client to GYBC [Great Yarmouth Borough Council] tomorrow to make payment offer, letter says client has only two days to do this.

Darius also had health issues. A GYROS adviser went with him to physiotherapy appointments. She also phoned his general practitioner (GP) and other health service providers on his behalf.

Accompanied client to health centre to help him to follow up his physiotherapy appt [appointment]. Client was advised at the reception that there is nothing on his notes about referral and that he needs to self-refer and was provided with leaflet. I helped client to call to book this, I was advised that client is on waiting list, max[imum] waiting time 18 weeks.

Darius often fell in and out of eligibility for benefits (mainly Universal Credit) depending on whether he could prove he was 'exercising his Treaty rights' (such as working). Not having a contract for work or for his tenancy when he first moved to the UK made it difficult for him to provide the paper trail needed to prove evidence of his entitlement to Universal Credit. Over the course of the last five years, GYROS has helped Darius to navigate his benefit entitlements at various points.

(2016) I accompanied client to GY [Great Yarmouth] Jobcentre. Client had a 'further evidence interview' at jobcentre today to provide his tenancy agreement and proof of his rent payments. He provided his bank statements to prove his rent payments to his landlord. Client also had his HRT [Habitual Residence Test] interview straight after. Client was able to provide documents to support his residence in the UK, like payslips, P45, employment contracts, GP letters, NINO [National Insurance number] letter. I advised client to come to GYROS walk-ins in future if he needs help maintaining his UC [Universal Credit] account online.

GYROS also provided Darius and his children with food parcels when he struggled to make ends meet, as well as helping him to register with other work agencies to find more hours.

(2020) The client contacted me and explained that he has no money to live. He received a message to his UC [Universal Credit]. I checked the message for him and added that his working hours have been reduced. He said his children received £15 vouchers for food (weekly). I explained he needs to go [to] the foodbank.

GYROS also helped Darius' children to access school places and helped him communicate with the school, because (initially) none of the family spoke English.

In 2021, GYROS helped the whole family make applications under the European Union Settlement Scheme (EUSS) to continue their legal residence in the UK after Brexit. They were all awarded settled status.

As subsequent chapters will show, the clustering of problems in Darius' case is typical for low-paid migrant workers in Great Yarmouth. Some do nothing and their problems often accumulate. Some resolve their own problems, sometimes with help from friends or family. Many, like Darius, go to GYROS for help. This brings us to our third research question: what does GYROS do? GYROS' advisers are skilled at getting their clients help across a range of matters (immigration, employment, housing, welfare). The help is solution-oriented, holistic and pragmatic. This is particularly important for EU migrant workers with a poor command of English and little understanding of the (legal) system in the UK. What we do not see is GYROS advisers encouraging their clients to go down formal legal routes, let alone going to court.

For us as lawyers, both academic and practitioner, GYROS' response made us reflect on our own understanding of the role of the law, law as a discipline and how law is practised. We know that when lawyers think about law, they think about statutes, cases, judges and courts. Issues are boxed up into legal categories and seen as legal problems which can ultimately be resolved through formal dispute resolution mechanisms. However, as Darius' case shows, GYROS' clients rarely saw their problems as *legal* problems. The advisers – most of whom were not qualified lawyers – also did not see their clients' problems as legal problems and so they did not think about the need to have recourse to legal avenues of dispute resolution.

This dissonance between lawyers' (especially academic lawyers') perception of law, which focuses on the law and formal legal structures,[4] and the reality of non-lawyers' (non-)engagement with the law, which focuses on the individual and the range of problems they face, which need

---

[4]   This is not a thesis on legal philosophy and this characterization might be seen as somewhat legal positivist, but we use it to provide a stark contrast to what is happening on the streets of Great Yarmouth. For criticism, see: L.L. Fuller, *Morality of Law* (New Haven, CT: Yale University Press, 1969); K.A. Rundle, *'Forms Liberate': Reclaiming the Legal Philosophy of Lon L. Fuller* (Oxford: Hart Publishing, 2013).

resolution in a holistic manner, was striking. Yet we found an absence of literature examining the very early, day-to-day and often unwitting engagement of people with the law and how they respond to it (particularly concerning migrant communities/those who do not speak English). There are notable works, literature and expertise in law, anthropology, sociology, critical legal studies and socio-legal studies that touch on these issues, and from which we have benefited. However, we do not think that the existing literature, outlined in Section D, adequately explains the data that we have analysed. Consequently, we explored grounded theory methodologies (Appendix I), and by analysing and re-analysing the data, we developed a new theoretical framework within which our material sits: what we call 'pragmatic law'.[5] This provides a lens to consider the deeply pragmatic responses to (legal) problems by both migrant workers and their (non-legal) advisers as well as the benefits and risks associated with this approach. Our case for a fresh theoretical framing is addressed in more detail in Chapter 8.

In this chapter, we set out the theoretical framing of the book (Section D). However, we begin by explaining why we located our research in Great Yarmouth and how our research was conducted. We then look at the themes that have emerged from our data before considering the overall structure of the book.

C. Place, precarity and pragmatism

1. Locating the research in Great Yarmouth

1.1 The Why

The book explores the lives of EU migrants in Great Yarmouth, the problems they experience, particularly through the eyes of those living in the HMO (the 'House' of our research) and through the records of GYROS' clients and how they respond to those problems. We draw on the evolving literature on legal geography to justify the location of our research in Great Yarmouth,

---

[5]   As distinct from 'legal pragmatism'; see: D. Luban, 'What's pragmatic about legal pragmatism' (1996) 18 *Cardoso Law Review* 43; R.S. Summers, 'Pragmatic instrumentalism in twentieth century American legal thought – a synthesis and critique of our dominant general theory about law and its use' (1981) 66 *Cornell Law Review* 861; S. Haack, 'On legal pragmatism: where does "the path of the law" lead us?' (2005) 50 *American Journal of Jurisprudence* 71. See also A.J. Morris, 'Some challenges for legal pragmatism: a closer look at pragmatic legal reasoning' (2007) 28 *Northern Illinois University Law Review* 1. Pragmatic law (as we set out) is distinct from legal pragmatism because pragmatic law focuses on how advisers do *not* expressly use/apply the law, but rather use law – or (legal) 'rules' – to shape the advice they give.

looking at how EU free movement law – and now Withdrawal Agreement law – has brought EU migrant workers to the Town and provided the legal basis for their continued residence and right to work.

Orzeck and Hae define legal geography as 'the production of holistic knowlege about the place and function of law in contemporary (and historical) societies'.[6] Legal geographers note that 'nearly every aspect of law is located, takes place, is in motion, or has some spatial frame of reference'.[7] Legal geography uses concepts of scale,[8] jurisdiction,[9] territory and networks[10] to look at the interrelatedness of law and place. For us, the place is the declining seaside resort of Great Yarmouth in the East of England and the law is EU free movement law/Withdrawal Agreement law and its intersection with UK law on immigration, employment, housing, welfare and healthcare.

Why did we choose Great Yarmouth? Research to date on EU free movement to the UK has focused mainly on cities, such as London[11] or Manchester,[12] and 'urban citizenship',[13] often looking at high-skilled, English-speaking migrants. Central and Eastern Europeans (broadly defined), especially low-waged and low-skilled individuals with poor English,[14] are underrepresented in that research,[15] often because of language issues. Those working in rural farms and factories make up communities that are particularly invisible to researchers. Focusing our study in Great Yarmouth – a deprived coastal town that, in the 2016 referendum on the UK's membership

---

[6]   R. Orzeck and L. Hae, 'Restructuring legal geography' (2020) 44(5) *Progress in Human Geography* 832. See also F.de Witte, 'Here be Dragons: Legal Geography and EU law', *European Law Open*. 2022;1(1):113-125. doi:10.1017/elo.2021.2.

[7]   I. Braverman, N. Blomley, D. Delaney and A. Kedar, *The Expansion Spaces of Law* (Stanford, CA: Stanford University Press, 2014), 1.

[8]   B. de Sousa Santos, 'Law: a map of misreading. Toward a postmodern conception of law' (1987) 14(3) *Journal of Law and Society* 279; S.A. Marston, 'The social construction of scale' (2000) 24 *Progress in Human Geography* 219.

[9]   N. Blomley, 'What sort of legal space is a city?' *SSRN* (2012), available at: http://dx.doi.org/10.2139/ssrn.2165083, accessed 22 November 2023.

[10]   J. Painter, 'European citizenship and the regions' (2008) 15 *European Urban and Regional Studies* 5.

[11]   A. Lulle, L. Moroşanu and R. King, 'And then came Brexit: experiences and future plans of young EU migrants in the London region' (2018) 24 *Population, Space and Place* 1, 8–9.

[12]   A. Rzepnikowska, 'Racism and xenophobia experienced by Polish migrants in the UK before and after Brexit vote' (2019) 45 *Journal of Ethnic and Migration Studies* 61.

[13]   Painter, n 10, 8.

[14]   T. Guma and R. Dafydd Jones, ' "Where are we going to go now?" European Union migrants' experiences of hostility, anxiety, and (non-)belonging during Brexit' (2019) 25 *Population, Space and Place* e2198.

[15]   T. Bueltmann and A. Bulat, *EU Citizens, Identity, Belonging and Representation Post Brexit* (Glasgow: University of Strathclyde, 2021), available at: https://the3million.org.uk/sites/default/files/files/Bueltmann-Bulat_FullSurveyReport_0.pdf, accessed 17 March 2023.

of the EU recorded the fifth-highest Leave vote in the UK and where perhaps one in four of the population is an EU migrant – offers a different perspective on EU migration to the UK. This gives us a more rounded picture of EU free movement to the UK and its long-term implications for those who have exercised their rights (and, to a lesser extent, for the Town[16]).

1.2 The How

Our research was significantly helped by our partnership with the charity GYROS (see Chapter 2, Section E). One of the authors had worked in GYROS (during 2012–2019).[17] Access to GYROS – its dataset, its clients and its advisers – has allowed us to gain a deeper and richer understanding of both the experience of EU migrant workers in the Town and their approach to the (legal) problems they face. Specifically, we had access to the longitudinal dataset (covering 2015–2020) held by GYROS. Each client's attendance at their service is recorded under a relevant 'enquiry label' on that day; the label indicates the issue they were seeking help with – for instance, housing, employment and health. The dataset contains 3,018 unique enquiry labels with 6,856 unique case notes.

The GYROS dataset provides a helpful 'snapshot' of clients accessing help during the period 2015–2020. The largest nationality groups in the dataset were (in size order) Portuguese, Lithuanian, Romanian, Polish and Latvian and more recently Bulgarian. Additionally, there were clients from Guinea-Bissau, Cape Verde, Sao Tome and Principe, and East Timor, many also holding Portuguese nationality. Further, 3 per cent of the dataset were non-EU family members of EU nationals (NEFMs; see Chapter 3).

The dataset consists of 56 per cent women and 41 per cent men (3 per cent did not specify gender), spanning in age from 20 to over 70 with a median age of 45. The data show that most clients have arrived since 2000 (Table 1.1; this is described further in Chapter 2, Section B.3).

To add depth to the research, we also undertook an ethnographic study, which involved living in 'the House', an HMO just off St Peter's Road in Great Yarmouth for eight weeks (see Chapter 2). The eight residents of the HMO shared their stories and experiences of living and working in the Town, as did the British landlord, Frank. We also conducted focus groups with GYROS staff (a total of ten staff participated in four focus groups) and with

---

[16] C. Barnard and F. Costello, 'When (EU) migration came to Great Yarmouth' (2023) 18 *Contemporary Social Science* 150.

[17] By late 2019, one of the authors had worked in a research-related role within a tri-partner project – *Community Pathways Partnership* – that GYROS was involved in. She was not employed by GYROS, but worked for another project partner, spending one day per week throughout our fieldwork period working on the partnership.

Table 1.1: Year of arrival in the UK for clients on the GYROS database, 2015–2020

Year	Percentage of respondents
Pre-2000	2
2000–2005	12
2006–2010	19
2011–2015	35
2016–2019	19
Unknown	13
Total	100

GYROS clients (seven focus groups) as well as eight in-depth interviews with frontline staff, the strategic director and chair of the board of trustees (see Appendix II). We also analysed court data by attending hearings, undertaking interviews and examining case reports. Finally, we also conducted specific health data analysis in light of the COVID-19 pandemic. A full description of our methodology – a mixed methods, grounded theory approach to the data – and its limitations can be found in Appendix I.

Two overriding themes emerged from our data – precarity and pragmatism – themes to which we now turn.

2. Themes

In respect of precarity, many EU migrant workers experience precarious finances, housing and employment. As Darius' story (Box 1.1) shows, it takes very little to go wrong – ill health, reduction in hours, an unexpected bill, not to mention exploitation by landlords, employers and even advice sharks – for an individual to end up in debt and face losing their home. They may even come to the attention of social services, particularly if they have children. Sometimes the state can help, through payment of benefits and even provision of basic furniture for a family. However, more often the state is seen as a threat, with powers to remove children or encourage (and pay for) voluntary returns to the home state.[18]

The other theme is pragmatism, which emerged somewhat unwittingly from the case notes in the GYROS database, specifically the pragmatic way GYROS' advisers help their clients. As Darius' story shows, GYROS advisers

---

[18] V. Mantouvalou, *Structural Injustice and Workers' Rights* (Oxford: Oxford University Press, 2023), 21, identifies a related issue of the state 'creating concrete rules which ... allocate power in a way that increases and entrenches workers' vulnerability to exploitation'.

will: obtain the necessary paperwork for EUSS applications; contact employers, landlords and the council; translate letters; accompany clients to healthcare visits; give them small sums of money to attend job interviews; and give out food vouchers. We also see them trying to explain the position of their EU clients to 'street-level bureaucrats'[19] such as local authority representatives at Great Yarmouth Borough Council. In other words, GYROS acts as advocate, translator, sponsor, de facto safety net, broker and trusted adviser (and sometimes all of these at once). In those multiple roles, problem resolution is, perhaps of necessity, pragmatic and holistic. It is very different to the more siloed, specialized approach taken by lawyers when giving formal legal advice.

Access to advice and problem resolution of this sort at street level is a lifeline for those living in areas of high deprivation, such as Great Yarmouth, where there is little free legal advice. It is, however, very different to the ways that lawyers traditionally operate, with its emphasis on problem resolution rather than legal resolution. This is an issue we return to in our discussion on pragmatic law (Section D.3).

3. Structure of the book

These themes – precarity in the lives of EU migrant workers and pragmatism in response to problems that arise – are played out across the chapters that follow.

Chapter 2 introduces the Town, the Street and the House where our research takes place. It also introduces the charity GYROS. Specifically, we meet the individuals living in the House, a multistorey HMO typical of the accommodation lived in by migrant workers like Darius. The House is a common thread through the research. The stories of the lives of the residents of the House are interwoven with findings from the GYROS data. The House provides a physical symbol of deprivation (the roof leaks, there is no central heating, the bathroom is mouldy). The arrangements for those living in the House (the informality of the tenancy arrangements, the absence of names on bills) make it more difficult for these migrant workers to prove their residence and status, especially when applying to the EUSS, which is a precondition for EU migrant workers and their family members to continue to live, work, claim benefits and receive healthcare in the UK post-Brexit. This is just one example of 'paper trails'[20] and the 'bureaucratic bordering'[21] experienced

---

[19] M. Lipsky, *Street-Level Bureaucracy: Dilemmas of the Individual in Public Services* (New York: Russell Sage Foundation, 1980).

[20] S. Horton and J. Heyman (eds) *Paper Trails: Migrants, Documents, and Legal Insecurity* (Durham, NC: Duke University Press, 2020).

[21] P. Manolova, 'Inclusion through irregularisation? Exploring the politics and realities of internal bordering in managing post-crisis labour migration in the EU' (2021) 48 *Journal of Ethnic and Migration Studies* 3687.

by EU migrant workers: paperwork requirements prove a real challenge for low-skilled EU nationals and may sometimes defeat them altogether.

Chapter 3 considers the advent of the EUSS and the creation of two statuses: pre-settled status (EU (PS)) for those with less than five years' residence; and settled status (EU (SS)) for those with more than five years' residence. Specifically, Chapter 3 looks at the problems EU migrant workers have faced with the operation of the scheme. It shows how a combination of poor English language skills, intermittent employment history and a lack of access to Wi-Fi, smartphones and digital IT skills make it more difficult for this group of EU migrant workers to apply for pre-settled or settled status.

Chapters 4 to 7 consider the common (legal) problems experienced by EU migrant communities in Great Yarmouth, grouped thematically: employment (Chapter 4); housing (Chapter 5); welfare benefits and debt (Chapter 6); and health and healthcare (Chapter 7). These thematic areas follow the labels used in the GYROS database of issues for which clients seek support. In each themed chapter, we examine both the experiences of those living in the House and the issues faced by those seeking help from GYROS. We quote directly from the interviews we conducted and from the case notes written by GYROS' advisers (mainly EU migrants themselves). We therefore hear the migrants and their advisers explaining their situations and actions in their own words (as in, for example, the case study in Box 1.1). Those voices tell of precarious lives, uncertain working hours, money troubles, poor housing and difficulties with paperwork for accessing services. We also hear how GYROS advisers respond to the issues presented to them.

Chapter 4 looks at the issues that arise in the GYROS database around employment, specifically the precarious position of agency workers and those on zero-hours contracts.[22] It also considers the (legal) problems migrant workers face in the workplace[23] – for instance, bullying and harassment, and non-payment of wages and holiday pay – issues also seen in the handful of cases which have been brought to employment tribunals

---

[22] 'Migrants in the UK labour market: an overview' (2022) *The Migration Observatory at the University of Oxford*, available at: https://migrationobservatory.ox.ac.uk/resources/briefi ngs/migrants-in-the-uk-labour-market-an-overview/, accessed 22 November 2023; Migration Advisory Committee, *Migrants in Low-Paid Work* (London: Migration Advisory Committee, 2014), available at: https://assets.publishing.service.gov.uk/government/uplo ads/system/uploads/attachment_data/file/333083/MAC-Migrants_in_low-skilled_wor k__Full_report_2014.pdf, accessed 1 May 2020.

[23] A. Favell and R. Barbulescu, 'Brexit, "immigration" and anti-discrimination' in P. Diamond, P. Nedergaard and B. Rosamond (eds) *The Routledge Handbook of the Politics of Brexit* (London: Routledge, 2019), 118.

by EU migrant workers across the UK. Alongside these problems, which are familiar to lawyers, we also see informal working arrangements – for example, payslips not being provided. This makes it difficult to establish entitlement to employment protection and to the EUSS. We also learn of poor employment practices: denial of toilet breaks; a production line moving too fast; trays of frozen poultry which are too heavy to lift; and the need to 'pay' the supervisor to get extra shifts.

If EU migrant workers cannot work due to ill health, including cases of COVID-19, or if they lose their job, their problems quickly accumulate they cannot pay their bills, especially their rent; they get into debt in an attempt to pay their bills; and if they cannot pay their debts, they risk losing their home. This is particularly the case if the work comes with accommodation, as with jobs in tourist caravan parks. Problem clustering of this kind is an issue for all those on low incomes and zero-hours contracts;[24] however, for EU migrant workers, the position is exacerbated if they have pre-settled status, as their access to benefits and housing support is limited. This issue is considered in Chapter 5 on housing, a central strand of the research. Once again, we encounter precarious living arrangements – here, in the form of informal rental agreements, word of mouth referrals and poor-quality accommodation. We also see the issues which arise in the GYROS database: refusal to rent to EU migrant workers; poor-quality accommodation; eviction; and difficulty EU migrant workers have in accessing social housing.

Chapter 6 considers welfare benefits and debt. Provision of advice about welfare benefits is the most common category in the GYROS database. A large number of clients face in-work poverty, and Chapter 6 looks at the escalating use of foodbanks in the Town as well as the problems facing EU migrant workers attempting to access Universal Credit (often to top up low-paid work), because of bureaucratic bordering.[25] For example, those with pre-settled status must prove that they have been both 'habitually resident' and 'exercising a Treaty right' (such as working or being self-employed) in order to claim access to welfare benefits.[26] If

---

[24] See, for example, 'Nearly a million older people just one big bill away from financial disaster as new report shows reality of trying to meet the extra costs of ageing on a low income' *Age UK* (6 April 2019), available at: www.ageuk.org.uk/latest-press/articles/2019/april2/nearly-a-million-older-people-just-one-big-bill-away-from-financial-disaster-as-new-report-shows-reality-of-trying-to-meet-the-extra-costs-of-ageing-on-a-low-income/, accessed 22 November 2023).

[25] Manolova (2021), n 21.

[26] The Immigration (European Economic Area) Regulations 2016. See 'Check if you have the right to reside for benefits' *Citizens Advice*, available at: www.citizensadvice.org.uk/benefits/claiming-benefits-if-youre-from-the-EU/before-you-apply/check-if-you-have-the-right-to-reside-for-benefits/, accessed 19 October 2021.

they cannot access state support, the clients often get into debt, the other issue considered in the chapter.

Chapter 7 looks at migrant health, building on Hazel Genn's work on health justice.[27] Since much of the research was conducted during the COVID-19 pandemic, health (already an issue seen in the GYROS database) was a main priority. Migrant communities encounter barriers to accessing healthcare in the UK,[28] including language and cultural barriers. Health issues are also the starting point from which many of the other problems cascade to or from: ill health results from poor accommodation, limited finances and difficult work environments; or ill health means that working hours must be reduced, so difficulties arise in relation to money and accommodation.

Chapter 8 draws together the themes (precarity and pragmatism) that emerged from our data. It also looks at how to analyse how migrant communities interact with the law, and enforcement of that law, in Great Yarmouth. It argues that generally EU migrant workers turn to GYROS for help to resolve their problems and that the problems are not necessarily seen, by advisers or clients, as legal problems (albeit they are likely to be underpinned by law). How can this be theorized? As noted earlier, while the existing literature has helped our thinking, it did not always fit with our observations on the ground. Consequently, we returned to the themes and the data and drew on 'adaptive grounded theory' to explore a fresh theoretical framework,[29] what we call pragmatic law. In the next section, we outline the strands of existing legal and socio-legal scholarship around access to justice and legal needs, and legal consciousness and law in the everyday, and the difficulties we have identified with this scholarship for our work, together with a brief outline of other influences we have identified, before introducing our concept of 'pragmatic law'.

---

[27] H. Genn, 'When law is good for your health: mitigating the social determinants of health through access to justice' (2019) 72 *Current Legal Problems* 159.

[28] H. Jayaweera, 'Access to healthcare for vulnerable migrant women in England: a human security approach' (2018) 66 *Current Sociology* 273; S. Germain and A. Yong, 'COVID-19 highlighting inequalities in access to healthcare in England: a case study of ethnic minority and migrant women' (2020) 28 *Feminist Legal Studies* 301.

[29] D. Layder, *Sociological Practice: Linking Theory and Social Research* (London: Sage, 1998).

D. Framing of the book

This research project has been a voyage of discovery. We have read across a range of disciplines: anthropology,[30] ethnography,[31] sociology,[32] cultural studies[33] and geography.[34] We have benefited greatly from talking to colleagues in these disciplines, who have kindly given of their time. We draw together some of the material from these disciplines in Chapter 8. We are conscious, however, that we are intellectual magpies, rooting round for nuggets from other disciplines as we developed our work. While this may raise questions about our theoretical rigour, we think that some of the insights gained have given us the tools to address our first question (concerning what life is like for low-paid EU migrant workers in Great Yarmouth and what problems they experience), our second question (concerning the responses of EU nationals in Great Yarmouth to the (legal) problems they are experiencing) and part of our third question (concerning how GYROS helps EU migrants navigate and resolve their (legal) problems).

However, we found that a lacuna in the existing literature was how to address the fundamental part of our third question: what do the responses of the clients and GYROS tell us about how (legal) problems are addressed and resolved on the frontline? Is what we are witnessing in Great Yarmouth a different way of approaching law and lawyering? The two strands of literature which speak most closely to our work are access to justice (Section 1) and

---

[30] G. Ramsay, 'Time and the other in crisis: how anthropology makes its displaced object' (2020) 20 *Anthropological Theory* 385; L. Nader, *The Life of the Law* (Berkeley, CA: University of California Press, 2005); V. Das and D. Poole, *Anthropology in the Margins of the State* (New Delhi: Oxford University Press, 2004); N. De Genova, 'Migrant "illegality" and deportability in everyday life' (2002) 31 *Annual Review of Anthropology* 419.

[31] S. Bibler Coutin and E. Vogel, 'Migrant narratives and ethnographic tropes: navigating tragedy, creating possibilities' (2016) 45 *Journal of Contemporary Ethnography* 631; I. Koch, *Personalizing the State: An Anthropology of Law, Politics and Welfare in Austerity Britain* (Oxford: Oxford University Press, 2018); S. Holmes, *Fresh Fruit, Broken Bodies: Migrant Farmworkers in the United States* (Berkeley, CA: University of California Press, 2013); V. Dubois, 'Towards a critical policy ethnography: lessons from fieldwork on welfare control in France' (2009) 3 *Critical Policy Studies* 221.

[32] R. Gropas and A. Triandafyllidou (eds), *European Immigration: A Sourcebook* (Farnham: Ashgate, 2014); A. Triandafyllidou, *Immigrants and National Identity in Europe* (London: Routledge, 2003); F. Anthias, 'Interconnecting boundaries of identity and belonging and hierarchy-making within transnational mobility studies: framing inequalities' (2016) 64 *Current Sociology* 172.

[33] M. Bonn, 'Migrants' acquisition of cultural skills and selective immigration policies' (2015) 3 *Migration Studies* 32.

[34] See Orzeck and Hae (2020), n 6; Braverman et al (2014), n 7.

legal consciousness (Section 2). However, as we shall argue, neither of these frameworks capture what we have witnessed. This led us to develop the concept of pragmatic law (Section 3).

1. Access to justice

The socio-legal access to justice scholarship takes a largely bottom-up approach, looking at the prevalence of justiciable issues within the general population and specifically the access to justice pathways and legal needs of individuals. This bottom-up research employs a variety of methodologies and theoretical perspectives. It focuses on legal problems and considers people's response and advice-seeking behaviours in relation to these problems.[35] Specifically, it asks whether, and how, people access formal legal pathways to resolve their legal problems.[36]

The access to justice research identifies a relatively high incidence of justiciable problems within the general population and it shows that this is more pronounced among certain sociodemographic groups, including those we are considering.[37] It tells us that certain problems have a propensity to cluster together or 'cascade', whereby one problem directly leads to another (as in Darius' case, Box 1.1) when due to insufficient hours under his zero-hours contracts, he did not earn enough to pay his bills).[38] The research

---

[35] See, for example: R. Sandefur, 'What we know and need to know about the legal needs of the public' (2016) 67 *South Carolina Law Review* 339, 443; P. Pleasence and N.J. Balmer, 'Development of a general legal confidence scale: a first implementation of the Rasch measurement model in empirical legal studies' (2019) 16 *Journal of Empirical Legal Studies* 143; A. Buck, P. Pleasence and N.J. Balmer, 'Do citizens know how to deal with legal issues? Some empirical insights' (2008) 37 *Journal of Social Policy* 661.

[36] P.T. Pleasence and N.J. Balmer, *Legal Confidence and Attitudes to Law: Baseline Measures and Social Patterning* (London: Legal Education Foundation, 2018); H. Genn, *Paths to Justice: What People Do and Think about Going to Law* (Oxford: Hart Publishing, 1999).

[37] P. Pleasence and N.J. Balmer 'Caught in the middle: justiciable problems and the use of lawyers' in M. Trebilcock, A. Duggan and L. Sossin (eds) *Middle Income Access to Justice* (Toronto: University of Toronto Press, 2012), 27.

[38] P. Pleasence, N.J. Balmer, A. Buck, A. O'Grady and H. Genn, 'Multiple justiciable problems: common clusters and their social and demographic indicators' (2004) 1 *Journal of Empirical Legal Studies* 301. Among other identified clusters they found a large cluster, of nine problems, associated with: consumer rights, rented housing, money and debt, welfare benefits, personal injury, employment, owned housing, neighbours and those considering legal action (this problem cluster was particularly associated with younger respondents, those in receipt of benefits, those with academic qualifications, those who are long-term ill or disabled, those living in flats, those with mortgages, those renting and lone parents (pp 323–324). See also A. Buck, N. Balmer and P. Pleasence, 'Social exclusion and civil law: experience of civil justice problems among vulnerable groups' (2005) 39 *Social Policy and Administration* 302.

also identifies low legal capabilities – that is, low knowledge and confidence around legal issues – among the general population.[39]

Historically in the UK (and elsewhere), access to justice has also been facilitated by what is termed 'community lawyering', defined as grassroots access to legal advice and representation.[40] In the past, this was provided through a mix of pro bono legal advice and legal aid for those who could not pay. However, as we shall see in Chapter 8, the Legal Aid, Sentencing and Punishment of Offenders Act 2012 (LASPO 2012) undermined the provision of legal aid across England and Wales, leading to the expansion of huge 'advice deserts' throughout the country, including in the East of England. This led Robins and Newman to argue that '"access to justice", a conceptually elusive idea at the best of times, has been so debased as to be rendered meaningless'.[41] They say that early advice (needed at a hyperlocal level) prevents problems from snowballing (an issue we discuss throughout the book)[42] and that early legal advice in specialist areas must complement the generalist advice given, as they note, mostly by volunteers at Citizens Advice.[43] They advocate for 'the value of law centres as providers of specialist legal advice'.[44]

While we would agree with these observations, they show how access to justice scholarship often focuses on access to legal advice from lawyers and, ultimately, access to formal legal pathways. However, the participants in our research have not accessed Citizens Advice, let alone law centres; nor have they engaged with more formal legal access to justice pathways. We argue that EU migrant workers in Great Yarmouth do not see their problems as 'legal' issues, but as problems which need street-level (non-legal), pragmatic solutions (usually achieved with the help of GYROS) rather than more formal dispute resolution. For these reasons, our observations do not fit within the existing access to justice literature.

2. Legal consciousness and everyday law

The other obvious frame of reference for our work is the legal consciousness literature, including the work of Merry,[45] Conley and O'Barr (in the United

---

[39] Pleasence and Balmer (2019), n 35.

[40] J. Kinghan, 'The context and controversies of progressive lawyering' in *Lawyers, Networks and Progressive Social Change: Lawyers Changing Lives* (Oxford: Hart Publishing, 2021), 7.

[41] J. Robins and D. Newman, *Justice in a Time of Austerity: Stories from a System in Crisis* (Bristol: Bristol University Press, 2021), 172.

[42] Ibid, 179–180.

[43] Ibid, 181.

[44] Ibid, 181.

[45] S. Engle Merry, *Getting Justice and Getting Even, Legal Consciousness among Working Class Americans* (Chicago: University of Chicago Press, 1990).

States – US),[46] Cowan[47] and Halliday and Morgan (in the UK)[48] and Hertogh (in the Netherlands).[49] The field of legal consciousness scholarship, first elaborated in the US and more recently developed in the UK and Europe,[50] seeks to understand people's routine experiences and perceptions of law in everyday life.[51] Sally Engle Merry defines consciousness as 'the "natural" and normal way of doing things'.[52] This scholarship has provided various frameworks and strategies to describe how people 'define, think about, and use the law'.[53]

While our research is not directly a study of the legal consciousness of individuals accessing help from GYROS or of individuals living in the HMO resolving their problems without outside intervention, the legal consciousness literature nevertheless helped us to think about what we call 'pragmatic law'. This literature consistently highlights the inability of those with less socioeconomic power to navigate legal pathways as successfully as those with more socioeconomic power. Examples include those who are 'against the law' (Ewick and Silbey[54]) and those who take 'a relational approach' to the law (Conley and O'Barr[55]) or, as in the case of Sally Engle Merry's work (1999)[56], where the legal system has barriers too high for those more vulnerable or marginalized to navigate despite increased accessibility to the legal system. The common thread is that those who are more socially marginalized are least likely to be able to find expression in (formal) legal narrative and structure. We have seen this in our data as well.

However, where our work departs from the legal consciousness literature is that while that literature is predominantly focused on the formal legal system, what we observed was a group (EU migrant workers) who did not perceive their problems to be necessarily legal and who may be helped by (GYROS) advisers who did not consider they were necessarily providing

---

[46] J.M.M. Conley and W.M. O'Barr, *Rules vs Relationships: The Ethnography of Legal Discourse* (Chicago: University of Chicago Press, 1990).
[47] D. Cowan, 'Legal consciousness: some observations' (2004) 67 *The Modern Law Review* 928.
[48] S. Halliday and B. Morgan, 'I fought the law and the law won? Legal consciousness and the critical imagination' (2013) 66 *Current Legal Problems* 1.
[49] M. Hertogh, *Nobody's Law: Legal Consciousness and Legal Alienation in Everyday Life* (London: Palgrave, 2019).
[50] Cowan (2004), n 47.
[51] Ibid, 929.
[52] Merry (1990), n 45, 5.
[53] P. Ewick, and S. Silbey, *The Common Place of Law* (Chicago: University of Chicago Press, 1998), 28.
[54] Ibid.
[55] Conley and O'Barr (1990), n 46.
[56] Merry (1990), n 45.

'legal' advice, but rather holistic and pragmatic support. So how can this be described?

3. Pragmatic law

As explained earlier, while we have benefited very much from the existing literature, we do not think it fully captures either the approach of EU migrant workers to their problems or the approach of GYROS advisers to helping their clients. Consequently, we outline a new theoretical framework, arising out of our data, which we call 'pragmatic law', a term adapted from Boltanski's 'pragmatic sociology'.[57] Pragmatic sociology seeks to explore what happens when things go wrong for people in their everyday life and the 'values of worth' that are used to justify or explain actions. From a theoretical perspective, the focus of pragmatic sociology is on understanding the dynamics of action and how actors operate within a dispute situation. Like Boltanski, we are interested in how actors operate faced with a dispute situation, specifically the problems facing GYROS' clients and how they, with GYROS' support, respond to those problems outside the traditional pathways of the legal system.

Pragmatic law explores how legal problems are understood and resolved long before they undergo any legal framing or legalization. Pragmatic law therefore examines problem solution in the everyday. We are interested in this because by understanding the role of law in the everyday, we can further develop our understanding of law in action and people's experiences and awareness of law, as well as highlighting the extensive reach of law beyond what are traditionally considered (formal) boundaries. This enables us to build a more inclusive understanding of 'the law' and the response to that law, by widening its scope to include community-level advice and responses. The term pragmatic law is therefore a descriptive label for what is happening on the ground: to include people's response to their problems and advisers' response to their clients' problems.

However, our interest in pragmatic law is not merely in terms of typology and classification. We think that by understanding how one particularly vulnerable group, namely low-paid EU migrants and their advisers, respond to (legal) problems they are facing, this helps us to have a fuller understanding of the enforcement pyramid.[58] As lawyers, we think about legal problems being packaged into legal categories and then, where necessary, cases

---

[57] L. Boltanski, *De la critique. Précis de sociologie de l'émancipation* (Paris: Gallimard, 2009).

[58] Initially inspired by I. Ayres and J. Braithwaite, *Responsive Regulation: Transcending the Deregulation Debate* (Oxford: Oxford University Press, 1992), available at: http://john braithwaite.com/wp-content/uploads/2016/06/Responsive-Regulation-Transce.pdf, accessed 22 November 2023.

being started in the lower courts (for example, in employment tribunals) and proceeding up the pyramid to the higher appellate courts. Yet our earlier research showed enforcement levels of (employment) rights through traditional legal pathways were very low.[59] Pragmatic law helps to explain why, and in so doing it provides a broader understanding of what we prefer to call 'resolution pathways' (see Figure 8.1). Further, by describing and explaining what is happening on the ground, we can examine the benefits but also the risks associated with this pragmatic approach to the law and problem resolution (see Chapter 8).

E. Conclusion

In this book, we seek to describe the complex circumstances of EU migrant workers living in a deprived coastal town, doing jobs that the pandemic revealed were essential to provide (cheap) food for the public, and the (legal) problems they are experiencing. Others have documented the lives of 'Eurostars': those for whom EU free movement has been overwhelmingly beneficial.[60] The story we tell about EU migrants in Great Yarmouth is more complicated and nuanced. There is a rich geographical literature that sees communities such as Great Yarmouth as a product of the intersection between their histories and the legal frameworks they operate in. This helps to justify our focus on one particular town.

The role played by law in the lives of EU migrant workers is complex. It is threaded through the very fabric of people's daily lives, whether they are conscious of it or not. In fact, those from lower socioeconomic backgrounds with less social capital tend to encounter the rough edges of the law more than others.[61] Law is not always a protector; it is also a threat (the need to have EUSS status or face the risk of deportation; the need to have a television licence or face the risk of prosecution). And even when it offers protection (for example, against discrimination or unfair dismissal), its protective shield is rarely invoked, at least not through any formal legal resolution pathway.

With Engel, we have therefore 'pitch[ed] [our] tents on the side streets'[62] of Great Yarmouth and examined how law is experienced every day by the

---

[59] C. Barnard and A. Ludlow, 'Enforcement of employment rights by EU-8 migrant workers in employment tribunals' (2016) 45 *Industrial Law Journal* 1.

[60] A. Favell, *Eurostars and Eurocities: Free Movement and Mobility in an Integrating Europe* (Oxford: Blackwell Publishing, 2008).

[61] L. Clements, *Clustered Injustice and the Level Green* (London: Legal Action Group, 2020), 5.

[62] D. Engel, 'Law in the domains of everyday life: the construction of community and difference' in A. Sarat and T.R. Kearns (eds) *Law in Everyday Life* (Ann Arbor: University of Michigan Press, 1995). Engel says: 'Law academics generally prefer to pitch their tents in the shadow of the Supreme Court rather than on Main Street or in urban or suburban neighbourhoods', 124.

EU migrant workers in our book. We are interested in the 'journey' of (legal) issues in communities, identifying the waymarks of their journey with the clustering and cascading of problems and the advisers' pragmatic approaches to seeking solutions. This provides a thicker and more comprehensive understanding not only of the lives of more marginalized groups in a turbulent period of British history (low-paid EU migrant workers in the time of Brexit) but also of dispute resolution beyond the formal structures of the legal system. It shines light on the world of the law (whether recognized as such) and how it has an impact on a particular community, providing as true as possible a picture of what problems one group of vulnerable individuals are experiencing and how they are resolved.

2

The Town, the Street, the House
and the Advice Charity

A. Introduction

In this chapter, we describe the House, the Street and the Town of our research. We do this to paint a picture of the environment EU migrant workers encounter when they first arrived in the UK and the context in which they now work, live and socialize. As noted in Chapter 1, legal geographers say that 'nearly every aspect of law is located, takes place, is in motion, or has some spatial frame of reference'.[1] So, we describe the Town (Great Yarmouth), the Street (St Peter's Road) and the House (an HMO just off St Peter's Road) where we examine how the law – EU law, Withdrawal Agreement law and UK domestic law – plays out.

The lens of the House, the Street, the Town gives us unique insights into the everyday lives of EU nationals living in Great Yarmouth. These insights sit alongside and add depth to the data obtained through our analysis of the GYROS dataset and our interviews. What stands out vividly from our data is EU migrant workers' precarity – of work, of income, of tenancies – often exacerbated by poor English language and IT skills, lack of awareness of how UK systems work and, sometimes, uncertain immigration status. Our data also show the multiple problems experienced by this group, many of whom turn to GYROS for help. In Section E, we look in some detail at GYROS, the frontline advice charity which has been central in our research, considering what it is and what it does, together with its source of funding. We locate GYROS in the broader context of the community advice sector.

We begin, however, by looking at Great Yarmouth, particularly its socioeconomic situation, before considering the different phases of migration

---

[1]   I. Braverman, N. Blomley, D. Delaney and A. Kedar, *The Expansion Spaces of Law* (Stanford, CA: Stanford University Press, 2014), 1.

to the Town (Section B). We move on to look at the Street (Section C) and then consider in more detail the House, including its layout and how it is organized. We also meet its eight residents (all Lithuanian and Latvian citizens), Frank,[2] the landlord, and Edita, a former tenant (Section D). Their stories and experiences are woven into later chapters.

B. The Town

1. Introduction

Great Yarmouth is a coastal market town and port in Norfolk, in the East of England. It is a town with Roman and Saxon settlement origins.[3] Fishing became a key industry in the Town in the 19th century: Great Yarmouth was the world's leading herring fishing port, with the Town's smokehouses producing bloaters. During the fishing season, 'the town's population would be swelled by thousands – by fishermen, their wives and daughters (known as 'herring girls'[4]) who gutted and pickled the fish, and the coopers to make the barrels the fish were transported in'.[5] This was an early example of (temporary) migration to the Town.

With the first railway arriving in 1844, Great Yarmouth's fame as a seaside tourist attraction and holiday destination spread. This brought further economic prosperity and indeed 'the early 20th century was a boom time for Great Yarmouth'.[6] Travelling celebrity acts performed at the Great Yarmouth Pavilion and international circus acts at the Hippodrome, a purpose-built circus building with a sunken pool under the main stage, which is still fully operational today.[7] Residents remember, during their childhood, seeing elephants being 'walked' on the beach.[8] Houdini, Charlie Chaplin and the Beatles all performed in the Town. Authors visited too: most famously, Charles Dickens stayed in the Town in 1849, and Peggotty in *David Copperfield* (published in 1850) comes from the Town.

---

[2] All names have been changed to protect the anonymity of participants.

[3] F. Meeres, *A History of Great Yarmouth* (Chichester: Phillimore, 2007), 5–6.

[4] 'Fish wives and herring girls' *Seaboard History*, available at: www.seaboardhistory.com/gallery/herring-girls/, accessed 27 January 2022.

[5] Meeres (2007), n 3, 27.

[6] Ibid, 94.

[7] See the website of the Hippodrome, Great Yarmouth at: https://hippodromecircus.co.uk/heritage, accessed 17 January 2022.

[8] F. Wright, 'Did you ever see an elephant on Great Yarmouth beach? A look back on decades of fun at the seaside' *Eastern Daily Press* (31 July 2017), available at: www.edp24.co.uk/news/20830289.ever-see-elephant-great-yarmouth-beach-look-back-decades-fun-seaside/, accessed 27 January 2022.

However, this prosperity was not to last. As a port on the east coast, Great Yarmouth suffered badly in both world wars. In the First World War, Great Yarmouth experienced the first civilian casualties in the country (two residents who had gone into the street to catch sight of the Zeppelin overhead). The Street of this book, then called St Peter's Plain, was hit by Zeppelin raids with 'not a single building escaping damage'.[9] In the Second World War, the famous 'Rows', 145 narrow lanes with houses packed closely together, were seriously damaged.[10] The narrowest, Kittywitches Row, just 27 inches wide, was destroyed by enemy aircraft in 1942.[11] By 1945, 20,000 properties in Great Yarmouth had been destroyed or damaged and 217 people had been killed.[12]

Lots of housing, often of poor quality, was rapidly erected in the immediate postwar period, and this is still inhabited today. A substantial storm hit the East of England in 1953 and Great Yarmouth was particularly affected by the flooding. Ten people died and over 3,500 houses were directly affected.[13] Meanwhile, largely due to overfishing, the herring industry fell into decline. Tourism also suffered and that decline became acute in the 1970s following the expansion of package holidays to the sun in Spain and Italy. Once-flourishing bed and breakfasts (B&Bs) and hotels in Victorian and Edwardian villas in the Town struggled for business.[14] Many, including the House of this book, have been turned into HMOs, now lived in by EU migrant workers (see Section D).

2. Socioeconomic context of the Town

Today, Great Yarmouth experiences very high levels of deprivation. Thirteen of its neighbourhoods are ranked in the top 10 per cent of areas of relative deprivation nationally, with some central wards listed among the most deprived neighbourhoods in the UK.[15] Among working-age residents, 20 per cent are in receipt of at least one out-of-work benefit. In some urban areas such as Central Northgate and Nelson, this figure is more than 55 per

---

[9] Time and Tide Museum information display (August 2022).

[10] See, for example: A. Hedges, *Great Yarmouth as it Was* (Nelson: Hendon Publishing, 1973); F. Meeres, *Yarmouth & Gorleston through Time* (Stroud: Amberley Publishing, 2009), 17.

[11] Ibid.

[12] C. Tooke, *Great Yarmouth: A Second Selection* (Stroud: The History Press, 2013), 77.

[13] Time and Tide Museum information display, n 9.

[14] *Select Committee on Regenerating Seaside Towns and Communities Report of Session 2017–19. The Future of Seaside Towns* HL Paper 320, available at: https://publications.parliament. uk/pa/ld201719/ldselect/ldseaside/320/320.pdf, accessed 29 January 2022, 61.

[15] See the Norfolk Insight website, available at: www.norfolkinsight.org.uk/, accessed 2 February 2022.

cent.[16] The proportion of residents aged 16–64 years who claim benefits/
Universal Credit is almost double the national average.[17] The average income
in Great Yarmouth is £23,600, which compares unfavourably with areas just
ten kilometres inland where the average is £33,800.[18] Some 17 per cent of
households experience fuel poverty (this goes to up 25 per cent in the Nelson
ward[19]), compared with 15.6 per cent in Norfolk as a whole and 13.2 per
cent in England.[20] In the borough of Great Yarmouth, which includes the
Town and surrounding villages, 20 per cent of children are living in low-
income families[21] (24.4 per cent in the Nelson ward) compared with 12.0
per cent in Norfolk and 14.7 per cent in England.[22] Residents in the Town
also have low levels of educational attainment with 26.5 per cent having
no formal qualifications, ranking sixth worst in the country.[23] Similarly,
the Town was the lowest ranked in England and Wales for residents with
Education Level 4[24] or above, with only 18.2 per cent of residents holding
a university-level qualification.[25]

Research shows that the towns already experiencing deprivation were
hit the hardest by the UK's austerity policy, and seaside towns like Great
Yarmouth were particularly badly affected.[26] Beatty and Fothergill show
a £610 loss per resident (working-age adult) in Great Yarmouth (2014–
2015).[27] Funding for community development programmes almost entirely
dried up after 2010, meaning support for those most deprived and affected

---

[16] Ibid.
[17] See the Norfolk Insight website, available at: https://www.norfolkinsight.org.uk/econ
omy-and-employment/reports/#/view-report/215592c79f7843158bc3c89615cf60c4/
E07000145/G2 , accessed 01 December 2023.
[18] J. Treadwell, 'Troubled waters: tackling the crisis on England's coast' *Onward*, available
at: www.ukonward.com/wp-content/uploads/2023/09/Troubled-Waters-Tackling-the-
crisis-on-Englands-coast.pdf, accessed 22 September 2023, 20.
[19] 'Deprivation – Nelson ward – report builder' *Norfolk Insight* (2020), available at: www.
norfolkinsight.org.uk/deprivation/reports/#/view-report/e52c6f125f644323a2a9580ba
51f811e/E05005795/G7, accessed 10 February 2023.
[20] Ibid.
[21] Absolute low-income is defined as a family whose equivalized income is below 60 per
cent of the 2010/2011 median income adjusted for inflation.
[22] Norfolk Insight, n 15.
[23] 'Education, England and Wales: Census 2021' *Office for National Statistics* (2022), available
at: www.ons.gov.uk/peoplepopulationandcommunity/educationandchildcare/bulletins/
educationenglandandwales/census2021, accessed 10 February 2023.
[24] Level 4 sits above the highest level of secondary education.
[25] N 23.
[26] C. Beatty and S. Fothergill, 'The local and regional impact of the UK's welfare reforms'
(2014) 7 *Cambridge Journal of Regions, Economy and Society* 63.
[27] Ibid, 72.

by the cuts was lost.[28] Great Yarmouth was one of the pilot areas for the rollout of Universal Credit in 2014/2015. As we will discuss in Chapter 6, the impact of delays with payments and various problems with the new system had a serious impact on residents; foodbank usage in the Town increased by 200 per cent at that time.[29]

Employment is a particular issue in Great Yarmouth (see Chapter 4) since much of the work is seasonal: tourism in the summer months and turkey processing in winter. Those who do earn higher wages tend to live in the nearest city, Norwich, commuting in and out each day.[30] In addition, Great Yarmouth is poorly served by transport connections. There are no motorways in Norfolk (it is often said that the nearest motorway to the Town is in the Netherlands). A single arterial road, the nine-mile single carriageway Acle Straight, serves the Town and this is often jammed. All this adds to a sense of the Town being remote.

3. Phases of migration to the Town

3.1 Earlier migration to the Town

As we have seen, there is a long history of migration to the Town, including the Scottish 'herring girls' up to the 1950s. This was followed by Greek Cypriots in the postwar period whose arrival was viewed, at least with hindsight, as adding 'a welcome diversity to the modern town'.[31] The Socratous family 'established the Rainbow Corner and Café Au Lait restaurants in 1947, and Loucas Chryssafi who set up the Savoy restaurant in the 1950s'.[32] In 1967, the Church of England entrusted St Peter's Church (on the Street) to the growing Greek Orthodox community. The church, now dedicated to Saint Spyridon,[33] hosts a Greek and Greek Cypriot mass every week and community coffee mornings and other events, as well as running a Greek school for young children.[34]

---

[28] Interview with former community development worker in Great Yarmouth (online, March 2022).

[29] T. Bristow, 'We're being used as guinea pigs' – impact of universal credit welfare revolution felt hardest in Yarmouth' *Eastern Daily Press* (2 December 2016), available at: www.edp24. co.uk/news/we-re-being-used-as-guinea-pigs-impact-of-universal-936014, accessed 6 January 2023.

[30] See C. Barnard and F. Costello, 'When (EU) migration came to Great Yarmouth' (2023) 18 *Contemporary Social Science* 154.

[31] Meeres (2009), n 10, 9.

[32] Meeres, n 3, 198.

[33] A. Benns, B. Catchpole and C. Williams, *The Holy Church of St Spyridon in Great Yarmouth* (Great Yarmouth, The Holy Church of St Spyridon).

[34] Interview with church leader (Great Yarmouth, October 2021).

A different type of migration occurred in the late 1990s and very early 2000s: given the availability of cheap accommodation, Great Yarmouth became a dispersal area for London boroughs looking to relocate asylum seekers – predominantly from Kosovo but also from Russia, Kenya, Sri Lanka, Guinea-Bissau, Angola, Turkey, Afghanistan and Macedonia.[35] One previous asylum seeker said: "When we came, there were three rundown B&Bs filled with asylum seekers. And we were literally the only non-White population in Great Yarmouth."[36] She says she and her husband were put on a train in London to take them to Great Yarmouth, but they had no idea where in England that was.

The placing of vulnerable asylum seekers in the Town, without any wraparound support, prompted some community members to set up the charity GYROS in 1998.[37] GYROS has been working to support 'newcomers' to the Town ever since, now primarily EU migrants but also more recently other newly arrived asylum seekers. It is the charity we have been working with (Section E).

3.2 Portuguese migration to the Town

For some time following the UK's accession to the EU, there was little migration to and from the UK under the free movement rules, particularly Article 45 Treaty on the Functioning of the European Union (TFEU) on free movement of workers and Article 49 TFEU on freedom of establishment (see Chapter 3). This changed with the accession of Portugal to the EU in 1986. Local employers looking for farm and factory workers saw Portugal as an important source of labour. This recruitment 'coincided with a negative cycle in the Portuguese economy that started in 2001'.[38] The poultry producer Bernard Matthews opened recruitment offices in Lisbon due to its 'satisfaction with established Portuguese employees, Portugal's EU status and its high unemployment'.[39] The company offered workers 'a good salary, transport and accommodation'.[40] It even hired a housing officer

---

[35] Government is repeating this policy today. See D. Grimmer, 'Judge blocks Great Yarmouth hotel use for asylum seekers' *Great Yarmouth Mercury* (21 December 2022), available at: www.greatyarmouthmercury.co.uk/news/23206572.judge-blocks-great-yarmouth-hotel-use-asylum-seekers/, accessed 21 December 2022.

[36] Interview with a former asylum seeker housed in the Town (Great Yarmouth, September 2020).

[37] For more, see GYROS' website at: www.gyros.org.uk/, accessed 27 January 2022.

[38] J.C.P. Almeida and D. Corkill 'Portuguese migrant workers in the UK: a case study of Thetford, Norfolk' (2010) 26 *Portuguese Studies*, 28.

[39] ' "Bootiful" Portuguese boost Bernard Matthews' *The Times* (16 September 2004).

[40] Almeida and Corkhill (2010), n 38, 34, 30.

to support employees moving into B&B accommodation in towns such as Great Yarmouth.[41]

Unlike some of the later Eastern European communities, those migrating from Portugal tended to have relatively low standards of education and skills, including English language skills.[42] Bernard Matthews ensured 'all company literature is published in English and Portuguese. The company also organised language courses for Portuguese workers to learn English and for other nationalities to learn Portuguese.'[43] However, the GYROS data still shows significant demand for English language support for their Portuguese clients.[44]

It was not just Portuguese citizens coming from Portugal; the citizens of a number of African, South American and Southeast Asian countries with Portuguese nationality have exercised free movement rights too.[45] Some have never lived in Portugal, as was the case with Rosa, an East Timorese Portuguese national who came to the UK and found employment as a care worker (Box 2.1). The 'Portuguese' community, given the diversity of sending countries, is therefore not one homogenous group within Great Yarmouth. Nationals from each Lusophone country bring their own language, dialect, culture, heritage, customs and practices. This raises a number of different issues, including health-related issues. For example, the local James Paget Hospital appointed a specialist in female genital mutilation (FGM)[46] following the arrival of Portuguese nationals from countries in which FGM is practised.[47]

Box 2.1: Rosa's story

Rosa is an East Timorese Portuguese national. She and her family survived civil war in East Timor, though their lives were badly affected by it and the family was divided, with some living in Indonesia while Rosa, her mother and brother lived in East Timor. When she was 19, she was invited by the school priest at her Catholic boarding school to

---

41 *The Times*, n 39.
42 Almeida and Corkhill (2010), n 38, 30.
43 *The Times*, n 39.
44 Barnard and Costello (2023), n 30.
45 Such as Angola, Mozambique, Guinea-Bissau, East Timor and Brazil.
46 See James Paget University Hospitals NHS Foundation Trust, *Female Genital Mutilation (FGM) Reporting and Safeguarding Policy*, available at: www.jpaget.nhs.uk/media/472 540/Female-Genital-Mutilation-FGM-reporting-and-safeguarding-policy.pdf, accessed 2 February 2022.
47 On new cases of FGM in Norfolk, see: G. Scott, 'New cases of female genital mutilation in Norfolk' *Eastern Daily Press* (13 June 2018), available at: www.edp24.co.uk/news/hea lth/fgm-norfolk-1230014, accessed 2 February 2022.

study theology in the Philippines. From the Philippines, she travelled to Italy to become a nun. She studied for four years before deciding to work as a carer. At this point, her mother's cousin contacted her to ask if she would like to come to England. She travelled to Portugal, though only to organize her passport before flying to London Stansted Airport. Her cousin's friend met her at Stansted, using photographs to recognize each other as they had not met previously. They travelled together by bus to Great Yarmouth. Rosa has lived in Great Yarmouth for over ten years now, and she met her husband (also East Timorese) in the Town. They now have two children. Rosa speaks Tetum (an East Timorese language), Portuguese, Italian and now English. When she first arrived in Great Yarmouth, she worked as a care worker.

There is an unspoken hierarchy within the Portuguese community in Great Yarmouth. Mariana, a Mozambican Portuguese national, said that "there is always this idea, of [Portuguese] being better". She said that the East Timorese community can be seen as "not really Portuguese – they just have the passport. Because they don't even speak Portuguese."[48] This can lead to discrimination from within the nationality group. Mariana described the discrimination and abuse her family experienced from the Portuguese community when they first arrived in Lisbon after fleeing civil war in Mozambique.[49]

Within the county of Norfolk, 42 per cent of all Portuguese nationals who applied for EUSS status live in Great Yarmouth.[50] The Town has the highest percentage (32 per cent) of Portuguese nationality applications (relative to total applications) for the EUSS of any local authority area in the country.[51] The long-term impact of this Portuguese presence can be readily observed in Great Yarmouth, which now has numerous Portuguese cafes, restaurants, festivals, community groups and supermarkets. The cafes and supermarkets act as meeting points for the local Portuguese community. There is little evidence of cross-community involvement in these cafes (that is, neither Great Yarmouth locals nor other non-Portuguese nationals go to the cafes). Abranches et al note that Portuguese nationals often stand on the street, drinking coffee and smoking, and this creates fear, even among other migrant communities.[52] This point is also made by the police (Section C).

[48] Interview with Mariana (Great Yarmouth, August 2022).
[49] Ibid.
[50] Home Office, 'EU Settlement Scheme Statistics' *Gov.uk*, available at: www.gov.uk/government/collections/eu-settlement-scheme-statistics, accessed 3 October 22.
[51] Ibid.
[52] M. Abranches, U. Theuerkauf, C. Scott and C. White, 'Cultural violence in the aftermath of the Brexit Referendum: manifestations of post-racial xenoracism' (2021) 44 *Ethnic and Racial Studies* 2885.

Figure 2.1: Country of birth (excluding United Kingdom) of residents in Great Yarmouth, 2021

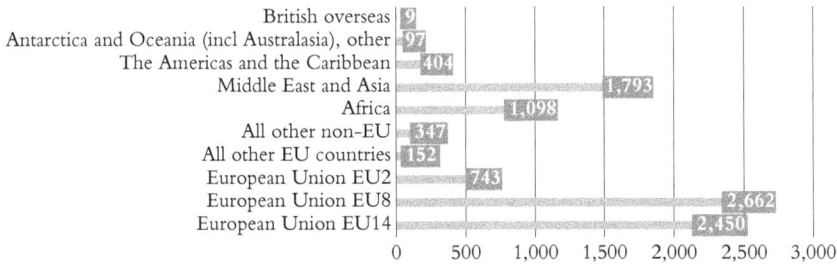

Source: Census, 2021

3.3 Central and Eastern European migration to the Town

In 2004, the EU8 countries joined the EU, namely Poland, Lithuania, Latvia, Estonia, the Czech Republic, Slovakia, Hungary and Slovenia (as well as Cyprus and Malta). While most EU member states introduced some form of restriction on their free movement until 2011, Sweden, Ireland and the UK did not and this led to a significant number of these EU migrants coming to the UK and Ireland, mainly for work.[53] According to Census data for 2021, in Great Yarmouth EU8 nationals represent the largest non-British group in the Town (Figure 2.1),[54] while EUSS applications data for June 2023 suggests the Portuguese represent the largest incoming group (Figure 2.2).

Those moving from Central and Eastern European countries tended to be better educated. Many believed in the 'any job, better job, dream job' migration–employment trajectory in the UK.[55] This meant they accepted jobs below their skills level when they first moved to the UK and then worked towards jobs more suited to their skills. For example, Lina gained a master's degree in linguistics in Lithuania but came to the UK to work in a chicken factory. Her English teacher (also from Lithuania) worked as a cleaner in the factory while, at the same time, working towards another postgraduate degree in the UK so that she could find work as a teacher.

Our Lithuanian and Latvian interviewees described paying someone in their home country anything from £300 to £1,000 to help them move to

---

[53] C. Barnard, *The Substantive Law of the EU: The Four Freedoms* (Oxford: Oxford University Press, 2022), 238–239.

[54] 'Country of birth (detailed)' *Office for National Statistics* (2021), available at: www.ons.gov.uk/datasets/TS012/editions/2021/versions/1, accessed 10 February 2023.

[55] V. Parutis, '"Economic migrants" or "middling transnationals"? East European migrants' experiences of work in the UK' (2012) 52 *International Migration* 36, 41.

Figure 2.2: Most numerous nationalities in applications to the EUSS from Great Yarmouth, June 2023

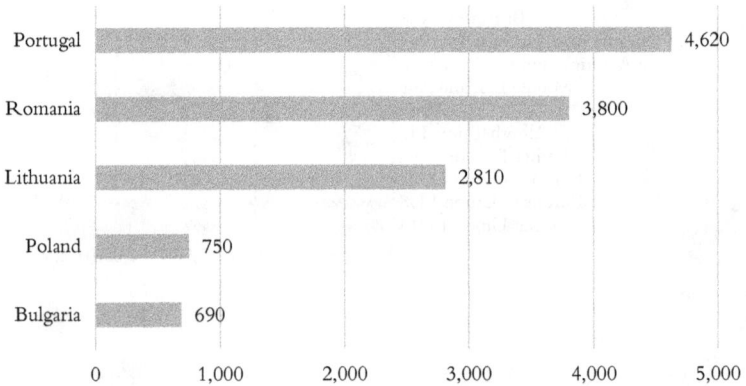

Source: EUSS Statistics https://www.gov.uk/government/collections/eu-settlement-scheme-statistics

the UK and find work. They would often be required to work off this debt after arrival in the UK. Like Darius (Box 1.1), they talk about being picked up in a van at Stansted and driven to Great Yarmouth, where they were placed in shared accommodation. In the House, Rasa, a Latvian woman in her sixties, said that on the night she arrived in the Town, she slept in the living room of a caravan with six other people – men and women – in the same clothes she had travelled in. At 4 am they were brought to the chicken factory to work. Her subsequent accommodation was a room in a 'hotel' shared with one other person (see chapters 4 and 5).

Like the Portuguese nationals before them, the Central and Eastern European communities living in Great Yarmouth are now much more established than in 2004. There are a number of Polish and Lithuanian supermarkets and shops and a Lithuanian letting agent, and for a time there was a Polish language Catholic mass. Yet these communities still largely keep themselves to themselves, due in part to the long hours they work (see Chapter 4).

3.4 Romanian and Bulgarian migration to the Town

When Romania and Bulgaria joined the EU in 2007, the UK placed transitional restrictions on free movement into the UK for these EU2 nationals;[56]

---

[56] 'Transitional controls had little impact on Romanians' and Bulgarians' access to UK benefits' *The Migration Observatory at the University of Oxford* (21 February 2014), available at: https://migrationobservatory.ox.ac.uk/press/transitional-controls-had-little-impact-on-romanians-and-bulgarians-access-to-uk-benefits/, accessed 2 February 2022.

those restrictions ended in 2014. After that, Romanians became an important source of labour for local factories and farms, particularly Roma Romanians,[57] mainly recruited in country by agencies. GYROS reports that of its total client group (covering Great Yarmouth and Ipswich, Suffolk) in 2021, about 6 per cent self-identified as Roma.[58] This group experiences significant vulnerability, including literacy issues. The Roma Support Group says illiteracy within the Roma community affects as many as 1 in 5 people[59] (with 3 in 5 'functionally illiterate'[60]), compared with 1 in 100 of their Romanian national counterparts.[61] As one police officer said:

> 'So, speaking to the management agency [which] brought the people over … [t]hey were basically saying because of Brexit looming, they couldn't recruit from Lithuania, Portugal, and, actually, this is where they would normally go. So, they went to Romania, and engaged with a community that they hadn't before, which was Romanian gypsies. That's how they identified themselves. And so they brought them over and they are a very identifiable community. And their education level was below the workers we normally have, their grasp of English just below, their social skills were below because of how Romanian gypsies are treated within their own country. They don't access education …. And what this gave us was a very identifiable new community within Great Yarmouth, who have their own cultural … identity.'[62]

Some of the issues raised by the arrival of Roma Romanians (and Bulgarians) in the Town are considered in Section 4.

As for Bulgarian workers, the two couples in our focus group said they had come to the UK following a call from a friend telling them there was work available through an agency operating in the Town centre. After they arrived, they were told they could receive a payment of £100 for each person they recruited from Bulgaria. Both couples were also Roma. Neither could read

---

[57] G. Wemyss and K. Cassidy, ' "People think that Romanians and Roma are the same": everyday bordering and the lifting of transitional controls' (2017) 40 *Ethnic and Racial Studies* 1132.

[58] GYROS database: equal opportunities monitoring, 2020–2021.

[59] House of Lords Public Services Committee, 'Uncorrected oral evidence: access to public services for the Gypsy, Roma and Traveller' (2 February 2022), available at: https://committees.parliament.uk/oralevidence/3402/pdf/, accessed 23 November 2023, 2.

[60] Ibid, 2. Functional illiteracy is defined as reading and writing skills that are inadequate to manage daily tasks involving reading skills beyond a basic level.

[61] 'Learning and skills | Youth and adult literacy rates' *UNICEF* (June 2022), available at: https://data.unicef.org/topic/education/learning-and-skills/, accessed 6 January 2022.

[62] Interview with local police officer (Great Yarmouth, November 2021).

or write in their own language, let alone speak or write any English. They did not understand their contracts but had been told they had to work 48 hours per week (although they were on zero-hours contracts). They said they lived in accommodation with approximately 100 people, each couple sharing a small room; they shared bathroom and kitchen facilities with 10–14 people on their floor.[63] They did not know how much their rent was, as it was taken directly from their pay, but they thought the room they shared cost approximately three hours' work per week each.

As Figure 2.2 shows, in Great Yarmouth, Romanian nationals now constitute the second largest group (after Portuguese nationals) who have made applications for EUSS. This fits with the national picture, as Romanian nationals are now the group with the highest number of applications to the EUSS in the UK, with more than 1.5 million applications. The national figure for Bulgarian nationals is 421,870.[64]

4. Effect of migration on the Town

Census data for 2021 shows that outside of London, the East of England has had the highest increase (3.9 per cent) in residents not born in the UK.[65] As we have noted, they came for work:[66] employers in East Anglia needed workers in agriculture, especially for fruit picking and work in food processing, particularly poultry factories.[67] These jobs entail labour-intensive, low-paid work with long, antisocial shifts. This is often agency work and (more recently) tends to be based on zero-hours contracts.[68] Local people have not wanted this often short-term and low-paid work,[69] and EU migrants have, up until Brexit, filled the gap.

Although the local communities and migrant communities lead separate – and largely segregated – lives, the arrival of large numbers of relatively poor EU migrants in a short space of time to a town already suffering significant

---

[63] Bulgarian factory worker focus group (Great Yarmouth, December 2022).

[64] 'EU Settlement Scheme quarterly statistics' *Gov.uk* (June 2023), available at: www.gov. uk/government/statistics/eu-settlement-scheme-quarterly-statistics-june-2023, accessed 22 September 2023.

[65] See 'The changing picture of long-term international migration, England and Wales: Census 2021' *Office for National Statistics* (2023), available at: www.ons.gov.uk/peopl epopulationandcommunity/populationandmigration/internationalmigration/articles/thec hangingpictureoflongterminternationalmigrationenglandandwales/census2021#main-poi nts, accessed 10 February 2023.

[66] Almeida and Corkill (2010), n 38, 30–31.

[67] Ibid, 30.

[68] C. Barnard and A. Ludlow 'Enforcement of employment rights by EU-8 migrant workers in employment tribunals' (2016) 45 *Industrial Law Journal* 1.

[69] Almeida and Corkhill (2010), n 38, 30.

deprivation added to the suspicion and hostility[70] which predated both Brexit and the referendum.[71] There were concerns among local people that already pressed public services would be spread even more thinly and that the identity of the Town was changing.[72] The Roma Romanian community was a particular source of concern for local people.[73] The local police cited an incident where banks reported that people were huddled around a cash machine but only one person was obtaining cash. This created suspicion, aggravated by rumours of a child abduction that was circulating on social media at the time:

> when we drilled down it was because of their maths and their English grasp, one person would know how to use the cash machine. So that one person was using multiple cards but obtaining the cash, and then we had ... baby-snatching rumours going around in the communities, which was driven mainly on Facebook. And, I mean, and that was just bizarre, because we had no reported children stolen.[74]

The police said that the Roma community were very visibly spending time together in the streets and in the Town centre, and this made suspicion worse. This was explained in part by the fact that their accommodation had little, if any, social space where residents could meet (see Chapter 5).[75]

The local hostility to Romanian nationals is also seen at national level. Fox et al say that Romanians have 'figured prominently in the public consciousness and (tabloid) media as objects of fear, scorn and contempt' and, as a community, they have often borne the brunt of public anxiety over 'East European' migration.[76] This reveals, in stark terms, the well-researched phenomenon of 'desirable' or 'undesirable' migrants.[77] While Eastern Europeans and particularly Romanians fell into the 'undesirable' category, Greek Cypriots are (now) seen as desirable.[78] For example, Abranches et al talk of William, a local government

---

[70] A. Rzepnikowska, 'Racism and xenophobia experienced by Polish migrants in the UK before and after Brexit vote' (2019) 45 *Journal of Ethnic and Migration Studies* 61.

[71] J.M. Lafleur and E. Mescoli 'Creating undocumented EU migrants through welfare: a conceptualization of undeserving and precarious citizenship' (2018) 52 *Sociology* 480.

[72] Interview with former Great Yarmouth Borough Council worker (online, March 2022).

[73] P. Clahane, 'The false child abduction rumours against Romanians in Great Yarmouth' *BBC News* (7 May 2019), available at: www.bbc.co.uk/news/av/uk-england-norfolk-48155614, accessed 22 September 2023.

[74] N 62; ibid.

[75] N 62; ibid.

[76] J.E. Fox, L. Moroşanu and E. Szilassy, 'Denying discrimination: status, "race" and the Whitening of Britain's new Europeans' (2015) 41 *Journal of Ethnic and Migration Studies* 729, 735.

[77] J.E. Fox, L. Moroşanu and E. Szilassy, 'The racialization of the new European migration to the UK' (2012) 46 *Sociology* 680, 682.

[78] Ibid.

officer, who recalled the arrival of Greek Cypriots during the 1970s as a positive source of cultural diversity and economic incentive:

> Near enough all the restaurants along the seafront were owned by Greek families and ... no hassle, no trouble. .... They brought the restaurants, they brought the gentlemen standing outside with the menus, you know .... They've brought lots of different skills to Great Yarmouth.[79]

The borough of Great Yarmouth had the fifth-highest Leave vote in the 2016 EU referendum. Free movement was not the only reason for the vote to leave the EU, but as Goodwin and Milazzo suggest, it was an important one.[80] The Brexit vote – and the UK government's 'levelling up' agenda – has brought renewed focus on, and money to, the Town.[81] The Venetian Waterways on the seafront (built in 1926) have been fully restored,[82] the Winter Gardens (built in 1904), which are the UK's only surviving winter gardens, are benefiting from a £10 million facelift,[83] the BBC Concert Orchestra has taken up a three-year residence in the Town,[84] Banksy left his footprint on the walls in summer 2021[85] and millions are being spent on the Market Place regeneration,[86] a Third River Crossing[87] and a new Marina Leisure Centre.[88] Meanwhile, the Town is developing expertise in

[79] Abranches et al (2021), n 52, 2885.
[80] M. Goodwin and C. Milazzo, 'Taking back control? Investigating the role of immigration in the 2016 vote for Brexit' (2017) 19 *The British Journal of Politics and International Relations* 450, 451.
[81] For more, see: A. Dickson, 'Brex on the beach: UK seaside revival gives hope to Leave voters' *Politico* (6 May 2021), available at: www.politico.eu/article/brexit-staycation-england-beaches-holiday-coronavirus-crisis-boris-johnson/, accessed 10 February 2023.
[82] For more, see 'Welcome to the waterways' *The Waterways, Great Yarmouth*, available at: https://venetianwaterways.com/, accessed 23 November 2023.
[83] See: 'Great Yarmouth Winter Gardens given £10m lottery funding' *BBC News* (13 July 2021), available at: www.bbc.co.uk/news/uk-england-norfolk-57807909, accessed 10 February 2023.
[84] For more, see: 'BBC Concert Orchestra to take up residency in Great Yarmouth' *BBC News* (January 2022), available at: www.bbc.co.uk/news/uk-england-norfolk-60163682, accessed 2 February 2022.
[85] 'New "Banksy" artwork appears at Great Yarmouth model village' *BBC News* (9 August 2021), available at: www.bbc.co.uk/news/uk-england-norfolk-58143164, accessed 10 February 2023.
[86] 'Your new marketplace: updated designs' *Great Yarmouth Borough Council* (20 March 2022), available at: www.great-yarmouth.gov.uk/market-place, accessed 10 February 2023.
[87] 'Project aims and funding' *Norfolk County Council*, available at: www.norfolk.gov.uk/roads-and-transport/major-projects-and-improvement-plans/great-yarmouth/third-river-crossing, accessed 10 February 2023.
[88] J. Weeds, 'Great Yarmouth's £26m Marina Centre officially opens', *Eastern Daily Press* (5 August 2022), available at: www.edp24.co.uk/news/20610688.great-yarmouths-26m-marina-centre-officially-opens/, accessed 17 March 2023.

Figure 2.3: Aerial view of Great Yarmouth and St Peter's Road

Note: The arrows, pointing to the road, were added by the authors.

Source: Copyright John Fielding Aerial Images (permission has been obtained from the photographer for use of this figure)

wind turbines, and this has brought higher-skilled EU migrants to Great Yarmouth,[89] at least temporarily.[90]

C. The Street

Having looked at the Town's history of migration and socioeconomic profile, we turn now to St Peter's Road, the Street of our research, where many EU migrant workers live in HMOs, like the House of our research, which is located just off the Street (see Section D). Situated at the heart of the Town, St Peter's Road leads directly from the seafront to the South Quay (Figure 2.3). It hosts a number of businesses (European and Kurdish as well as British), cafes (Portuguese), mini supermarkets (Lithuanian, Polish, Portuguese, English), hairdressers, barbers, newsagents (there are five on this road alone), fast food shops – including a chicken takeaway, a Vietnamese

---

[89] M. Shields, 'Great Yarmouth: how offshore wind is re-energising seaside town' *BBC News* (7 May 2019), available at: www.bbc.co.uk/news/uk-england-norfolk-48029440?intlink_ from_url=&link_location=live-reporting-story, accessed 10 February 2023.

[90] 'Great Yarmouth reveals aim to be "UK strategic offshore port"' *ReNewsBiz* (20 October 2020), available at: https://renews.biz/63890/great-yarmouth-reveals-ambition-to-be-uk-strategic-offshore-port/, accessed 7 February 2022.

Figure 2.4: St Peter's Road with a view of St Spyridon

Source: image authors' own

restaurant, a Chinese takeaway and a fish and chip shop (Roger's Fish and Chips, family owned since 1923) – some pubs, a primary school, a church (St Spyridon, mentioned in Section B.3.1 and visible in Figure 2.4), a betting shop, a letting agent (Lithuanian) and a brothel (English). There are a mix of houses, some privately owned but mainly rented accommodation, particularly HMOs.

The layout of the Street, as well as its diverse mix of businesses and uses, has created problems. The police officer we interviewed said:

> 'It's a long straight road which lends itself to fast acceleration. A tight bend at the top lends itself to conflict. The parking at the top lends itself to more conflict. The shop at the top is open if not 24 hours, then it's open late, which means there's people coming and going early hours. We've got, dare I say it, a brothel on there, which isn't technically a brothel, because there is only ever one girl in there, so it is not against the law … it's not that busy any more.'

The officer also said that the seafront end is "inherently noisy because of the arcades"[91] and that there is a "feeling of unsafety", which was exacerbated

---

[91] Interview with local police officer (Great Yarmouth, November 2021).

by the fatal stabbing of a 23-year-old Portuguese man in broad daylight in February 2023.[92] For some, St Peter's Road is considered a 'no-go' area, especially at night. The police officer also said that local people feel unsafe in the Street when they cannot understand the languages being spoken and they see groups of EU nationals gathered together.[93]

St Peter's Road sits within Nelson ward,[94] which, together with Central and Northgate ward, has the highest density of housing[95] and the highest proportion of rental properties in Great Yarmouth borough. Nelson is one of the most deprived wards in Great Yarmouth. Parts of Nelson rank as low as 39th worst of 32,844 wards in England in terms of deprivation.[96] This deprivation affects residents' life chances. For example, 'life expectancy among men in Nelson ward is 71.6 years, while among men in the nearby village of Fleggburgh, also in the borough but the least deprived ward, it is 82.2 years'.[97] Nelson ward also has higher levels of economically inactive residents, at 38.3 per cent compared with 31.9 per cent in Norfolk and 30 per cent in England.[98] Some 46.4 per cent of residents aged 16–64 in Nelson are in receipt of Universal Credit (see Chapter 6), compared with 13.2 per cent in Norfolk and 14.3 per cent in England.[99]

The deprivation and poverty of the Street is not just a matter of comparative statistics. It is tangible in the crumbling facades of shops and houses (see Figure 2.4), the quantities of litter and discarded rubbish in doorways and on street corners, and the availability of bootleg cigarettes in the various newsagents and supermarkets.[100] This poverty is in stark contrast to the

---

[92] 'Police launch murder probe after fatal stabbing in Great Yarmouth' *BBC News* (9 February 2023), available at: www.bbc.co.uk/news/uk-england-norfolk-64574132, accessed 10 February 2023.

[93] Interview with local police officer (Great Yarmouth, November 2021).

[94] A 'ward' is defined as an administrative division of a city or borough that typically elects and is represented by a councillor or councillors. There are 17 wards across the borough of Great Yarmouth.

[95] 'Demos for thriving local economies project' *Barclays* (2020), available at: https:// home.barclays/content/dam/home-barclays/documents/who-we-are/our-strategy/ GREAT%20Y ARMOUTH%20l ife%20chances%20Nov%2020%20Final.pdf, accessed 10 February 2023.

[96] 'English indices of deprivation' *Gov.uk* (2019), available at: www.gov.uk/government/sta tistics/english-indices-of-deprivation-2019, accessed 10 February 2023.

[97] N 95.

[98] 'Economy report for Nelson (Great Yarmouth)' *Norfolk Insight*, available at: www.norfolk insight.org.uk/economy-and-employment/reports/#/view-report/47200c8cfb7b433ca ad9af5019a1b1dc/E05005795/G7, accessed 23 November 2023.

[99] Ibid.

[100] For more, see L. Coates 'Thousands of illegal cigarettes and alcohol seized in raids in Great Yarmouth and Norwich' *Eastern Daily Press* (16 January 2020), available at: www. edp24.co.uk/news/20725456.thousands-illegal-cigarettes-alcohol-seized-raids-great- yarmouth-norwich/, accessed 6 January 2022.

development and superficial improvements happening just a stone's throw away on the seafront (Section B.4). One community adviser described this as the "doughnut effect".[101] Money is invested into the new leisure centre and in the offshore wind energy economy and enterprise zones (the ring of the doughnut), while inner areas of Nelson (the hole in the centre of the doughnut) are ignored. He said that those living on St Peter's Road cannot afford to use the new leisure centre and that the money from the offshore sector does not stay in the Town.

D. The House

We turn now to the House that was the setting for our ethnographic work, an HMO just off St Peter's Road. The House itself dates from the 1860s and is a Grade II listed building (similar in style to the picture on the front cover).[102] The House was registered as an HMO[103] (at least five tenants lived there, forming more than one household and sharing a toilet, bathroom or kitchen facilities with other tenants), licensed over a decade ago, although its life as a shared rented house predates this. The House is central to our project (the researcher lived there and interviewed its residents and the landlord) and, of course, to the lives of its residents.[104] In this section, we describe the layout of the House and meet its residents (two couples and four individuals – all Lithuanian and Latvian nationals; Section 1). We also meet the landlord (Section 2).

1. The House and its residents

The House has three storeys. The ground floor had five rooms as well as an unused basement area, reached by a set of stairs, and an unfinished upstairs flat, reached via a back stairway, which had a cardboard sign saying 'construction site, no unauthorised entry'. The rooms were set out as follows: a studio (Room 1), a workshop/junk room, a shared bathroom[105] (Figure 2.5) and a communal laundry space. The House also had a guest room on the ground floor – an unusual feature for an HMO[106] – allowing

---

[101] Interview with former community development worker (online, March 2022).
[102] To respect the privacy of tenants living there, we have chosen not to reveal the exact location of the House.
[103] See 'Private Renting' *Gov.uk*, available at: www.gov.uk/private-renting/houses-in-multiple-occupation, accessed 23 October 2021.
[104] J. Moran, *Reading the Everyday* (Abingdon: Routledge, 2005) 132.
[105] S. Heath, K. Davies, G. Edwards and R. Scicluna, *Shared Housing, Shared Lives. Everyday Experiences Across the Life Course* (London: Routledge, 2018), 97; they note this scenario could cause conflict – and it did.
[106] Ibid, 89.

Figure 2.5: Bathroom on the ground floor, shared by tenants in Rooms 1, 3 and 4

Source: image authors' own

tenants to have friends and family (or indeed researchers) visit. The tenants took a previously unused room, cleared and painted it, and salvaged other furniture from around the House to turn it into a guest room that was available to all tenants and booked using a calendar which hung on the guest room door. This is a good example of a phenomenon witnessed elsewhere – tenants improving their space and ultimately the living conditions in the place where they live (see Chapter 5). Apart from the guest room there was no other communal space.[107] The space by the back door was used as a smoking area, although the residents also smoked in their rooms, leaning out of the windows as they did so. Five of the eight residents were smokers. People in the House lived quite separate lives, mostly keeping to their own (locked) rooms while not at work. Adomas said: "in our situation,

---

[107] Ibid, 83.

Figure 2.6: Unfinished flat on the first floor – Rasa (Room 3) has put one of her plants here for light

Source: image authors' own

we have a separate flat. There is nothing we share. We just share the washing machines. It's the only thing. We barely see them. All of them, they're working."

There was a single tenant (Ivo – male, fifties) living on the ground floor of the House, at the front, in a studio room with kitchen cupboards, a microwave and a kettle (Room 1). Ivo used the communal downstairs bathroom. On the first floor, there were two flats, one unfinished and in a state of disrepair (Figure 2.6) and the other occupied by a Lithuanian couple (Lina and Adomas, Room 2) and their cat. Lina (female, thirties) had lived in the House for more than three years and had been in the UK for more than five. Her partner, Adomas (thirties), had only recently joined the household (less than six months previously) after 11 years in the UK, having moved to Great Yarmouth from London after meeting Lina. Their flat had an en suite bathroom and separate kitchen/living area.

On the second floor, there was a self-contained studio room (Room 3), occupied by Camilla (female, fifties), a Lithuanian who had been in the UK for 16 years, and a flat (which we refer to as Room 4) with two rooms – a separate galley kitchen and a large bedroom/living room – occupied by Rasa (female, sixties), a Latvian who had been in the UK for 18 years. Rasa had lived in the House for ten years and Camilla for four years. Both women were single. Rasa and Camilla used the bathroom on the ground floor, sharing shower facilities with Ivo. However, in September 2021, they added a single toilet on their floor, with the help of Ivo, who had become the House handyman.[108] Rasa had recently repainted and recarpeted both her rooms, and Rasa and Camilla had put slip-prevention carpet tiles on the wooden stairs when Camilla was injured after tripping. Rasa said that the improvements were paid for by the landlord. She kept all paint cans and other decorating items so that she could use what was left over. To paint over the black mould on her kitchen ceiling, she created a colour by mixing all the paint pots left in the workshop room. Her view was: "It's better for me [and] it's not magnolia anyway – everything in England is magnolia!"[109] Edita noted the difference Rasa had made to the House since she moved in ten years earlier: "She's really made that house look cosy. You know. It's been a constant fight with Frank [the landlord] over it. Like, you know, it's not that he doesn't want to [make improvements] – I think he's just too poorly and old, I guess."

The top floor mirrored the layout of the floor below it. Vida (female, thirties), a Lithuanian tenant occupied a self-contained studio (which we call Room 5). She had lived in the UK, and the House, for less than two years, with a break in residency during the COVID-19 pandemic, when she returned to Lithuania. The final flat (which we call Room 6) contained two rooms – as on the lower floor, a galley kitchen and a large bedroom. This was occupied by a Latvian couple (Domantas – male, fifties; Terese – female, fifties) who had lived in the House for six years and had been in the UK for seven years. There was a shared toilet on this floor for the three residents on this level.

There was no Wi-Fi or central heating in the House. Residents relied on portable electric heaters. They shared laundry facilities – a single washing machine and a dryer, the latter being a more recent, and much-praised, addition. There was a bucket on top of the dryer to collect contributions of 50p per use.

The average age of residents in the House was 45, with ages ranging from 30 to over 60. One resident had pre-settled status; the rest had settled status.

---

[108] Interview with Rasa (Great Yarmouth, September 2021).
[109] Ibid.

Residents' view of their lives varied. Vida said: "My life is quite boring. Just working and living." Domantas said: "I quite enjoy my life in Great Yarmouth – I have work, I have somewhere to live and I visit places on weekends to have a rest from work life. During the week, it does feel as if it is only work and home." As we shall see later in the book, despite the poor condition of the House and the lack of facilities for residents, it was seen as a place of safety, and they feared being forced to leave if Frank was not able to accommodate them anymore.[110]

The researcher lived in the House for two months and was able to interview the residents and, to a limited degree, socialize with them. Given the importance of these interviews to our research, she was supported by Edita, a multilingual (English, Lithuanian, Latvian, Polish, Russian speaker) former resident, who had lived in the House for ten years, having left in 2019. Edita was also interviewed about her experiences of living in the House. Domantas and Terese's interviews were conducted in Lithuanian and translated into English. Terese said:

> 'I am not able to speak any English and I really wish it was otherwise. I have managed to learn some basic phrases, but that is all. I have bought CDs and books to study, but I have a feeling that the English language just doesn't want to "stick" to me.'[111]

Lack of opportunity to practise English was a common experience for those in low-skilled, low-paid work in the UK, because they mainly worked with other non-English speakers.[112] In fact, both Edita and Lina learnt another language – Polish for Lina/Lithuanian for Edita – while they were working in chicken factories, largely because their colleagues were Polish/Lithuanian speakers.

Rasa brought her Latvian–English dictionary to the interview. She had bought the dictionary when she came to the UK 18 years earlier; it is now well worn, with tape holding the spine together. Rasa said she did not even know the word 'hello' in English when she first arrived in the UK. She used to work her way through her dictionary whenever she was not at work, learning words page by page, cover to cover: "I came

---

[110] In fact, their concerns were realized the following year when Frank died and all the tenants were served notice to vacate the property. See the postscript to this book.

[111] Interview with Terese (Great Yarmouth, October 2021).

[112] A. Grzymala-Kazlowska, 'From connecting to social anchoring: adaptation and "settlement" of Polish migrants in the UK' (2018) 44 *Journal of Ethnic and Migration Studies* 252; C. Barnard, S. Fraser Butlin and F. Costello, 'The changing status of European Union nationals in the United Kingdom following Brexit: The lived experience of the European Union Settlement Scheme' (2021) 31 *Social & Legal Studies* 365, 370.

Figure 2.7: Rasa's English–Latvian dictionary

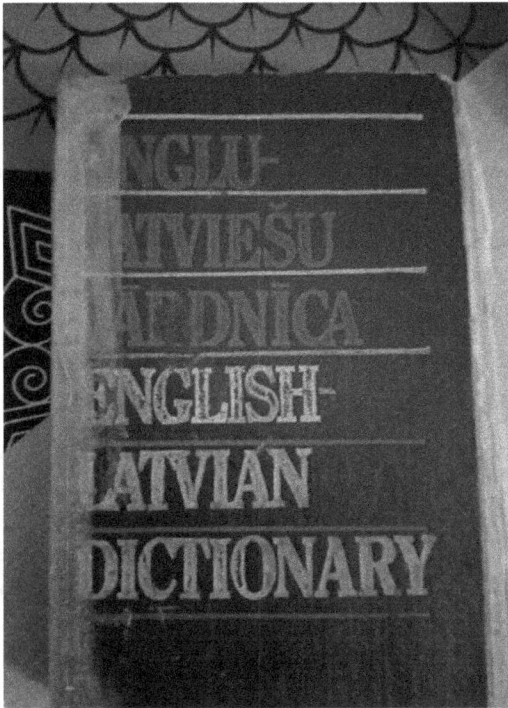

Source: image authors' own

with [a] brand new dictionary and now my dictionary looks like a Bible" (see Figure 2.7).[113]

During interviews, both Rasa and Camilla spoke in English, with a translator helping when they got stuck on a word or had difficulty explaining something. Lina, in her interview, mentioned that although she spoke fluent English, she got nervous when speaking to native English speakers and this led her to struggle to communicate. The younger Lithuanian residents (Lina, Adomas, Vida) had all learnt English at school in Lithuania; the older Lithuanian residents had learned Russian. However, Adomas said he struggled with English when he first came to the UK, although he did pick up functional English quickly: "I was studying [English] in Lithuania, but [it] didn't help me much when I came here. I was thinking [that] I know the language. When I came here, I was like … I know nothing."[114]

---

[113] Interview with Rasa (Great Yarmouth, September 2021).
[114] Interview with Adomas (Great Yarmouth, November 2021).

Irrespective of their English language skills, all residents were at a minimum bilingual, speaking Latvian/Lithuanian and Russian/English. As noted above, Lina, who had worked in a chicken factory for three years, had gained a master's in applied linguistics in Lithuania and spoke four languages. Edita spoke five languages, two of which she learned after moving to the UK.

Apart from Adomas, who worked in a bar on the seafront, all the residents had worked or were currently working in food processing factories – mostly chicken factories – in the surrounding areas. The time spent working in factories ranged from 3 to 13 years. Camilla and Edita met at work, and Lina and Vida worked together at chicken factories at different times. Their experiences are discussed in more detail in Chapter 4.

2. The landlord

The landlord, Frank, was British, born and raised in Birmingham but with Norfolk roots. His mother was from Norfolk, having moved away "during the war when she was 18 to work at the Spitfire factory in Birmingham as a draft woman".[115] He moved back to Norfolk with his wife when he was 30. He said he bought the House using money he inherited from his mother.[116] At the time of our research, he was in his eighties and very unwell, suffering from cancer and needing an oxygen tank throughout the day. Frank's wife was bed-bound. Both lived about 20 miles outside Great Yarmouth and were unable to visit the House. They had no children.

Frank said he was determined to have Eastern Europeans in the House, explaining that "the only worthwhile people were Eastern Europeans. They are always hard-working, conscientious, helpful, and no trouble." He said "they have fitted into England and English ways, want to learn the language, want to progress, and I feel I am part of their family in a lot of ways. But it all helps with good relationships." Frank had visited Latvia a number of times and was particularly close to both Edita and Rasa. Rasa helped Frank with the garden at his house. In Latvia, Frank had worked on the plumbing in the farmhouse of Edita's parents, and he had been a guest at her wedding. He had also taken Edita and her husband (Rasa's son) out 'beating' (that is, hunting/shooting) in Norfolk. In Frank's living room (where our interview took place) he displayed a framed picture of Edita and her husband sharing Christmas with him and his wife. He was happy with the makeup of the residents, saying "long may it continue to be little Lithuania. And little Latvia." Frank supported, and voted for, Brexit.

---

[115] Interview with Frank (Suffolk, September 2021).

[116] Although it later transpired that Frank may not have legally owned the House – see the postscript to this book.

Other groups did not fare so well in the House. Frank described more than one physical altercation he had had with previous tenants, who were non-EU nationals:

'Well, I must say I chucked a man out who was six foot something tall and as broad as the doorway, and I believe now he was, he had overstayed his working visa in England. His visa had run out. And if I had got on to the border authorities, he'd have been turned away. But I had to evict him over rent. And he was so slow in going, I kicked his shoes down the stairs and he turned to me, and I said: "Do you know what is going to happen next? You are going to follow them." Shaking I was. I wasn't really, but I, you know, I had that advantage that I didn't know at the time – he was illegal.'

He described another encounter with a resident who was also behind on his rent. Frank called the police in advance to let them know he was going to evict this tenant and was expecting some trouble. In the end, the tenant also phoned the police, reporting an assault after the altercation with Frank. Frank continued:

'So, I went up, knocked on his door. "I want you out now." I had already given him notice – he was behind with the rent. I was well within my rights. He wouldn't go. We ended up having a bit of a fight. I tried to throw him down the stairs, but he was like an eel. And from that, I did get a couple of good ones in. He went back into his room and shut himself in and phoned the police [to say] that he's been assaulted.'

Frank said that when he bought the House, he removed all the non-European (non-White) tenants, describing the House at the time as the "United Nations". Referring broadly to "Africans" in the House, he said he engaged in "ethnic cleansing … well, I got rid of everybody, but since then we have only had good people in there, who have been Latvian, Lithuanian and Eastern European."

Most tenants had moved in following personal recommendation from other residents. Work colleagues had lived in the House for many years. Frank said that this informal "buddy" referral system worked for the House. He left it up to his tenants to decide who lived there, "because ultimately it's them that's got to live with them, not me".[117] The residents paid between £60 and £125 per week in rent, depending on room size. This was collected in cash each week by Rasa, who acted as an informal manager and matriarch

---

[117] Interview with Frank (Suffolk, 20 September 2021).

of the block. All bills (electricity, water, Council Tax and television licence) were included in the rent, and Frank dealt with those. Rasa's rent was reduced in return for maintaining the communal areas, collecting the rent and sorting out any bills. Residents could ask for a rent receipt and even a tenancy agreement, but they rarely did.

E. The advice charity

Having described the Town, the Street, the House and its residents, we now turn to look at GYROS, the charity we have been working with. We begin by outlining its work (Section 1), before situating it in the broader context of the community advice sector in the UK (Section 2).

1. What is GYROS?

As noted earlier, GYROS was established in 1998 to provide help to asylum seekers placed by London boroughs in Great Yarmouth pending a decision on their application. Its client group is now predominantly EU nationals and their family members. GYROS offers a free holistic, multidisciplinary, multilingual advice service. It has (at the time of writing) 2 full-time staff (immigration advisers), 14 part-time staff and 5 volunteers (this number fluctuates). In Great Yarmouth, it offers a weekly drop-in (on Tuesdays), held in the disused Debenhams (department store) building in the Town centre, where clients are triaged and assigned a case worker based on their language requirements or, in more limited cases, on the specialism they need, such as an immigration adviser. Individual issues may be sorted out there and then (within a 15- to 30-minute window), but where this is not possible, clients are asked to come back for a follow-up appointment (lasting 40 to 60 minutes) the following Friday in the GYROS offices in the Town. On average, 30–50 people attend these drop-ins each week and about 20 follow-up appointments take place.

Every interaction with each client is entered into the GYROS database, which is now hosted by Charitylog.[118] Clients are asked to provide feedback and rate the service they received during every visit. Complex cases are discussed by staff in a weekly online meeting dedicated to these cases; this has also been attended by another charity, ACCESS (based in King's Lynn, Norfolk).[119] ACCESS and GYROS were in a delivery partnership, funded by the National Lottery during the life of this research. These hour-long meetings serve as a peer development exercise in which workers discuss

---

[118] See Charitylog's website at: www.charitylog.co.uk/, accessed 16 March 2023.
[119] 'About us' *ACCESS*, available at: www.accessmigrantsupport.org.uk/about-us/, accessed 10 February 2023.

what needs to be done to resolve their clients' issues and get advice from more senior workers.

GYROS advisers are not legally trained. Save for specialist immigration advice (accredited by the OISC), GYROS is a generalist advice and community service. Its staff have often come via the same migration pathways as their clients and they worked in the same factories as their clients when they first arrived in the UK. Many start as volunteers before being taken on as permanent staff. GYROS' largest client nationality groups are (in order) Portuguese, Romanian and Lithuanian, followed by (in much smaller numbers) Polish, Bulgarian and Latvian EU migrants; advice is offered in these languages. However, the most senior immigration advisers at GYROS, who work on more complex immigration cases, are English/Russian speakers only, so clients needing Level 2 OISC immigration advice will be assigned to one of these workers with a GYROS adviser to translate.

GYROS operates largely on a word-of-mouth basis: clients may refer friends and family members. Other professional agencies also refer clients to GYROS. During the COVID-19 pandemic, GYROS services went online, and during this time it had clients seeking advice from as far afield as Folkestone and Newcastle (other cities in England), and even Lisbon and Tunisia. In these cases, GYROS attempted to refer clients to support more local to them.

GYROS has a part-time director and a five-member board of trustees, which sets strategy. It holds Matrix accreditation for its general advice service. As noted earlier, two of its advisers have Level 2 OISC accreditation for immigration advice, two hold Level 1 accreditation and six hold Level 1 accreditation limited to the EUSS (Chapter 3). GYROS is also registered with the Financial Conduct Authority for debt advice but for some areas, such as Personal Independence Payment applications, it refers cases to DIAL, another specialist charity in Great Yarmouth (see Chapter 6). The quality of advice is checked via internal and external mechanisms. For general advice, case notes are subject to supervision and audit by the adviser's line manager; for accredited (OISC or Financial Conduct Authority) advice, quality is checked by the subject lead. In addition, annual or biannual audits of case work are undertaken by accrediting bodies – OISC for immigration advice and Matrix for advice work.

One of the biggest challenges facing GYROS is funding. Senior management in the charity speak of the constant need for "plate-spinning",[120] with GYROS running up to 20 funds in any 12-month period, spanning small grants to large, multi-partner ones. It receives money from charity funders such as the National Lottery or through funding hosted by the

---

[120] Interview with GYROS director (Great Yarmouth, February 2022).

Community Foundation (Norfolk, Suffolk). It also receives small grants from local authority budgets, such as recent funding to support Ukrainian nationals, and some limited private donations. It has one member of staff whose principal task is to raise funds. GYROS' annual running costs are between £300,000 and £350,000. There have been times where its advice service has stopped, albeit briefly, in Great Yarmouth when the money ran out. More frequently, GYROS has had to tweak the service it offers, depending on the funding received. For example, GYROS might receive funding to run a 'job club', meaning that all employment-related enquiries had to be diverted to it, hence removing 'employment' from its general advice service. This can also lead to gaps in the GYROS database as job club outcomes might have to be recorded separately in line with the needs of the funder of that service. GYROS also runs a café, previously in the Town's library but now in the Time and Tide Museum just off St Peter's Road. This generates 'unrestricted funds' that are used for a hardship fund for GYROS clients (Chapter 6).

The precarity of funding, while not uncommon in the third sector, raises the paradox that the more precarious the lives of those that GYROS helps, the more they need GYROS' service, a service which could be withdrawn at any time due to lack of funding.

2. GYROS and the community advice sector

In the UK, the general community advice sector is, to a large extent, synonymous with Citizens Advice (formerly Citizens Advice Bureau) and questions regarding use of Citizens Advice feature prominently in empirical research. For example, in Hazel Genn's *Paths to Justice*, most of the participants said they knew about Citizens Advice.[121] However, while most were aware of it, few knew about the breadth of its service; fewer still knew of any other advice centres that could be accessed, including law centres.[122] The scale of Citizens Advice's operation is completely different to that of GYROS. It is a multimillion-pound charity with a nationwide network of 265 independent local centres, which can access resources and back office support, including legal advice, from the central organization. Nevertheless, their 2020–2021 annual report reveals similarities and differences with GYROS in the types of help people sought. While their main inquiry, consumer problems (930,000), does not feature in the GYROS data at all, this was followed by inquiries with striking similarities to the GYROS data: benefits (700,000),

---

[121] H. Genn, *Paths to Justice: What People Do and Think about Going to Law* (Oxford: Hart Publishing, 1999), 76.
[122] Ibid.

debt (258,000), housing (256,000) and employment (247,000).[123] While Citizens Advice is the best-known advice charity in England, there are many others. Advice UK, the UK's largest support network for independent advice organizations, has almost 800 members. Their 2020–2021 impact report lists (in order) welfare benefits, debt, housing, immigration and employment as the most prevalent inquiries dealt with by their network members,[124] again showing a striking similarity with GYROS.

As mentioned, Citizens Advice advisers have access to legal advice (albeit sometimes only at a national, as opposed to local, level). GYROS, by contrast, does not, although they have in the past referred some cases to local Law Centres. GYROS therefore falls within the broader community advice sector, which gains its legitimacy from its cultural and biographical proximity to those it supports; GYROS advisers are trusted and embedded within communities, so more likely to work with individuals in more marginalized groups or those less likely to seek 'mainstream' legal advice, particularly due to language barriers.

F. Conclusion

In this chapter, we have provided the context for our research, describing the Town, the Street, the House. We have shown a declining seaside resort where the local residents face high levels of deprivation, and a street in a ward which is among the most deprived nationally, diverse in terms of ethnicity and nationality, with residents living mainly in poor-quality rented HMO accommodation, such as the House of our research. We also described the work of frontline advice charity GYROS, which supports EU migrant workers in Great Yarmouth, providing general advice. We saw that the absence of alternative, more formal, legal advice has meant that EU migrants are reliant on GYROS for specialized advice on immigration.

The reasons for setting the scene in this way[125] is to provide context for the results of interview and focus group research, combining to give rich data and 'thick' description.[126] The details of day-to-day living are what we heard, saw and sensed while gathering data.[127] We turn now to the thematic

---

[123] Citizens Advice, *Annual Report 2020/21*, available at: www.citizensadvice.org.uk/about-us/our-work/annual-reports/, accessed 22 September 2023.

[124] 'Our impact' *Advice UK*, available at: www.adviceuk.org.uk/influencing/our-impact/, accessed 22 September 2023.

[125] Following the grounded theory idea that 'all is data'; B. Glaser, *The Grounded Theory Perspective: Conceptualization Contrasted with Description* (Mill Valley, CA: Sociology Press, 2001), 145.

[126] K. Charmaz, *Constructing Grounded Theory* (Sage Publications, 2014), 23.

[127] Ibid, 3.

chapters: immigration, employment, housing, welfare and debt, and health. For our cohort, the everyday is punctuated with another commonality, their immigration status. Brexit brought intense focus on, and change for, EU nationals living in the UK. In the next chapter, we look at the introduction of the EUSS in 2019, which offers a new immigration status for EU nationals already living in the UK post Brexit, now a prerequisite for EU migrant workers to continue to live and work in the UK. The chapter discusses the issues with the operation of the scheme for low-skilled EU migrants with little English, such as the Roma Romanians referred to in this chapter, and what GYROS does to help.

3

Immigration and the European Union Settlement Scheme

A. Introduction

Prior to Brexit, because EU nationals living in the UK were exercising their EU right to free movement, they were not subject to any UK immigration control, except in limited circumstances.[1] While for some, free movement, mainly under Article 45 TFEU, had an aspirational element, since it allowed 'citizens to move to Warsaw, Marseille or Berlin for love, work, to learn a language',[2] many of GYROS' clients came for work in the chicken factories (chapters 4 to 7). EU free movement to the UK has now ended, following Brexit.[3] However, under Part Two of the UK–EU Withdrawal Agreement (WA), those who had already exercised their free movement rights by the time of Brexit would have their rights protected. In the UK, the formal mechanism to protect those rights – the EUSS[4] – was introduced in March 2019 in anticipation of the obligations under the WA to protect the residence rights of EU nationals (together with those from Norway, Iceland, Liechtenstein and Switzerland) and some non-EU family members (NEFMs) of EU nationals who had already exercised their free movement

---

[1]   While EU nationals were not subject to any limits on their free movement, member states could place controls on access to their public services.

[2]   F. De Witte, 'Freedom of movement is not simply an economic good but a bulwark against oppression' *LSE* (3 February 2016), available at: https://blogs.lse.ac.uk/brexit/2016/02/03/freedom-of-movement-is-not-simply-an-economic-good-but-a-bulwark-against-oppression/, accessed 10 March 2023.

[3]   Section 1 Immigration and Social Security Co-ordination (EU Withdrawal) Act 2020. J. Dennison and A. Geddes, 'Brexit and the perils of "Europeanised" migration' (2018) 25 *Journal of European Public Policy* 1137, 1141.

[4]   See Home Office, 'EU Settlement Scheme' *Gov.uk*, available at: https://www.gov.uk/government/collections/eu-settlement-scheme-applicant-information, accessed 17 November 2023.

to the UK. It allowed these groups (who we shall call 'EU+') to apply for settled status, while those with less than five years of residence could apply for pre-settled status up to 30 June 2021. Having one or other of these statuses – and maintaining that status – is now mandatory for lawful residence in the UK, and the gateway to accessing (or continuing) employment (which we discuss in Chapter 4), housing (Chapter 5), welfare benefits (Chapter 6) and healthcare (Chapter 7).

For the residents in the House, the EUSS had not been an issue (during fieldwork in Autumn 2021, post the deadline). Apart from one resident (Vida, who was fluent in English and was digitally literate), each of the other residents had already lived in the UK for more than five years, and all were working. This meant that they had been able to make applications for settled status, which they did either on their own or with the help of family members (Edita, for example, helped Rasa to make her application).[5] Vida was able to apply for pre-settled status. Our focus in this chapter is, therefore, on the people who went to GYROS for help with their applications. We draw on data throughout the life of the EUSS (pre and post deadline)[6] and catalogue the practical issues applicants experienced when navigating the scheme, both in the early days and presently.

One of the themes running throughout this book is the issue of paper trails and bureaucratic bordering of migrant communities, particularly for those whose lives are precarious. In relation to the EUSS, these issues are particularly stark, as individuals struggle both to generate the right documents (due to lack of payslips or informal tenancy agreements) and to cope with the digital EUSS application. How GYROS advisers respond to these difficulties – helping their clients understand the requirements of the EUSS, giving practical advice, translating documents, contacting the relevant people – also shines light on how frontline community organizations operate.

This chapter therefore looks at the obligations in respect of Citizens' Rights under the WA (Section B), and the legal foundations of the EUSS, the process of making an application under EUSS and how this fits with the 'hostile environment' that EU nationals feel they are exposed to (Section C). It then considers the issues facing EU+ nationals in Great Yarmouth who have applied/are applying for the scheme, and the help they sought from

---

[5]   None of the residents underwent any form of immigration check from the landlord, Frank; nor did the researcher (an EU national).

[6]   For more, see C. Barnard, S. Fraser Butlin and F. Costello, 'The changing status of European Union nationals in the United Kingdom following Brexit: the lived experience of the European Union Settlement Scheme' (2022) 31 *Social and Legal Studies* 365. See also C. Barnard and F. Costello's blog series on the EUSS (2019–2022), published by The UK in a Changing Europe.

GYROS for difficulties in obtaining and maintaining their new status and how GYROS responds (Section D).

B. Withdrawal Agreement

After the UK left the EU on 31 January 2020, EU law continued to apply until the end of the transition period (11 pm GMT on 31 December 2020).[7] So the EU rules under Article 45 TFEU on free movement of workers, Article 49 TFEU on freedom of establishment and Article 21 TFEU on free movement of EU citizens applied until the end of 2020, as did the Workers Regulation 492/11[8] and the Citizens' Rights Directive (CRD) 2004/38/EC.[9] The CRD gives every EU citizen the right to reside in another member state for an initial period of three months with no conditions on their stay (apart from holding a passport or ID card).[10] The right to reside for more than three months remains subject to certain conditions, such as exercising Treaty rights as a worker, jobseeker or self-employed person.[11] EU or third country national family members can reside with the EU migrant.[12] Article 45 TFEU and Regulation 492/11 give EU migrants the right to 'look for a job in another EU country; work there without needing a work permit; reside there for that purpose; stay there even after employment has finished; enjoy equal treatment with nationals in access to employment, working conditions and all other social and tax advantages'.[13]

If there had been no agreement between the EU and the UK, EU free movement rights would have ended on 31 December 2020 and all EU nationals would have become subject to the Immigration Act 1971 (hereafter 'the 1971 Act'), irrespective of whether they were already in the UK or seeking to enter the UK. Section 1 of the 1971 Act provides that those without the 'right of abode' in the UK are subject to a system of control; Section 3 provides for the grant of leave to enter or remain for either a limited or for an indefinite period. Indeed, that is the legal position for EU nationals seeking to enter the UK after the end of the transition period: EU

---

[7]   These rights had been given effect in UK law via SI 2016/1052 The Immigration (European Economic Area) Regulations 2016, now repealed by paragraph 2(2) of Schedule 1(1) to the Immigration and Social Security Co-Ordination (EU Withdrawal) Act 2020.

[8]   OJ [2011] L141/1.

[9]   OJ [2004] L158/77.

[10] Article 6 CRD.

[11] Article 7 CRD.

[12] Articles 2 and 3 CRD.

[13] See 'Free movement – EU nationals' *European Commission*, available at: https://ec.europa.eu/social/main.jsp?catId=457, accessed 23 November 2023.

citizens are therefore now subject to the 1971 Act in the same way as anyone else who lacks the right of abode.

However, Part Two of the WA, given legal effect in the UK via Section 7A of the European Union (Withdrawal) Act 2018,[14] provides residence rights for 'Union citizens who exercise their right to reside in the United Kingdom in accordance with Union law before the end of the transition period and continue to reside there thereafter' (Article 10(1)(a)).[15] Article 16 WA says that EU nationals can acquire the right to reside permanently in the UK once they have completed the necessary period of five years of residence. Periods of legal residence or work, in accordance with EU free movement provisions, both before and after the end of the transition period, count towards the five years.

Article 18 WA provides for residence documents to be issued and confers a power on the UK to require EU citizens, their respective family members and others who reside in the UK, to apply for a new residence status and a document evidencing such status, which may be in digital form (Article 18(1)), will be issued. That scheme is the EUSS, which we consider in the next section.[16]

Alongside the residence rights, the WA guaranteed the continuation of rights to equal treatment as set out in the CRD and the Workers' Regulation 492/11. Rights to equal treatment also apply to NEFMs. This means EU citizens and their NEFMs are entitled to enjoy the same rights as UK nationals in respect of, for example, employment, housing, access to the National Health Service (NHS) – for both settled and pre-settled holders – and welfare benefits (though this is more complex in relation to holders of pre-settled status; see Chapter 6). Social security rights are preserved: Article 30 WA provides that EU regulations concerning social security coordination continue to apply to those who fall within the scope of the agreement. This means, for example, that periods of insurance, employment or residence completed under the legislation of one member

---

[14]   Inserted by Section 5 of the European Union (Withdrawal Agreement) Act 2020.

[15]   The provisions apply bilaterally so similar provision is made in relation to UK nationals in other member states, but for the purposes of this book, reference is made only to EU nationals in the UK.

[16]   Separate agreements were made in relation to citizens of Iceland, Liechtenstein and Norway, and of Switzerland. In relation to Iceland, Liechtenstein and Norway, an agreement was concluded between them and the UK on 20 December 2018: the EEA (European Economic Area) EFTA (European Free Trade Association) Separation Agreement. Part Two of the Separation Agreement is materially the same as the residence provisions of the WA. A separate Swiss Citizens Rights Agreement was concluded, and the provisions are the same as for the WA and the Separation Agreement. These agreements will not be discussed further since nationals from these countries have not been GYROS clients.

state are taken into account, where necessary, when determining entitlement to a benefit under the legislation of another member state.

In addition, Part Two of the WA confers residence rights on family members, who may or may not be EU citizens.[17] Those who are not EU citizens are described here as NEFMs. They are not EU nationals but are married to, or in a 'durable' relationship with, an EU citizen (for example, a Brazilian husband and a Polish wife) or are the family member of an EU national living in the UK (a child or parent, for example). They must also make an application under the EUSS to regularize their status in the UK.

There is a further group who can apply under the EUSS: 'derivative rights holders'. These are 'applicants who did not qualify for a right of residence under the CRD but may have had a right to reside in the UK derived from other EU law'.[18] Broadly, these are non-EU, non-British nationals whose residence rights in the UK derive from another EU, European Economic Area (EEA) or British national. An example might be an Argentinian mother who is the primary carer of a British child resident in the UK; she would be a '*Zambrano* carer', after the Court of Justice of the European Union (CJEU) case of the same name, which held that where children would otherwise be deprived of their rights as EU citizens if the carer was forced to leave (as correspondingly the child would be denied 'genuine enjoyment'[19] of their EU citizenship rights), then their carer must be granted a right of residence.[20] The Court of Appeal held that applicants will be eligible to make an application as a *Zambrano* carer only where, by the end of the transition period (on 31 December 2020) and throughout the relevant period, they had a derivative right to reside but did not have any other leave to enter or remain in the UK (unless the only other leave they had was the EUSS under Appendix EU).[21] This group must submit paper applications to the EUSS; they cannot access the digital platform.

Implementing Part Two of the WA on citizens' rights is the responsibility of the UK (and individual member states with oversight by the European Commission). The UK government committed to – and has set up – an independent oversight body, the Independent Monitoring Authority for the Citizens' Rights Agreements.[22] UK courts can continue to hear cases and can make references to the CJEU for eight years after the implementation

---

[17] Article 13(2) and (3) WA.

[18] See Home Office, 'EU Settlement Scheme Statistics' Gov.uk, available at: www.gov.uk/government/collections/eu-settlement-scheme-statistics, accessed 17 November 2023.

[19] Case C-34/09 *Ruiz Zambrano v Office National de L'Emploi* EU:C:2011:124 [42].

[20] Case C-34/09 *Ruiz Zambrano v Office National de L'Emploi* EU:C:2011:124.

[21] *Akinsanya v Secretary of State for the Home Department* [2022] EWCA Civ 37.

[22] For more, see 'Welcome to the Independent Monitoring Authority for the Citizens' Rights Agreements' *IMA*, available at: https://ima-citizensrights.org.uk/, accessed 23 November 2023.

of the WA. Concerns about implementation can be raised in the Joint Committee, established to oversee the WA, or the specialized committee on citizens' rights.

C. European Union Settlement Scheme

1. Legal provisions

The specific arrangements established in the UK as required by the WA are set out in 'Appendix EU' to the 1971 Act[23] and called the European Union Settlement Scheme (EUSS). It is a 'constitutive scheme', meaning that the rights must be conferred by a grant of residence status (rather than a 'declaratory scheme', whereby the rights automatically arise once the conditions are fulfilled[24]). The two statuses of pre-settled and settled status were established within the UK scheme.

Settled status is the grant of indefinite leave to remain where an applicant, at the date of application, has resided legally in the UK for a continuous period of five years.[25] Pre-settled status is the grant of limited leave to remain for five years, to those who could not satisfy the five-year continuous residence requirement for settled status.[26] The EUSS does not require the person to have been exercising a Treaty right, such as being a worker or being a student or a person of independent means with sufficient resources and comprehensive sickness insurance as required by Article 7 CRD. Rather they simply had to be resident. This was a considerable concession by the UK government. However, the consequence of having pre-settled status (that is, time-limited leave to remain) is that at the end of the five years, the individual would have had no lawful status in the UK, unless that limited leave was extended or the individual successfully applied for settled status. Many pre-settled status holders are not aware of this requirement, which is particularly difficult to communicate because the deadline is set on an individual basis according to when the holder was granted pre-settled status. Further, unlike under the initial scheme, there is no safety net in the form of a late application or a further status to fall back on (such as pre-settled status for those who did not get settled status). Without leave to remain,

---

[23] 'Immigration rules' *Gov.uk*, available at: www.gov.uk/guidance/immigration-rules/immigration-rules-appendix-eu, accessed 23 November 2023. See also Home Office, *EU Settlement Scheme: EU, Other EE and Swiss Citizens and their Family Members* (Home Office, 2023), available at: https://assets.publishing.service.gov.uk/media/6527a44c2 44f8e000d8e7453/EU_Settlement_Scheme_EU_other_EEA_Swiss_citizens_and_fam ily_members.pdf, accessed 23 November 2023.

[24] Article 18 WA.

[25] Appendix EU 2 and EU 11.

[26] Appendix EU 3 and EU 14.

the individual would not be permitted to work or access benefits, and they would have been an illegal overstayer if they did not leave the UK.

This requirement to 'upgrade' from pre-settled to settled status, in order to be permitted to remain in the UK, was challenged in *R (Independent Monitoring Authority) v Secretary of State for the Home Department*.[27] The Divisional Court held that the requirement for pre-settled status holders to apply for settled status was precluded by Article 13(4) WA because the WA offered lifelong protection for those individuals who had been granted residence rights in the UK under the WA. Once the rights had been given, they could not lose them due to a failure to apply for further rights at the end of the five-year period. Article 18 WA meant that the rights conferred by the grant of new residence status under the WA (in this case pre-settled status) to those who did not have the requisite five-year residence period for permanent residence had to include a right to reside permanently once the five-year period had been satisfied. Consequently, the High Court declared that the EUSS was unlawful insofar as it abrogated the right of permanent residence for those granted limited leave to remain. The Home Office did not appeal the decision[28] and has introduced steps to implement the ruling, including a two-year extension of the pre-settled status (Section D.2.4).

Finally, the rights provided by settled status are also not permanent: where an individual is absent from the host state for a period exceeding five consecutive years, then that status will be lost. For pre-settled status holders, it will be lost where the person is absent for a period of two consecutive years. However, for those with pre-settled status, while status is only *lost* after two years of absence from the UK, regular absences could affect their application to 'upgrade' to settled status: in order to apply for settled status, they must show that they have had continuous residence for the previous five years, which requires no absences of more than 6 months in any rolling 12 months (either in one stretch or as separate absences adding up to 6 months).

2. Applications to the scheme

There was considerable uncertainty for EU nationals in the UK between June 2016 (when the referendum was held) and March 2019 (when the EUSS was introduced) as to whether and how their residence rights would be protected.[29] Some applied for the EEA

---

[27] *R (Independent Monitoring Authority) v Secretary of State for the Home Department* [2022] EWHC 3274.

[28] For more, see 'IMA welcomes confirmation that Home Office will not pursue appeal in EU Settlement Scheme case' *IMA* (16 February 2023), available at: https://ima-citizen srights.org.uk/news_events/ima-welcomes-confirmation-that-home-office-will-not-pur sue-appeal-in-eu-settlement-scheme-case/, accessed 23 November 2023.

[29] This section is drawn from an earlier paper: Barnard et al (2022), n 6.

Figure 3.1: Permanent residence documents issued to EU nationals, 2012–2018

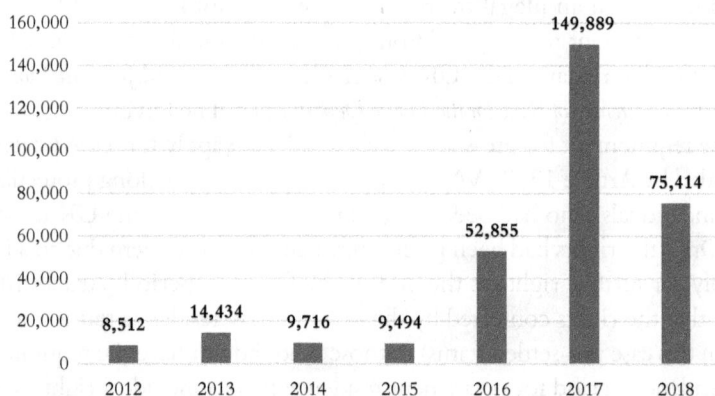

Source: Home Office, 'European Economic Area (EEA)' *Gov.uk*, available at: www.gov.uk/gov ernment/statistics/immigration-statistics-year-ending-september-2019/list-of-tables#european-economic-area-eea

(PR),[30] the permanent residence application, which had been available to EU nationals prior to the introduction of the EUSS on an optional basis (there was a spike in applications after the referendum, as shown by the number of documents issued; Figure 3.1). This gave permanent residence once a person could provide evidence of five years' continuous residence (as a 'qualified person'[31]) already in the UK. However, the cost of the application (£65.00) was prohibitive for some. EEA(PR) status became defunct after 30 June 2021, and all those who had applied still needed to apply for the EUSS.

The EUSS is by far the largest ever administrative exercise in respect of immigration undertaken by the Home Office. To date it has had over seven million applications,[32] despite initial estimates putting the EU national population in the UK at about 3.4 million (and later Census data returning about the same figure).[33] The scheme marked a step change in

---

[30] For more, see: 'Permanent residence documents for EU, EEA or Swiss citizens' *Gov. uk*, available at: www.gov.uk/permanent-residence-document-eu-eea, accessed 23 November 2023.

[31] A 'qualified person', as defined in the Immigration (European Economic Area) Regulations 2016, is an EEA national living in the UK as a jobseeker, a worker, a self-employed person, a self-sufficient person or a student; available at: www.legislation.gov.uk/uksi/2016/1052/regulation/6/made, accessed 23 November 2023.

[32] Note this figure relates to applications and not applicants, so could include repeat applications from the same person.

[33] G. Sturge, *Migration Statistics* House of Commons Library Research Briefing (November 2022), available at: https://researchbriefings.files.parliament.uk/documents/SN06077/SN06077.pdf, accessed 24 January 2023; see also 'Census' *Office for National Statistics*,

the administration of immigration status by the Home Office. First, the evidence requirements were more flexible (though for many of those attending GYROS, they were still too challenging to meet). Second, criminal records checks were undertaken for all those applying. Third, the Home Office set up an EUSS Resolution Centre, which individual applicants and professional advisers could call directly to enquire about an application. Save for a brief closure during the first COVID-19 lockdown, the availability of case workers to discuss applications was seen as a positive step by the advisers on the part of the Home Office. Fourth, and perhaps most importantly, it is a digital scheme in terms of the application process, the status granted and its maintenance.[34]

The EUSS was first piloted in 2018, with 230,000 applications from EU+ employed in various settings, including universities and hospitals.[35] At this point, the scheme still had the £65 application fee attached to it. This fee was later abolished,[36] and refunds were granted automatically. The scheme was rolled out fully from March 2019 with an application deadline of 30 June 2021, albeit with the possibility of making a late application if reasonable grounds are shown.[37] Of the six million plus applications received before the deadline, 52 per cent obtained settled status, 43 per cent obtained pre-settled status and 4 per cent obtained another status (including refused, withdrawn and void outcomes).[38] Figure 3.2 shows that the majority of applicants pre deadline[39] were in the 18–64 age category. However, as we note later, the applications from older people and from the young were fewer than expected, indicating a lower take-up rate among these groups.

Figure 3.3 shows applications by nationality for the most numerous five countries (in terms of application numbers). The highest numbers of pre-deadline applications were from (in order) Polish, Romanian, Italian, Portuguese and Bulgarian nationals. Post deadline, there was a much higher

---

available at: https://www.ons.gov.uk/peoplepopulationandcommunity/populationandmi gration/internationalmigration/bulletins/ukpopulationbycountryofbirthandnationality/ yearendingjune2021 accessed 02 December 2023.

[34] A paper application may be granted for limited reasons.

[35] UK Visas and Immigration, 'EU Settlement Scheme public beta testing phase report' *Gov. uk* (2 May 2019), available at: www.gov.uk/government/publications/eu-settlement-sch eme-public-beta-testing-phase-report, accessed 23 November 2023.

[36] UK Visas and Immigration, 'EU Settlement Scheme: application fee refunds' (28 March 2019), available at: www.gov.uk/guidance/eu-settlement-scheme-application-fee-refu nds, accessed 23 November 2023.

[37] 'Apply to the EU Settlement Scheme (settled and pre-settled status)' *Gov.uk*, available at: www.gov.uk/settled-status-eu-citizens-families/eligibility, accessed 23 November 2023.

[38] Home Office, n 18.

[39] Ibid.

Figure 3.2: Age range of applicants to the EUSS up to the June 2021 deadline

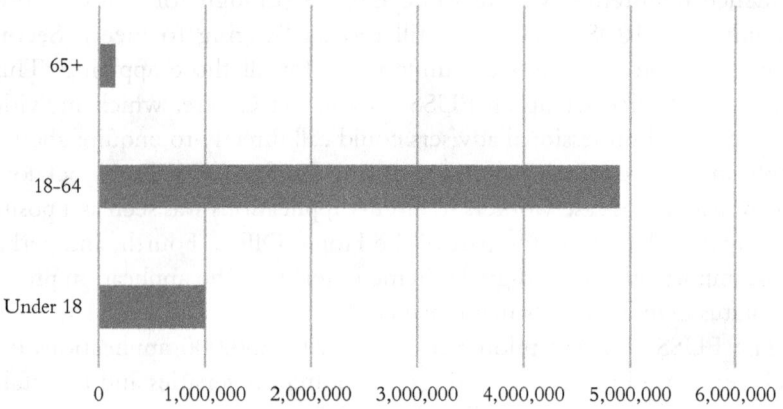

Figure 3.3: Most numerous nationalities of applicants to the EUSS pre and post deadline

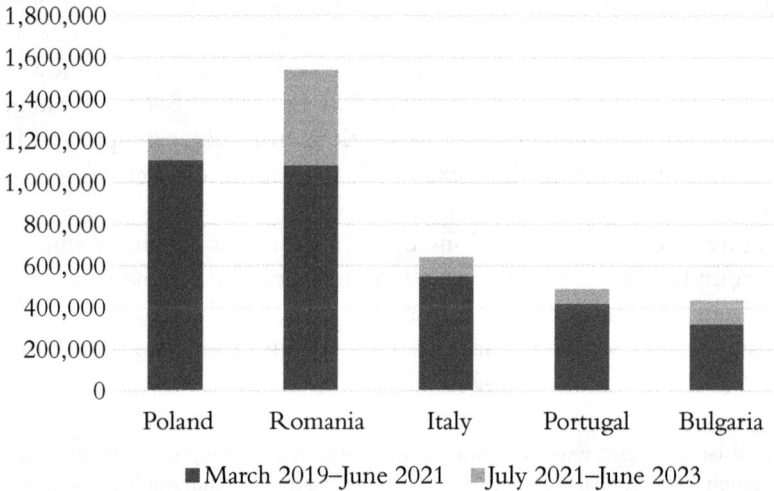

■ March 2019–June 2021 ▩ July 2021–June 2023

Source: Home Office, 'EU Settlement Scheme Statistics' *Gov.uk*, available at: www.gov.uk/gov ernment/collections/eu-settlement-scheme-statistics

share of late applications coming from Romanians (closely followed by Bulgarians) compared to the other nationalities.

The scheme also includes non-EEA national EUSS application data. At the time of writing the total number of non-EEA applications to the scheme was 418,340 pre deadline, with over 44,000 (10 per cent), of these in June

2021 alone and 160,710 (28 per cent) post deadline (June 2023).[40] The high number may be linked to the reality of the ongoing applications of (joining) family members of EU nationals (see Section D.2.3).

A certificate of application (CoA) is provided to each applicant once their application is submitted. This can be used to provide evidence of eligibility to work and rent accommodation until a decision on the application has been made. A CoA is also given to those who have pending late applications.[41] Although the decision process was very quick for many people, the average length now is six to eight weeks,[42] and in some complicated cases, it can take months.[43] The CoA, which can be viewed online, allows the applicant to continue to live and work in the UK pending an outcome. However, as discussed later, it can give a false sense of security for those who make an ineligible application (Section D.2.1). Refusals of applications to the scheme have been relatively low to date – 8 per cent of applications by EU nationals and 10 per cent of applications by non-EEA nationals. However, although these percentages are relatively small, they still equate to about 567,700 applications. The number of refusals has been increasing recently, particularly in the context of late ineligible applications (see Section D.2.1). Refusals of 'derivative rights' holders are also higher (see Section D.2.3).

When an application is refused, the individual may seek an administrative review of the decision (within 28 days of receiving the decision, at a cost of £80) or appeal the refusal to the First Tier Tribunal (within 14 days of the decision date or 28 days if the individual is not in the UK). They could also submit a new application, previously a route often seen as easier and quicker, particularly while late applications were permissible (see Lara's case, Section D.1.3). While 'reasonable grounds' were necessary to submit a late application, the threshold for acceptance was still high. However, this more generous test for 'reasonable grounds' changed on 9 August 2023 when stricter rules were introduced. From 9 August 2023, reasonable grounds for making a late application have become a validity requirement instead of an eligibility requirement. If the Home Office finds that the grounds for a late application are not reasonable, they will reject rather than refuse the application. This rejection means that the applicant will not have the right to an Administrative Review or an appeal. This is considered further in

---

[40]   Ibid.

[41]   'Summary of EU citizens' rights' *the3million*, available at: https://the3million.org.uk/summary-eu-citizens-rights, accessed 23 November 2023.

[42]   www.gov.uk/settled-status-eu-citizens-families/after-youve-applied

[43]   Home Office, 'EU Settlement Scheme: current estimated processing times for applications' *Gov.uk* (May 2022), available at: www.gov.uk/government/publications/eu-settlement-scheme-application-processing-times/eu-settlement-scheme-pilot-current-expected-processing-times-for-applications, accessed 23 November 2023.

Section D.2.1. For those who are unsuccessful in any review or appeal and do not have any other immigration status to permit them to remain in the UK, they will then have no entitlement to reside in the UK: the hostile environment makes it particularly difficult to continue living and working in the UK. While there does not, yet, appear to be a widespread system of deportations, if an individual has contact with a body that has a duty to report (such as the local council, health services, Department for Work and Pensions), then they may receive a letter saying they need to make an application to the EUSS or they may be offered help to voluntarily return to their home state.

3. Feeling unwelcome

So far, we have concentrated on the legal rules underpinning the EUSS and the numbers involved, but what about the impact of the scheme on EU+ nationals? We were struck by how many of our interviewees said how unsettled and unwelcome the EUSS process had made them feel. Some EU nationals left the UK because of Brexit,[44] and in earlier work with EU nationals, we noted a difference between EU14 nationals on one hand and EU8 and EU2 nationals on the other.[45] For many EU14 nationals, Brexit was the first time they had felt 'othered'[46] in the UK. Previously, they had identified as equal EU citizens exercising their right to move to the UK or, for those who had been here for many years, they had felt they belonged. A German national commented: 'Before the referendum, I felt British. It's since been made clear to me via media and individuals that I am not part of this country.'[47]

By contrast, for many of the EU8 and EU2 nationals we spoke to (and the Portuguese nationals in low-paid work in Great Yarmouth), this feeling of not being welcome was simply a continuation of rhetoric they experienced before, during and after the referendum.[48] Everyone in our focus groups had experienced some form of 'go home' rhetoric in their time in Great Yarmouth.[49] As Portes notes in relation to migration trends from the EU to the UK between the referendum and 2020: 'It does appear

---

[44] J. Portes, 'Immigration and the UK economy after Brexit' (2022) 38 *Oxford Review of Economic Policy* 82, 85.

[45] Barnard et al (2022), n 6.

[46] T. Guma and R.D. Jones, ' "Where are we going to go now?" European Union migrants' experiences of hostility, anxiety, and (non-)belonging during Brexit' (2019) 25(1) *Population, Space and Place* 1, 2.

[47] Barnard et al (2022), n 6, 369.

[48] Ibid.

[49] Ibid.

that the psychological impact of Brexit on past and prospective migrants from elsewhere in the EU was considerable.'[50] This is, in part, to do with the 'bureaucratic bordering' that the EUSS entails and the onus to prove eligibility and legitimacy shouldered by many EU migrants in the everyday:

> 'It very much feels … not eligible until you, as a client, provide evidence and explain the complex law so we can prove your eligibility yourself. So, my feeling is you need to be more or at the same level of knowledge as the decision makers to be able to explain how you are eligible, and why those immigration/EU regulations 2016 apply in your case.'[51]

For many EU nationals, the introduction of the need to document their right to live in the UK and access employment, housing, welfare and health services meant that, for the first time, they encountered the 'hostile environment'. This term was first used by then Home Secretary Theresa May to describe a raft of new migration policies seeking 'to create, here in Britain, a really hostile environment for illegal immigrants'.[52] Although announced in 2012, the 'hostile environment' policy dates back much further, with governments of all political parties taking cumulative steps to make it more difficult for people (including those in former British colonies) to move to the UK or hold British citizenship, including in some instances pressuring colonial governments to limit those it gave British passports to.[53]

The hostile environment of today, now rebranded the 'compliant environment', is expressed in high fees for immigration visa applications, limited appeal opportunities and inaccessible Home Office decision makers (unlike the context of the EUSS where, as we have noted, individuals and agencies could contact the Resolution Centre). However, the hostile environment affects the everyday, and this is where it meets the EUSS – in the need to prove immigration status to employers, landlords, health officials and banks. Consequently, the external borders of the state bleed into the interactions of everyday life and place a burden on individuals, such as employers and landlords, to deal with immigration issues. Employers[54] might face fines of £45,000 per worker for not undertaking the correct right to work checks, and landlords can be fined £5,000–£10,000 or receive

---

[50] Portes (2022) n 44, 84.
[51] Interview with council worker (online, October 2021).
[52] 'The hostile environment explained' *The Joint Council for the Welfare of Immigrants*, available at: www.jcwi.org.uk/the-hostile-environment-explained, accessed 17 November 2023.
[53] M. Goodfellow, *Hostile Environment: How Immigrants became Scapegoats* (London: Verso, 2019), 56.
[54] Section 21, Immigration, Asylum and Nationality Act 2006.

a criminal conviction, or both for failing to carry out checks.[55] Although there have been concerns about the discriminatory impact of the EUSS, the Court of Appeal rejected a claim by The Joint Council for Welfare of Immigrants[56] that the scheme breached Article 8 (right to a family life) and Article 14 (non-discrimination) of the European Convention on Human Rights.[57] Having assumed without deciding the point that Article 8 was engaged, the Court held that the objective of the EUSS was sufficiently important to justify the limitation on individuals' rights under articles 8 and 14. Moreover, the scheme could be operated by landlords in a proportionate way, which was a complete answer to the claim that rights under articles 8 and 14 were breached.

Another aspect of feeling unwelcome is the question of no recourse to public funds (NRPF).[58] In order to claim certain welfare benefits in the UK, such as UC (or other public resources), an applicant must pass a two stage test, first proving that they have a 'right to reside' and that they are 'habitually resident' (Chapter 6). As we move through the chapters of the book, we highlight instances in the GYROS data whereby EU nationals were incorrectly labelled 'NRPF' and GYROS needed to work to provide evidence of these individuals' right to make a claim. The complexity of the law does not help, and it is not just the clients that struggle. As one council housing worker commented, they had no training around the EUSS to help them understand which status gives rise to which rights.[59] This is particularly difficult in relation to the distinction between pre-settled and settled status and the ability to access public funds, such as housing support or welfare benefits (Chapter 6), and the council sometimes comes to GYROS for advice. The hostile environment can make it difficult for clients to gather the information needed to prove they are not in fact NRPF: 'there is that level of hostile environment in the air'.[60] And this barrier can manifest as difficulties in gathering bank statements or letters from GPs.

---

[55] Immigration Act 2014. See also Immigration Enforcement, 'Tripling of fines for those supporting illegal migrants' *Gov.uk* (7 August 2023), available at: www.gov.uk/government/news/tripling-of-fines-for-those-supporting-illegal-migrants#:~:text=Fines%20are%20to%20be%20more,them%20or%20rent%20their%20properties, accessed 23 November 2023.

[56] See The Joint Council for the Welfare of Immigrants' website at: www.jcwi.org.uk/, accessed 23 November 2023.

[57] *R. (on the application of Joint Council for the Welfare of Immigrants) v Secretary of State for the Home Department* [2020] EWCA Civ 542.

[58] As opposed to its proper meaning, which is when someone has an 'NRPF' condition attached to their temporary leave in the UK.

[59] Interview with council worker (online, November 2021).

[60] Interview with council worker (online, October 2021).

Having outlined the establishment of the EUSS and the impact it has had on EU+ nationals, we turn now to consider how the scheme has been operating on the ground – specifically, what issues GYROS' clients have faced (sections D.1 and D.2) and how GYROS has responded to those difficulties and helped clients (Section D.3).

D. Issues faced by GYROS' clients when applying under the European Union Settlement Scheme

Our longitudinal dataset from GYROS (2015–2020) and our fieldwork in Great Yarmouth (2019–2022) span the pre-Brexit period (2015), the referendum (2016), the introduction of the EUSS (2019), the deadline to apply for the scheme (June 2021) and the period for late and repeat applications (June 2021 onwards). GYROS recorded 1,636 contacts relating to the EUSS from 1 April 2019 to 30 June 2021 (before the deadline) and significantly more, 6,414, from 1 July 2021 to 31 July 2023 (after the deadline).[61]

A significant number of practical issues have arisen from the EUSS, which we address in subsequent chapters, including insecure work (Chapter 4) and informal renting (Chapter 5), making it difficult to provide formal evidence of, respectively, the work and rental history necessary to prove residence for the purpose of the EUSS application. In this section, we consider some of the issues that can be seen in the GYROS data in the early stages of the operation of the scheme (Section 1) and ongoing issues (Section 2). We also identify how GYROS' clients understood, and understand, issues arising with the scheme and GYROS' approach to tackling these issues.

1. Early days

'Early' issues seen in the GYROS dataset included, perhaps unsurprisingly, lack of awareness of the Home Office's requirements and then a fear about how the Home Office might use data provided for the purpose of the scheme. There was also confusion over whether Brexit was actually going to happen. Bureaucratic bordering, a theme that we identify throughout this book, came to the fore in relation to issues over proof of residence and employment in respect of EUSS applications, with challenges for people to prove residence and deal with a digital system. We look at these issues in turn.

---

[61]   GYROS contact monitoring data up to July 2023. In August 2020 GYROS were awarded partnership funding by the National Lottery to continue and increase their service delivery across Great Yarmouth, Ipswich, Thetford and later, Lincoln.

1.1 Lack of awareness and confusion over Brexit dates

Lack of awareness of the requirement to apply for the EUSS was acute in more marginalized and isolated groups, including those who could not speak English (much of the communication about the scheme was in English), people experiencing street homelessness, older people and those living in rural areas (particularly isolated rural farm workers with little or no Wi-Fi access[62]). The GYROS dataset indicated a particular lack of awareness of the scheme among older and younger people (this is reflected in the number of applications nationally, as shown in Figure 3.2). People who had lived in the UK for decades were unaware that they too had to make an application, as were those who had already received permanent residence (see Figure 3.1). Take, for example, the case of Sofia[63] (Lithuanian, fifties, lived in the UK for 18 years), who sought help from GYROS to apply for the EUSS almost a year after the scheme had been open for applications. As indicated in the GYROS case note, she heard about it by chance:

> 08/10/2019 Client has PR [permanent residence] but has not done EUSS yet. She did not even know about it until someone in ESOL [English for Speakers of Other Languages] class talked about it. I did her app[lication] today and explained that all EU national[s] and their families living in the UK should do it. The rest of her family are British. Client does not know how to use email, so the app was done with my email.[64]

Four months later, Sofia received her settled status.

> 07/02/2020 Client's EUSS award letter came. I passed the information to client along with printed status outcome letter and settled status page that HO [Home Office] holds for her (the page with her photo in). I stressed again the importance of updating personal info as it changes. We changed her phone number today as she has a new number now.[65]

GYROS also saw examples of older people who had come to the UK to provide childcare for their grandchildren not knowing that they needed to apply. There were also cases, especially among the Romanian community, of parents not being aware that they needed to make applications for their

---

[62] C. Barnard and F. Costello, 'EU settled status: what's occurring?' *UK in a changing Europe* (27 February 2020), available at: https://ukandeu.ac.uk/eu-settled-status-whats-occurring/, accessed 24 January 2023.

[63] Pseudonyms are used throughout the book.

[64] Client ID 1149.

[65] Ibid.

children and assuming children's applications would be linked to those of the parents.[66] Some of this confusion was created by the government itself. This was explained by a council worker:

'the scheme has been advertised poorly. The families were not aware that every child has to apply. The other issue was ... that's related, that the Home Office announced that children will get the status of the parents. Which cannot be more misleading, because each child has to make their own application.'[67]

The timings of Brexit also caused some confusion and further uncertainty. When the UK did not leave the EU in March 2019, but rather sought an extension to its membership, initially to 31 October 2019[68] and subsequently to 31 December 2020, many EU nationals delayed completing their EUSS applications. One organization in Wisbech (Cambridgeshire) 'reported that their clients were waiting for Brexit to happen as there was "no point" in doing anything before then'.[69]

1.2 Digital-only application and data concerns

As we have noted, the EUSS is a digital immigration scheme. An application is made online and the identity check for the application can be done via the 'EU Exit: ID document check' app, available on smartphones; the check can also be done at document scanning centres at various locations throughout the UK or by posting ID documents for verification. Prospective applicants can also request a paper application form in lieu of the digital application from the EUSS Resolution Centre, but paper applications are only permissible in limited circumstances.[70] Applicants receive digital-only

---

[66] C. Barnard and F. Costello, '"Even children born in the UK need to apply" – one week left to apply for the EU Settlement Scheme (EUSS)' *Mumsnet* (2021), available at: www.mums net.com/talk/guest_posts/4276860-Even-children-born-in-the-UK-need-to-apply-one-week-left-to-apply-for-the-EU-Settlement-Scheme-EUSS, accessed 24 January 2023.

[67] Interview with council worker (online, October 2021).

[68] G. Cowie, 'Parliament and the three extensions of Article 50' (31 October 2029), *House of Commons Library*, available at: https://commonslibrary.parliament.uk/research-briefi ngs/cbp-8725/, accessed 24 November 2023.

[69] C. Barnard, S. Fraser Butlin and F. Costello, 'Unsettled status? Vulnerable EU citizens may lose their UK residence overnight' *LSE* (27 November 2019), available at: https:// blogs.lse.ac.uk/brexit/2019/11/27/long-read-unsettled-status-vulnerable-eu-citizens-may-lose-their-uk-residence-overnight/, accessed 24 November 2023.

[70] The circumstances are: (1) they are applying based on a derivative right to reside; (2) they do not hold a valid identity document and are unable to obtain one; and (3) they are unable to apply using the online application form and cannot be supported to do so.

proof of status, accessed with unique log-in details via the Gov.uk portal. Groups like the3million[71] campaigned, ultimately unsuccessfully, for physical proof of status. Further, as we saw in the adviser's reminder to Sofia, for those with pre-settled or settled status, there is an obligation to keep personal details up to date, and this is done online too.

Inevitably, those who lack both the basic hardware, such as a smartphone, and the necessary digital skills have struggled to navigate the online EUSS application process and provide subsequent updates. The Office for National Statistics has estimated that 9 per cent of adults in the UK are non-internet users.[72] Digital literacy has been found to be especially low among GYROS clients, with more than 60 per cent rating their IT skills lower than 5 out of 10 (where 1 is non-existent and 10 is excellent).[73] So to apply for or maintain their status, these clients often need digital support, sometimes at the most basic level.

Some clients were unable to understand the outcome of their application, or were not aware there was an outcome. In one example: '02/03/2020 Client came over to check if she was awarded Settled Status. Client had deleted emails from them[.] I have checked online, and client was awarded Settled Status.'[74] This client had made her application in November 2019, at which point she had already been living in the UK for 12 years. However, she described her English language skills as "none". In another example:

29/05/2019 I called client to ask about her EUSS settlement application and dates. Client said she didn't receive any email and that she received only the certificate of application .... I went to www.gov.uk 'view and prove your status rights' and checked for info regarding outcome. Client and her children all have settled status and unlimited leave to remain.[75]

This client had already been through the process of making an application for EEA(PR), which, as mentioned, became defunct two years later, requiring her to prove, once again, five years of residence for her and her children.

Another issue for many clients is that they did not have email addresses – we saw this with Sofia and see it again here: '21/10/2019 A client came to apply for settled status, she couldn't use her email and phone, so we gave her our details.'[76]

---

[71] See the website of the3million at: https://the3million.org.uk/, accessed 24 January 2023.
[72] 'Internet users, UK: 2020' *Office for National Statistics*, available at: www.ons.gov.uk/businessindustryandtrade/itandinternetindustry/bulletins/internetusers/2020, accessed 24 January 2023.
[73] Barnard et al (2022), n 6, 380.
[74] Client ID 234.
[75] Client ID 331.
[76] Client ID 1214.

The digital-first approach also applies to providing proof of status: individuals generate a shareable digital code which third parties (for example, employers or landlords) use to verify the person's immigration status. This caused considerable anxiety among GYROS clients:

> 27/05/2020 Emailed client asking about the outcome of her application. She replied saying that she received it on 09/12/2019 but is having trouble getting the proof – her employer wants to see it. I offered our help with it, and she was really happy to hear that we could help her remotely. ... We did appt [appointment] via Skype. I accessed client's EUSS record, saved and emailed it to her, so she can show that as proof if an employer asks. She asked about the code for the employer. I explained that she can generate and share it with her employer, when she has one. Client was worried that she won't be able to herself, even after my explanation, so I reassured her that she can always call us back and we will help her with it.[77]

The obligation to engage with the digital scheme applies equally to landlords and employers. The Public Law Project has outlined the nine-step process a third party has to undertake in order to check the status of an EU+ citizen.[78] It is not yet known what impact this process and additional responsibilities regarding immigration checks will have on employers, landlords and others, although early research suggests it does disincentivize renting to EU nationals.[79] And for some, it is a serious barrier. Take Frank, the landlord of the House. He did not have a smartphone and he was not digitally confident; moreover, the House did not have Wi-Fi.

Frank was not alone. Jacob, a Dutch national who had lived in the UK for nearly 40 years, was a landlord of various HMOs. He accessed GYROS services in June 2021 for help with his own EUSS application. He was not an internet user and did not own a PC or laptop. He came to GYROS with his Nokia 3210,[80] his only phone, which he rarely switched on. He

---

[77] Client ID 533.
[78] J. Tomlinson and A. Welsh, 'Digital immigration status: a monitoring framework' (2020) *Public Law Project*, available at: https://publiclawproject.org.uk/resources/digital-only-status/ accessed 24 January 2023, 6. See also J. Meers, J. Tomlinson, A. Welsh and C. O'Brian, 'Rights on paper? The discriminatory effects of immigration status on private landlord decision' (14 March 2023) *UK Constitutional Law Association*, available at: https://ukconstitutionallaw.org/2023/03/14/jed-meers-joe-tomlinson-alice-welsh-and-charlotte-obrien-rights-on-paper-the-discriminatory-effects-of-digital-immigration-status-on-private-landlord-decisions/, accessed 3 October 2023.
[79] Ibid.
[80] This model is dated, and is not a smartphone.

said he struggled with the digital march of most applications and mentioned that his utility providers had not believed that he could not take and send a picture of his meter reading because his phone did not have this facility. So he was unable to apply for or manage his own status without help from GYROS, let alone navigate the immigration checks he had to undertake as a landlord, via a share code provided by his tenants.

Applicants, who generally had had no previous interaction with the Home Office, also had concerns about submitting their data to a digital system run by the Home Office. Their fear in relation to data protection was exacerbated by an exemption clause in the Data Protection Act 2018 preventing EU citizens living in Britain from finding out what data the Home Office held on them.[81] The Court of Appeal made a declaration that the exemption was incompatible with the General Data Protection Regulation (Regulation 2016/679),[82] but suspended the declaration until 31 January 2022 to give the UK government reasonable time to make legislative amendments to remedy the incompatibility.[83] However, the deadline for EUSS was 30 June 2021 and therefore EU nationals had to go ahead and apply, irrespective of their concerns. In an early survey we conducted on the EUSS, one German respondent said:

> EUSS in practical terms was reasonably straight forward. I found it upsetting that I had to do it at all. I had to borrow a phone. I am worried about the biometric data where it is going and what they will do with it. Being on a Home Office database and doing God knows what with it.[84]

1.3 Establishing proof of residence
Some of GYROS' clients struggled to meet the evidence requirements for EUSS, despite the fact that these were very flexible. As one external worker who attended the GYROS complex case discussion meetings told us:

> 'I think generally people from abroad, especially people from so-called Eastern Europe, they are very used to bureaucracy, providing information, confirmation of the identity, such as passport, national ID card, bank statements. They understand that you need to provide

---

[81] Paragraph 4, Schedule 2, Data Protection Act 2018.
[82] OJ 2016 L 119/1.
[83] *R (on the application of Open Rights Group Ltd) v Secretary of State for the Home Department* [2021] EWCA Civ 1573.
[84] Barnard et al (2022), n 6, 374.

a lot of evidence to be able to access certain provisions. So that in itself is not as much of a problem. The problem is how people can navigate the system in the UK to obtain the correct evidence. They come across some ridiculous hurdles for no apparent reason. It is almost like a systemic discrimination against them because they are from abroad. I mean, again, I came across occasions where clients were telling me: "No, I can't possibly obtain my bank statements, or my bank will charge me for that. They won't give them to me." I go to the bank with the client as their adviser and suddenly the conversation is very different. All the statements are printed there and no questions about the money. It's the same when asking for confirmation from [the] GP that families are registered at – I heard stories where they won't issue that letter, or they will want to charge for issuing that letter. So yes, there is ... there is that level of hostile environment in the air.'[85]

The lack of a paper trail to prove residence is a theme that frequently arises in our data, particularly for those working without employment contracts and living (sometimes for years) without any tenancy agreements. For some, the evidential burden was a struggle because a cost was involved:

12/05/2020 Client said that she wanted to apply for EUPS [EU Pre Settled] for her 2 children, but children don't have birth certificates. I explained that we could ask for them online, but that client needs to be able to pay for them. Cost £11 + £3 for post costs. Client said she doesn't have money now, but that she will get paid on Friday by Midnight. We will do it next week.[86]

For others, it is that no paper trail exists. Take the case of Lara[87] (Box 3.1), who was not listed on any utility bills, because when she first moved to the UK, she was living in 'hotel' accommodation. She also had a OnePay[88] bank account, which does not require proof of residence. OnePay positions itself as 'solv[ing] the problem of paying temporary workers without UK bank accounts', and many employment agencies and employers are registered with OnePay because it offers an easy and quick way to pay staff.

---

85 Interview with council worker.
86 Client ID 864.
87 Client ID 809.
88 See the OnePay website at: www.onepay.co.uk/forbusiness, accessed 23 November 2023.

Box 3.1: Lara's story

Lara is a Portuguese woman with four children who moved to the UK in 2020 to find work. She worked part-time, on a zero-hours contract, in one of the local chicken factories; she found the job via a recruitment agency based in Great Yarmouth. In February 2022, Lara had to stop working due to illness (related to blood pressure and diabetes). Without any income, the family's problems began to accumulate. Lara first approached GYROS for help with applying for welfare benefits in March 2022. She had already tried to submit an application for EUPS. The notes said: 'She said that she had tried before but was not successful, her ID was expired, and she also had tried to get help but as she didn't have enough money, she was not able to apply before the deadline.'

This suggests Lara had approached advice sharks operating in the Town (see Section 2.2) to help her make an application for EUPS, but as she was unable to pay, she was refused the service. When Lara approached GYROS, she had to submit a new application for EUPS. It also became clear she had been working without a National Insurance number. In 2020, during the COVID-19 pandemic, the government stopped issuing National Insurance numbers to EU nationals.[89] This was due to capacity issues, as staff had to be redeployed to process benefit claims. Processing of National Insurance number applications reopened in December 2020.[90] These numbers allow individuals to work and pay National Insurance contributions. They also act as a personal identification/reference number when communicating with the Department for Work and Pensions and His Majesty's Revenue & Customs (HMRC).

GYROS made a new EUPS application for Lara in April 2022. In May, she sent GYROS her (expired) ID to accompany her application. In October 2022, she was asked for more evidence to support her case for residence since 2020. The GYROS adviser spoke to the Resolution Centre on 19 October 2022:

> 19.10.2022. I explained that we have uploaded evidence regarding her residence, payslips and that EU settlement keeps asking for evidence. [Resolution Centre worker] said that the caseworker ... was treating her case like a [settled status] application when it clearly showed in the application she was applying for Pre-settled status. The only reason he could see for this request of evidence ... might be because payslips don't have NINo [National Insurance number]. I explained that during lockdown they were not being issued, and she only probably got the Nino recently. Which was later confirmed by client. Regarding bank accounts,

---

[89] C. Barnard and F. Costello, 'EU nationals face new barriers for COVID-19 support' *UK in a Changing Europe* (8 April 2021), available at: https://ukandeu.ac.uk/eu-nationals-new-barriers-for-covid-19-support/, accessed 7 March 2023.

[90] D. Graham, 'Thousands unable to get an NI number because of coronavirus' *BBC News* (21 October 2020), available at: www.bbc.co.uk/news/business-54619548, accessed 7 March 2023.

I explained that when people arrive in the UK and start working, they are not able to get bank accounts straight away, only online banking and One Pay card for wages.

[Resolution Centre worker] understood and advised to get other evidence, such as utility bills. I believe client was living in hotels and does not have utility bills in her name.

[Resolution Centre worker] will put a note down for her caseworker and hopefully we will get an update soon.

The GYROS adviser called the Resolution Centre again the next day, after the client had received another request for more evidence. Lara was advised 'to get Company registration number on employer's letter'. GYROS also asked her to "send me P45 and NIN[o] letter", so this can be added to evidence supporting her employment in 2020. On 25 November 2022, Lara's application was refused: 'Client emailed me, email received from Home Office with refusal letter dated 16.11.2022. I called client and we decided to ask for an administrative review as client (now) has all evidence apart from the payslips with the National Insurance number.'

As we saw in Section C.2, applicants have 28 days to lodge an administrative review (AR), and this costs £80.00. Lara's case notes record: '12.12.22 called client several times last week without success. I have called today, and client said she didn't come to drop-in because she didn't have money to pay for AR. Client said she would have money this Friday.' Ultimately, the AR is not undertaken; a new application is seen as the quicker (and cheaper) route. This would entitle her to a CoA, giving her the right to work straightaway: '16.12.22 Client came for appointment to submit AR but after conversation with client we decided to submit a new application as client needs to be able to work as soon as possible. New application submitted today 16.12.2022.'

At the time of writing (March 2023), almost a year after GYROS first started helping her with her second, and then her third, application, the client has still not received an update on her case.

Lara's case (Box 3.1) shows some of the issues for vulnerable individuals applying for EUPS. Without EUPS, it became difficult for her to access other support. GYROS worked intensively with her over the course of the year (see Table 3.1).

Lara also sought help to apply for welfare benefits (Universal Credit and child benefit, both dependent on her claim of pre-settled status), food parcels, help via the Norfolk Assistance Scheme, a Council Tax reduction and debt and money advice (because of an inability to work or to claim benefits) as well as education support for her children in school. GYROS also helped her write to the employment agency as she was owed two days' pay. Lara's case is just one example of the issues we return to throughout

Table 3.1: Lara's interactions with GYROS (a snapshot)

Date case was opened	Project	Subcategory	Complete?	Date case was closed	Time spent on case by staff and volunteers
8 March 2022	IAG	Benefits	Yes	25 October 2022	3 hours, 19 minutes
11 March 2022	IAG	Safeguarding	Yes	6 July 2022	45 minutes
11 March 2022	IAG	Safeguarding	Yes	11 July 2022	20 minutes
11 March 2022	IAG	EUSS/EUPS	Yes	21 June 2022	57 minutes
11 March 2022	IAG	Debt and money advice	Yes	21 June 2022	2 hours, 20 minutes
23 March 2022	IAG	Other	Yes	23 March 2022	15 minutes
29 March 2022	IAG	Safeguarding	Yes	29 March 2022	10 minutes
11 April 2022	IAG	Safeguarding	Yes	26 July 2022	15 minutes
25 April 2022	IAG	Employment	Yes	19 May 2022	27 minutes
25 April 2022	IAG	Safeguarding	Yes	26 July 2022	18 minutes
26 April 2022	Immigration	EUSS/EUPS	No	Not closed	6 hours, 57 minutes
10 May 2022	Immigration	EUSS/EUPS	Yes	1 September 2022	15 minutes
30 May 2022	IAG	Education	Yes	25 October 2022	1 hour, 27 minutes
21 June 2022	IAG	Housing	Yes	25 October 2022	1 hour
27 June 2022	IAG	Safeguarding	Yes	26 July 2022	5 minutes
27 June 2022	IAG	Safeguarding	Yes	26 July 2022	20 minutes
23 August 2022	IAG	Education	Yes	25 October 2022	34 minutes
23 August /2022	IAG	Education	Yes	8 November 2022	27 minutes
23 August 2022	IAG	Education	Yes	8 November 2022	11 minutes
15 December 2022	Immigration	EUSS/EUPS	No	Not closed	1 hour, 24 minutes

Note: IAG = information, advice and guidance

this book – bureaucratic bordering (the need for paperwork) and problem clustering (not having pre-settled status meant she could not receive benefits), often due to issues beyond the individual's control (such as the suspension of the issuing of National Insurance numbers due to the COVID-19 pandemic).

Lockdown also saw a period of closure of the EUSS Resolution Centre and all local scanning centres, plus the suspension of the ability to send documents by post.[91] The processing of EUSS applications also took longer:

> 16-06-20 Called the client regarding their EUSS application. They have not heard anything. I called the resolution centre on their behalf and was advised that everything was ok, the application has passed the criminal conviction stage, which had been the holdup previously, and was just taking longer due to Covid19. I told the client, they were overjoyed and said it was a big weight off to know that things were ok with the application.[92]

For those who did not have valid ID documents to make an application for EUSS, the closure of embassies and consulates during this time created a backlog for appointments for those needing, for example, new passports, which in turn delayed applications to the EUSS. In addition, specialist support agencies, such as GYROS, moved to virtual support, which limited their capacity to help the very people who needed them most due to problems of digital access.

> 28/04/2020 Client messaged me asking me to call her. I called her this morning and client was worried as she hasn't got EUSS. Client said she has been living in the UK for 7 years and wanted to apply now. I asked her if client has a smartphone and client said that no she hasn't. She has a valid passport. Client is willing to wait until after the lockdown and I said I could help her when she is ready.[93]

2. Current issues

At the time of writing, the EUSS application system had been live for over four years and the status itself has been in use for more than two years. While some of the early issues persist, others have also come to light.

---

[91] C. Barnard and F. Costello 'The EU Settlement Scheme: a resounding success or a perfect storm?' *UK in a Changing Europe* (10 July 2020), available at: https://ukandeu. ac.uk/the-eu-settlement-scheme-a-resounding-success-or-a-perfect-storm/, accessed 23 November 2023.

[92] Client ID 748.

[93] Client ID 982.

2.1 Late applications

While the deadline to apply was 30 June 2021, it was always known that some people would miss this. Provision was made for individuals to apply late if they have 'reasonable grounds'. The guidance requires caseworkers to take a flexible and pragmatic approach to assessing claims of reasonable grounds. Examples given by the guidance include children whose carers have not applied for them, people with reduced mental and physical capacity, people with EEA residence documents, victims of modern slavery and victims of abuse. The guidance makes it clear that this list is not exhaustive and there is a wide, catch-all category of 'other compelling practical or compassionate reasons'.[94] As of June 2023, there were almost 505,330 late applications to the scheme.[95]

However, the Statement of Changes in Immigration Rules HC 1496[96] added a 'required date' to Appendix EU (EU 9(e)) for validity assessments of applications made on or after 09 August 2023. This means that from 09 August 2023, reasonable grounds for making a late application have become a validity requirement instead of an eligibility requirement. In fact, this two-step process was outlined in the Withdrawal Agreement,[97] bringing the Home Office approach more in line with the process outlined in the WA. If the Home Office finds that the grounds for a late application are not reasonable, they will reject rather than refuse the application. As we have seen, this rejection means that the applicant will not have the right to an Administrative Review or an appeal.

One reason given for this change[98] was the fact that within this group of late applicants were those ineligible to apply for the EUSS because they arrived in the UK *after* 31 December 2020. Previously, however, submitting an application and receiving a CoA meant that they had the right to work until they received a rejection of their application. For example, one family in Great Yarmouth arrived in June 2021 and then applied for EUSS and

---

[94] Home Office and UK Visa and Immigration, 'EU Settlement Scheme: case worker guidance' *Gov.uk*, available at: www.gov.uk/government/publications/eu-settlement-sch eme-caseworker-guidance, accessed 20 January 2023.

[95] Home Office, n 4.

[96] Statement of Changes in Immigration Rules HC 1496: https://www.gov.uk/government/ publications/statement-of-changes-to-the-immigration-rules-hc-1496-17-july-2023/ statement-of-changes-to-the-immigration-rules-hc-1496-17-july-2023-accessible#chan ges-to-appendix-eu changes to Appendix EU, accessed 03 December 2023.

[97] Article 18(1)(d)

[98] The Lord Murray of Blidworth letter to the Home Affairs Select Committee 09 July 2023, available here: https://data.parliament.uk/DepositedPapers/Files/DEP2023-0609/ Murray.pdf, accessed 03 December 2023.

received a CoA. With this, the mother started working and her children were enrolled in the local school, but her application will be refused when it is processed because she arrived after the deadline of 31 December 2020. Meanwhile, the CoA has given her a false sense of security of a future life in the UK.[99] The most recent changes mean that an applicant now does not receive a CoA until after they have passed the first validity check stage of their application. GYROS does not help those who arrived after the deadline to make late applications to the scheme, but it does provide them with other practical support, such as food vouchers.

There are other consequences for those who arrived after 31 December 2020. For example, when Paula arrived in the UK after the deadline, she was seven months pregnant; she submitted a late EUSS application with the help of an advice shark, who advised that she would be successful. She gave birth in the UK, so when her application is ultimately refused, she will face medical bills of up to £10,000, in accordance with NHS overseas visitor charges (see Chapter 7). When she interacts with a body such as the local council, she will be asked to prove her eligibility for support, but will not be entitled.[100] She could also face removal from the UK.

The continued stream of late EUSS applications has had a knock-on effect on those who applied by the June 2021 deadline. The spike in applications just before the deadline and the continued pace of applications since mean that there is now a significant processing delay, often with serious consequences for individuals. Take, for example, Ines, a Lithuanian woman who applied to EUSS on 28 June 2021 (pre deadline) but did not receive her CoA for a month, during which time the agency did not allow her to work. As a result, she fell behind on her rent, could not pay her utility bills and had to rely on food parcels. She also struggled to pay for medication. She had been living in the UK for 16 years.[101] Now the Home Office no longer issues a CoA until after it has decided on the validity criteria, genuine applicants – like Ines' – may face further significant delays in their ability to evidence their rights.

GYROS has been busier with EUSS applications and enquiries after the 30 June 2021 deadline than it was prior to that. This is because it is not only dealing with late applications but also chasing up submitted applications, generating share codes, undertaking joining family member applications,

---

[99] C. Barnard and F. Costello, 'EUSS applications: "meritorious" ones suffer from processing delays; "unmeritorious" ones benefit' *UK in a Changing Europe* (14 March 2022), available at: https://ukandeu.ac.uk/euss-applications-meritorious-suffer-from-processing-delays-unmeritorious-ones-benefit/, accessed 23 November 2023.

[100] Ibid.

[101] C. Barnard and F. Costello, 'EUSS beyond the cliff's edge' *UK in a Changing Europe* (17 August 2021), available at: https://ukandeu.ac.uk/euss-beyond-the-cliffs-edge/, accessed 23 November 2023.

'upgrading' applications and updating details online for those clients who cannot do so themselves. Also, in cases like Paula's, it helps to sort out issues generated by advice sharks.

2.2 Advice sharks

'Advice sharks' – so called because of the similarity in their mode of operation to 'loan sharks' – have also profited from those needing help with their EUSS applications, especially during the lockdowns, when regulated advice services, such as GYROS, went online and thus became inaccessible to those without internet access. They often charge significant fees (£30–£500 per visit) for their 'services', and they use intimidation tactics to elicit payment, even when the advice they have provided is wrong. Take Pieter, who paid £150 to an advice shark for help with his (free) EUSS application and was charged £40–£80 each time he returned to the advice shark for an update on his application – he paid £700 in total. He eventually discovered that the advice shark had lost his documents, including his ID card. The advice shark told Pieter that she would call the police if he contacted her again and threatened that she could have him deported as he no longer had a legal right to be in the UK. Pieter was left without any form of ID and had to apply late to the scheme via a paper application. He was unable to work or claim Universal Credit, because he had no ID and he had not submitted an EUSS application.[102]

2.3 Non-EU family members of EU nationals

Non-EEA nationals represent 6 per cent (607,960 applications) of the total EUSS applications up to June 2023.[103] The most numerous non–EEA nationalities applying to the scheme come from India (95,810), Pakistan (83,070), Brazil (66,370), Ghana (39,890) and Albania (39,800). Only 28 per cent of NEFMs received settled status when they applied – much lower than the percentage for EU nationals – a greater proportion having received pre-settled outcomes (54 per cent). Refusals for non-EEA nationals were slightly higher among this group than EU nationals, at 10 per cent compared

---

[102] F. Costello and C. Barnard, 'Advice sharks are benefitting from the cost-of-living crisis' *UK in a Changing Europe* (3 November 2022), available at: https://ukandeu.ac.uk/adv ice-sharks-are-benefitting-from-the-cost-of-living-crisis/, accessed 18 February 2023.

[103] The Home Office also holds data on EUSS Family Permit Applications. Home Office, n 4, 'EUSS family permits enable family members of EU, other EEA and Swiss citizens, resident in the UK by the end of the transition period (and who, with some exceptions, have pre-settled or settled status under the EUSS), and of qualifying British citizens returning to the UK after living in the EEA or Switzerland, to join them in the UK'. See also: https:// www.gov.uk/government/statistics/immigration-system-statistics-year-ending-june-2023/ why-do-people-come-to-the-uk-for-family-reasons, accessed 12 December 2023.

to 8 per cent. A further 7 per cent of applications were withdrawn, void or invalid. The higher level of pre-settled status could be because of the increased evidential requirements on this group to prove their relationship with the EU family member. The easiest mechanism for making a successful application was for the NEFM to link their application to an application for pre-settled or settled status by their EU family member.

Derivative rights holders and *Zambrano* carers also feature in our data. A freedom of information request to the Home Office about application numbers and outcomes for this group showed that:

- The largest groups of applicants were from Nigeria, Pakistan and Ghana.[104]
- Refusal rates for derivative rights holders (those whose rights are derived from another) were much higher than for the rest of the scheme, at for example 22 per cent for *Chen* carers[105] and 21 per cent for *Ibrahim/Teixeira* carers,[106] increasing to 81 per cent for *Zambrano* carers.
- For the paper application route, 59 per cent of applicants were women.

GYROS needed to navigate cases where other immigration routes were sought after an EUSS refusal (for derivative rights holders):

'My client AA★ had desperately tried to get under Zambrano EUSS and was refused twice. I have now just applied for FLR FP,[107] and I am sure she will get it, but it is such a long wait, and she will only be granted 2.5 years of leave, so it is very different.'[108]

2.4 Upgrading from pre-settled to settled status

As we have outlined, when the EUSS was first established, those with pre-settled status had to make another application to 'upgrade' their status to settled status after the initial five-year period. Among the effects of a

---

[104] C. Barnard and F. Costello, 'Paper applications to a digital scheme' *UK in a Changing Europe* (23 February 2022), available at: https://ukandeu.ac.uk/paper-applications-to-a-digital-scheme/, accessed 23 November 2023.

[105] Primary carer of a 'self-sufficient' EEA national child: Case C-480/08 *Chen v Secretary of State for the Home Department* EU:C:2010:83.

[106] Child of an EEA national worker/former worker where they are the primary carer of the child and the child is in education in the UK. Case C-310/08 *London Borough of Harrow v Nimco Hassan Ibrahim and Secretary of State for the Home Department* EU:C:2010:80.

[107] FLR (FP) stands for Further Leave to Remain under the F and P categories of the UK Immigration Rules, which are based on the Family Life (under the Appendix FM) or the Private Life (under Part 7). For more, see 'Immigration rules' *Gov.uk*, available at: www.gov.uk/guidance/immigration-rules, accessed 24 January 2023.

[108] Immigration adviser (Norfolk, June 2021).

loss of status are the inability to rent accommodation, accept job offers, open a bank account and access certain forms of healthcare for free. The EU+ national would also come face to face with the full force of the UK's hostile environment towards 'illegal' migrants. Concerns have long been raised that those more vulnerable and marginalized will once again struggle to make this second fresh application.[109] Others still (an unknowable number) will have received pre-settled status when they were in fact entitled to settled status, because of difficulty providing evidence to prove their residence in the UK – this is particularly the case for those who were street homeless and did not have access to their paperwork for the EUSS.

Following the High Court's *IMA* decision, the Home Office has announced that it would implement a two-year automatic extension for pre-settled status holders from September 2023.[110] However, the High Court held that once the relevant conditions are met, the right of permanent residence under the WA is acquired automatically. How does the two-year extension sit with the automatic accrual of permanent residence rights? For example, if someone fails to upgrade after an initial two-year extension, will a further two years be granted? The Home Office has not clarified this. From 2024, the Home Office intends to automatically convert the status of some individuals from pre-settled to settled status via automated digital checks (for example, using HMRC records). But for many low-paid migrant workers on precarious zero-hours contracts or working in informal employment contexts, like Darius in Box 1.1, or those not working, like Lara in Box 3.1, this digital footprint may not be generated. Further, there have been more than 1.2 million applications for children (aged under 18) to the scheme,[111] many of whom will not be generating the required footprint for an automatic upgrade. All of this is important because there are significant differences between the rights and entitlements of those with pre-settled and settled status. For example, as we shall see in Chapter 5, the *Fratila* judgment[112] confirmed that someone

[109] M. Sumption and M. Fernandez-Reino, 'Unsettled Status – 2020: which EU citizens are at risk of failing to secure their rights after Brexit?' *The Migration Observatory at the University of Oxford* (24 September 2020), available at: https://migrationobservatory.ox.ac.uk/resources/reports/unsettled-status-2020/, accessed 4 October 2023.

[110] Home Office and Lord Murray of Bildworth, 'EU Settlement Scheme enhancements confirmed' *Gov.uk* (7 July 2023), available at: www.gov.uk/government/news/eu-settlement-scheme-enhancements-confirmed, accessed 24 November 2023.

[111] Home Office 'EU Settlement Scheme quarterly statistics, June 2023' *Gov.uk* (24 August 2023), available at: www.gov.uk/government/statistics/eu-settlement-scheme-quarterly-statistics-june-2023, accessed 24 November 2023.

[112] *Fratila v Secretary of State for Work and Pensions* [2021] UKSC 53.

with pre-settled status but no other 'qualifying right to reside'[113] (such as being in work or self-employed) may not be able to claim Universal Credit.

3. GYROS' approach

As we have seen, having pre-settled or settled status is now the gateway to the rights discussed in the subsequent chapters: to work, rent accommodation, claim benefits and access healthcare. 'Have you got EUSS?' is the first question GYROS advisers ask clients, (although sometimes it has to be explained using other terms, such as: 'Do you have residency?'[114]). The previous sections have shown some of the issues facing GYROS' clients in navigating the EUSS application process. Through the discussion, we have also shown, almost incidentally, how GYROS' advisers interact with clients – one of the recurrent issues in this book. GYROS' approach can be characterized by pragmatism (sorting out an email address, upgrading a status online, ringing the Resolution Centre). It is informed by an understanding of the law, not least because, as we saw in Chapter 1, GYROS advisers are qualified to OISC Level 1 and Level 2 to give immigration advice.

Six GYROS advisers are OISC Level 1 (Limited to EUSS), a new advice route to increase the number of advisers within advice agencies who could help with the more straightforward EUSS applications. Changes to the scheme for late applications as outlined above, mean that most late applications are now more complex and will likely fall to level 2 advisers. GYROS have two Level 2 advisers. The OISC guidance says (regarding Level 1 [Limited to EUSS]):

> Such advisers can make applications for EU Citizens and their family members under the EU Settlement Scheme, where such applications rely on the straightforward presentation of facts to meet the criteria set out by the Home Office under the scheme. Such applications will not be discretionary or concessionary in nature and applicants will not have an immigration history that is likely to adversely affect the application in question. Where a case becomes complicated, or an application is refused an adviser must refer the client as soon as possible to an adviser authorised to practise at OISC Level 2 or 3.[115]

---

[113] 'Check if you have the right to reside for benefits' *Citizens Advice*, available at: www.cit izensadvice.org.uk/benefits/check-if-you-have-the-right-to-reside-for-benefits/, accessed 24 November 2023.

[114] Interview with council worker.

[115] For more, see 'Application for Level 1 EU Settlement Scheme registration' *Gov.uk*, available at: www.gov.uk/government/publications/application-for-level-1-eu-settlem ent-scheme-registration, accessed 24 November 2023.

E. Conclusion

This chapter has shown how the EUSS has operated in practice. The Home Office put considerable resources into setting up the scheme and was generous when it came to application requirements (in the sense that it was sufficient to show residence and not that the individual was exercising a Treaty right). The digital nature of the scheme also made it user-friendly and easily accessible for many, especially the Eurostars of other research, namely the high skilled, English speaking and digitally literate, working in universities and hospitals, who could demonstrate a clear footprint with the state (for example, through regular employment and payment of taxes). This has not been the case for the many EU migrant workers in Great Yarmouth who lack the language and IT skills to apply and manage their status and often lack any regular footprint of engagement with the state and do not have paperwork to prove their residence. They have, therefore, needed, and continue to need, help from advisers. Some find their way to OISC-qualified advisers; others fall into the hands of advice sharks.

This chapter has also shown how every aspect of GYROS' work is affected by the EUSS. GYROS has a standalone workstream that helps clients and their families apply for, maintain and use their status. But it is also a gateway to employment, housing and welfare rights. It is an aspect of GYROS' work which makes it unique as an advice charity: the general advice they offer must always be immigration led or grounded in immigration law and knowledge. It is not simply a matter of advising on, for example, eligibility for Universal Credit, but rather eligibility for Universal Credit as an EU national and the separate rules which apply. It is likely that GYROS' clients will need help for at least the next five years until they qualify for settled status, and beyond for help with joining family members, new(born) family members and those less digitally literate and in need of ongoing help to use their status, update it and provide it to relevant third parties as required.

The common themes of precarity and problem clustering that we will see in each chapter often find their root in immigration status. The additional hurdles EU migrants face in providing evidence of their immigration status, proving 'continuous residence' as a 'qualified person' and dealing with the mistakes of third parties through a lack of understanding of immigration regulations mean that the fingerprints of immigration status are found in every problem cluster.

Having set out the EUSS as a fundamental requirement to show the right to work in the UK (since July 2021), in the next chapter, we explore the work experiences of EU migrant workers in and around Great Yarmouth. We start in the early 2000s, when Edita and others from the House first moved to Great Yarmouth, exercising their free movement rights, and started working in a chicken factory in the local area, and come up to today to see if and how their situations have changed.

4

Employment

A. Introduction

Virtually all the participants in our research had come to the UK to look for work, exercising their free movement rights under Article 45 TFEU. The work they found, either directly from an employer in Great Yarmouth or via an agency, was mainly low paid and 'low-skilled',[1] and often precarious, frequently based on zero-hours contracts,[2] as was the case for Darius (introduced in Box 1.1). The main employers in and around Great Yarmouth are farms – where the work includes berry picking, pig farming and cultivating vegetable crops, such as asparagus and sugar beets – and poultry factories, including Bernard Matthews, Cranswick plc, Banham Poultry and the 2 Sisters Food Group. Some of these companies are poultry giants; for instance, the 2 Sisters Food Group produces one third of all poultry products consumed daily in the UK,[3] Banham Poultry sells more than 650,000 chickens per week[4] and Bernard Matthews, a household name in the UK (known for the advertising slogan, 'bootiful'), was once the biggest turkey

---

[1] A. Bulat 'High-skilled good, low-skilled bad?' British, Polish and Romanian attitudes towards low-skilled EU migration' (2019) 248 *National Institute Economic Review* 49.

[2] 'Migrants in the UK labour market: an overview' *The Migration Observatory at the University of Oxford* (6 January 2022), available at: https://migrationobservatory.ox.ac.uk/resources/briefings/migrants-in-the-uk-labour-market-an-overview/, accessed 11 February 2023; Migration Advisory Committee, *Migrants in Low-Skilled Work: The Growth of EU and non-EU Labour in Low-Skilled Jobs and Its Impact on the UK* (London: Migration Advisory Committee, 2014), available at: https://assets.publishing.service.gov.uk/government/uploads/system/uploads/attachment_data/file/333083/MAC-Migrants_in_low-skilled _work__Full_report_2014.pdf, accessed 1 May 2020.

[3] https://www.2sfg.com/About-Us

[4] See the website at: https://banhampoultry.co.uk/, accessed 17 March 2023.

farmer in Europe.[5] In 2016, Bernard Matthews was sold to 2 Sisters Food Group.[6]

As with the construction sector, where 'temporary, project-based labour, informal recruitment and casualised employment'[7] is the norm, making it an unattractive employment pathway for 'local' people,[8] so too the '3 Ps' (picking, packing and plucking) sectors described in this chapter. We begin by looking at the experience of working in chicken factories in Great Yarmouth, largely as described by those living in the House and participants in focus groups and interviews (Section B). We then consider the issues that have arisen in the GYROS data on employment problems (Section C) and reflect on focus group participants' experiences during the COVID-19 pandemic. Section D looks at formal enforcement routes and examines cases with similar facts which have made it to a tribunal. Finally, Section E looks at EU law requirements on equal treatment and enforcement, and what happens in reality with the help of GYROS advisers.

Apart from one resident, all of those living in our HMO have experience (either prior to the research or at the time of the research) of working in chicken factories. As one focus group participant recognized, as newcomers, the factories gave them "the opportunity to start earning money"; but they also saw disadvantages: "From the other side, it's really cold. It's very hard work. And the attitudes towards workers are not the best."[9] This view was supported by other data showing that working conditions were poor and bullying and sexual harassment appeared to be widespread. Problems were also evident in the few cases that have been taken to employment tribunals by EU migrant workers elsewhere in the UK. However, the GYROS data show that EU migrants tend to come to GYROS not for advice on these serious issues, but for help with more practical matters, such as writing and printing CVs to enable them look for work (and claim benefits). GYROS' response is pragmatic. They do not address the fundamental issues of, say, bullying and harassment, but they will help a client get a P45 if and when their job comes to an end, and they will help them find another job.

---

5   See the website at: www.bernardmatthews.com/, accessed 11 February 2023.

6   S. Goodley, 'The secretive "chicken king": inside the empire of Ranjit Singh Boparan' *The Guardian* (28 September 2017), available at: www.theguardian.com/business/2017/sep/28/chicken-king-empire-ranjit-singh-boparan, accessed 4 January 2023.

7   M. Ruhs, 'Immigration and labour market protectionism: protecting local workers' preferential access to the national labour market' in C. Costello and M. Freedland (eds) *Migrants at Work* (Oxford: Oxford University Press, 2014), 67.

8   Ibid, 67.

9   Focus group (Great Yarmouth, November 2021).

The need for 'paper trails'[10] and the problems of 'bureaucratic bordering',[11] discussed in Chapter 1, are constant themes in the employment context. The lack of payslips or a P45 leads to other difficulties, such as challenges in claiming benefits, applying for a place in adult education or, latterly, proving UK residency for EUSS post Brexit. So pragmatic law is important in delivering practical, short-term help to individuals. However, as noted, this does not address more structural issues (this is discussed further in Chapter 8).

We turn now to consider working life in the factories, as described by our interviewees. We cover their first impressions, the day-to-day working life and the effect of the pandemic.

B. Working life in the factories

1. Arrival and first impressions

As described in Chapter 2, many EU migrants working in and around Great Yarmouth were recruited in their own country. They describe being picked up in a van at Stansted airport and driven to Great Yarmouth, where they were placed in shared accommodation. We have already seen how Rasa (Latvian, sixties), on her first night in the country, slept in the living room of a caravan with six men and women. At 4 am, they were brought to the chicken factory to work. She was not shown to her permanent accommodation (a shared room in a hotel) until after she had worked her first shift in the factory.

A number of our interviewees had bad memories of their initial experiences in the factory: the time it took to travel to work, the size of the factory and the wet, cold environment. For example, Edita,[12] describing her first day at work, 16 years earlier, said the shared car ride "felt like we were driving there forever and ever and ever" and mentioned how "huge" the factory seemed, the constantly wet floor making her feet wet and cold through, the Wellington boots she was given, which had holes in, and the speed of the production line: "it was so fast paced. That's how it felt – everything was aching." Then, without any discussion, she was moved to a different room to do other work. "You don't know when you're gonna finish. You completely lose any control," she said. Edita's first shift was ten hours long. She wasn't offered any training, and there was just her friend to induct her. Edita also remembers the pain in her hands the next day:

---

[10] S. Horton and J. Heyman (eds), *Paper Trails: Migrants, Documents, and Legal Insecurity* (Durham, NC: Duke University Press, 2020).

[11] P. Manolova, 'Inclusion through irregularisation? Exploring the politics and realities of internal bordering in managing post-crisis labour migration in the EU' (2021) *Journal of Ethnic and Migration Studies* 3687.

[12] Interview with Edita (Great Yarmouth, September 2021).

'Waking up the next morning, I feel this, this finger was so swollen. I couldn't bend it, I couldn't move it, it was massive. It was so painful. That's how I woke up from the pain, because we kept like banding those [chicken] legs …. It was dreadful, honestly, the size of my finger. I really thought I'd damaged it.'

Lack of training and having to learn fast on the job was a common experience. Dorota (a Polish worker in a food processing factory) said:

'Thursday, when I went to work in the factory, they never showed me what to do … they put a basket of potatoes and scale and boxes. I am like, ok, how much? 50 grams. Ok. So, the first day I am like, 50, 47, 48, 49, 50. And then she comes to me and she, like, mimes "no" and "faster" hand gestures. Not even saying it to me, not even speaking to me. "Faster, Faster" [hand gestures] … nobody explained to me [on the] first day: "So this is what you do. You've got a scale here and you can put 40–60 grams in the box." No one told me this, so I am trying to do exactly 50.'[13]

Edita and Dorota were recalling their factory work in the period from 2004 to 2008. In our fieldwork we also spoke to individuals from one of the UK's largest recruitment agencies, which (though no longer involved in poultry factory recruitment in Norfolk) said they did have a robust induction and training plan for workers.[14] However, more recent arrivals tell much the same story. For example, Ana (a Romanian national) had a panic attack on her first day, in June 2021. She had spent four hours standing in one spot sorting through a constant, fast stream of chicken breasts.

2. Day-to-day working life in factories

As noted above, chicken factories are cold, wet places. Camilla (Lithuanian, fifties, Room 3 of the House) said that "2 Sisters is cold chicken, Banham is wet chicken"; she prefers the cold chicken. On the other hand, Vida (Lithuanian, thirties, in Room 5 of the House) found Banham too cold and preferred Bernard Matthews. With time, workers say they learned some 'tricks' to feel warmer, such as doubling up on gloves. They also said that the quality of their working lives in the factories depended on two factors: the section they worked in and the treatment from their supervisor/line manager (the 'white helmets').

---

[13] Interview with Dorota (Norwich, November 2021).
[14] Telephone conversation with a UK Recruitment Agency (online, 14 February 2022).

All agreed that the worst sections to work on were those that involved lifting heavy weights – they were expected to lift trays of poultry weighing between 30 and 60 kilos. One focus group participant said she had enjoyed working in the factory till she was moved to a section where she was expected to lift "very heavy cold turkeys and heavy bones from one area to another".[15] Some women in a focus group said they were required to lift weights similar to those lifted by much larger men. Regina (a Lithuanian focus group participant with 15 plus years in a chicken factory[16]) said that in the past there were more men who could do the lifting, but now, with staff shortages, "young girls or women … are expected to lift, like, metal wheels and trays of 50 kilos". Edita (Latvian, thirties, a previous tenant in the House) agreed:

'I know by law there's a certain amount that one person can lift, and I've never seen in factories that anyone ever weighs the tray full of [chicken] fillets. So, if you, if you take something like inner fillets, they go in a metal tray … I don't know, it's like 50/60 kilos, and you're expected to lift it, because it comes in very solid, doesn't it? And they're wet and they are really heavy.'[17]

Regina said that she often offered to do the heavier lifting: "I want to offer myself. I say, you know, I lived my life. I had my children. I do what I want to, you know. I'll pick it up. It doesn't matter. You know, I just, you know … looking out for younger colleagues or female colleagues." She is in her mid-sixties and has advanced arthritis in her hands. She said that she planned to retire soon and had nothing to lose by sharing her experiences. She commented: "It's just, it's just dreadful to watch young girls lifting that and damaging their health."

Another issue which came up repeatedly in the focus groups was the speed of the production line. Dorota, who later worked for a recruitment agency providing staff to poultry factories, said that people are "given jobs that they physically cannot do. It's too hard for them or too quick in the factories. People are complaining it is too quick. Sometimes the lines are making them sick. It must be so quick that when the line stops, people are [dizzy]." Ana recalled that when she was promoted to quality technician, she was able to stand back from the factory line and observe what was happening. She said team leaders hoping to make record numbers each day did not consider the toll it was having on the people who were working the lines. She explained:

[15]   Portuguese focus group (Great Yarmouth, July 2022).
[16]   Focus group (Great Yarmouth, November 2021).
[17]   Ibid.

'I was like, oh my God, poor things. Their hands was like this [shaking] and always doing like this [mimics shaking] ... like, oh my God! I tried to help of course but you cannot, you cannot. You cannot help everyone. Yeah, and they are always pushing them, always pushing them, always pushing them, faster, faster, faster. And the line managers ... I was just like, seeing, like, how are they looking at that screen. "And oh, we have 3,000 crates. So, if I do another 500, I'm gonna be number one this weekend. So let's pump it, go, go, go, work faster, faster", and then: "Oh, I've made it. I have 3,500." It doesn't matter that the people are like: "Oh my God!" [mimes being slumped over/collapsed].'

In a Portuguese focus group with six participants, three were off work with health issues, all related to the physicality of work on the factory floor.[18]

Line managers or supervisors would be 'promoted' based not on their management skills, but their language skills – that is, an ability to speak English plus the main language of workers on the line, enabling them to bridge communication gaps with management. A theme of poor management skills emerged. Dorota said: "The worst thing is when people are being shouted at, and it is happening constantly." Another interviewee complained that a Portuguese national was promoted to a managerial role and she caused "problems to the Portuguese ... she causes a lot of problems ... discrimination. ... [She is] very strict with people and demeans them."[19] One participant in a care worker focus group said that she believed her British manager "hates foreigners" and noted that she "visibly shakes in anger [about foreigners]. She voted for Brexit."[20]

Other factors affecting the quality of working life include the short period of time for breaks and overcrowding in canteens. By the time workers took off their personal protective equipment (PPE) and maybe went outside to smoke or went to the canteen, their break was over. Being late back was not an option. Ana said that "if you are too late with your hands [washing] and with whatever you're doing, you're going to be punished."[21] She said they "yell at you and call you names", and for her (a former primary school teacher from Romania), that is "the worst form of humiliation".

Workers often talked about being refused toilet breaks. For example, when Ana asked for a five-minute toilet break on her first day, she was told "Shut up or I will throw you out." Once again, line managers were abusing their

---

[18] Portuguese focus group (Great Yarmouth, July 2022).
[19] Ibid.
[20] Focus group (Great Yarmouth, March 2020).
[21] Focus group (Great Yarmouth, November 2021).

power. Ana commented: "If you want to go to toilet, yeah, you need to ask: "Can I please?" And if your eyes are beautiful, maybe they will give you a thumbs up. If not, you're gonna just go over there and do your job. They will say no."[22] She said she now suffers from bladder problems. Dorota said that for women, especially during their periods, the lack of toilet breaks, the provision of Portaloos and the physical distance to the toilets were issues, but this was rarely discussed. When we spoke to a recruitment agency, they said that people should be allowed toilet breaks. However, they also recognized that taking off all of the PPE and then putting it back on would have a significant impact on factory lines measured by speed and targets.

Beyond being denied toilet breaks, the women spoke of sexual abuse and harassment in the factories. Dorota recalled women being "pinched" and having chicken heads thrown at them. Edita said her male line manager expected that "something would happen between them". She said giving sexual favours was a commonly accepted way to get more or better shifts. Lina said a manager would touch "my friend and me like that, you know, inappropriately, and then that … then I didn't know what to do. I was, like, afraid to say so to someone to complain. And I said: 'Don't, don't do this.'"[23] The manager did stop but she was penalized, with changes to her timetable and fewer shifts, for not acquiescing.

The question of shift allocation came up repeatedly. Dorota told us that in her work in a recruitment agency, she had witnessed managers accepting payment for guaranteed factory shifts. She described people coming into the office saying:

'"My manager said I would be working all week." And I'm like, but the manager is not the one who makes this decision. We make these decisions. And then suddenly we will get an email from the manager the next day saying: "I want x, x and x person to work only."'

Workers on zero-hours contracts and precarious work arrangements were particularly vulnerable. Sickness or childcare issues were often given as reasons for a person being replaced or not offered hours. One research participant said that some workers pay line managers up to £20 cash per week in order to "guarantee" their shifts.

The poor working conditions have impacts beyond the factory floor. Many work 'continental' shifts (that is, 12 hours on/12 hours off, rotating days and nights) in the factories. This is tiring, especially when combined with travel time to the factory, which can take well over an hour each way; some buses

---

[22] Focus group (Great Yarmouth, November 2021).
[23] Interview with Lina (Great Yarmouth, September 2021).

left Great Yarmouth at 3.30 am for the 5 am shift. One mother said she used to drop her child off with the childminder at 2.30 am every day so that she could catch the bus to the factory.[24] All said they were exhausted and spend their days off sleeping. As Regina (Lithuanian) said: "It's impossible. ... If you work 12 and a half hours plus ... travel, if you've got children at home and family to look after, cook for them. Your brain just goes all, all ... just exhausted."[25] Edita agreed: "Like you completely lose any control. You have no say. That's how you feel – you have no say. Okay... Mentally it was very difficult." [26] Camilla (Lithuanian, fifties) said: "You need to work, work, work. No holiday, no weekend, no nothing, just pay money for rent and for water, for everything."[27] The long shifts, combined with the tiredness, meant that migrant workers had little time to connect with their (new) local community. The result, as we saw in Chapter 2, is that these migrant communities largely keep themselves to themselves.

We discussed with interviewees how they might improve their position. Edita spoke of her goal of becoming a directly employed factory worker rather than an agency worker, as this would give increased security. She, and Lina and Dorota, learned English and were able to be promoted in the factory. They subsequently moved into other jobs more relevant to their qualifications, following the 'first job, any job, dream job' progression.[28] However, this progression is more difficult for those who do not speak any English. Factories are informally delineated by nationality groups, and that can affect who is sent to work there by the recruitment agencies. Dorota said that she has "even had managers who said: 'I only want Polish, Lithuanian and Latvian. I don't want any other [nationalities].' I have this email from my manager ... probably [from] 2016. I couldn't believe I am actually being told by my boss: 'Listen, you employ only this, this and this [nationality].'" This meant that workers often learned another European language before learning any English, which, in turn, made employment progression and navigating issues in the workplace even more difficult. The GYROS database indicates that 86 per cent of their clients rate their English language skills as either limited, very limited or none.[29]

---

[24] Portuguese focus group (Great Yarmouth, July 2022).

[25] Focus group (Great Yarmouth, November 2021).

[26] Interview with Edita (Great Yarmouth, September 2021).

[27] Interview with Camilla (Great Yarmouth, November 2021).

[28] V. Parutis ' "Economic Migrants" or "Middling Transnationals"? East European migrants' experiences of work in the UK' (2011) 52(1) *International Migration* 36, 41.

[29] C. Barnard, S. Fraser Butlin and F. Costello, 'The changing status of European Union nationals in the United Kingdom following Brexit: the lived experience of the European Union Settlement Scheme' (2022) 31 *Social and Legal Studies* 365, 381.

3. The COVID-19 pandemic

The COVID-19 pandemic occurred during our fieldwork, so we looked at how lockdown and the pandemic restrictions affected low-paid EU migrant communities.[30] The 'key worker' status (assigned to those working in factories, farms, care homes and so on) of many in this group meant that they continued to work throughout lockdown. A Lithuanian care worker said her employer introduced a pay rise of £1 per hour in the early days of the pandemic, but she also noted:

> 'There hasn't been any social distancing introduced. We have been asked to wash our hands more often. Employer gave us ... a face mask to be worn outside the work and [a] box of gloves each. I have bought some masks and gloves online too, that I use outside the work.'[31]

Many said they felt unable to say no to overtime, given the increased pressure to get food onto supermarket shelves.[32] As one Lithuanian worker said:

> 'Yes, I have been asked to work on weekends, and managers really insist that we do. There are more orders, and we are expected to work at a faster pace [than] usual. As I work for [a] work agency ... our work coordinators do insist we need to come to work. People are worried to say no to overtime, as this might mean that there will be no hours offered.[33]

Some were glad to be in work and to have extra shifts: "I work more hours because [the] factory increased the time schedule. Everything is fine. I'm happy I have a job in this crisis period."[34] However, the long hours took their toll:

> 'I could not see my daughters. I didn't want to see them. I felt like to see them and hear them after 12 hours of working, it was just too hard.

---

[30] See M. Morris 'Migrant workers and coronavirus: risks and responses' *IPPR* (25 March 2020), available at: www.ippr.org/blog/migrant-workers-and-coronavirus, accessed 16 January 2023.

[31] Coronavirus telephone conversation (2020).

[32] C. Barnard and F. Costello, 'Working conditions of migrant "key workers" in the Covid-19 crisis' *UK in a Changing Europe* (8 April 2020), available at: https://ukandeu.ac.uk/working-conditions-of-migrant-key-workers-in-the-covid-19-crisis/, accessed 16 January 2023.

[33] Covid telephone conversations (April 2020).

[34] Telephone conversation (April 2020).

And they were like: "Mom, please can you spend some time with us?" "No. Leave me alone. I'm sleepy. I can't. I'm tired." Like it's awful.'[35]

The approach of management to COVID-19 restrictions, especially social distancing, varied. One worker said: "Only need to keep one metre distance between workers. Hand washing has been reinforced. If manager sees people working too close to each other, he asks them to increase distance. We all have been told at the meeting about social distancing."[36] Another said: "We need to keep social distance everywhere. We need to wear plastic facial mask, which gets wet quickly. However, people keep social distance in front of management, but when nobody see them, they do not keep it. It is a nightmare."[37] A worker in another factory said: "Management has not told us anything. Some people are trying to keep their distance as much as possible. We did have general advice when government introduced lockdown – only what to do for outside of work."[38]

Social distancing was a practical problem in some factories, because of the number of staff on site at any one time and the close proximity of workers on the factory line. Even where social distancing was implemented on the shop floor, workers would sit in the cafeteria together, smoke together and travel to work together, either car sharing or on buses. As one interviewee put it: "at the end of the night, everyone in a big pile to escape the factory, so what did [social distancing] matter?"[39] And given that many migrant workers in Great Yarmouth live in overcrowded shared rental accommodation and HMOs, with shared facilities – such as the kitchen, bathroom and laundry – social distancing, let alone isolation, was all but impossible.

A common complaint, especially from poultry factory workers, was about PPE, especially masks. One worker said: "[The manager] says that they have masks and PPE, but they're saying that if they go after two hours to take another mask, a clean mask, they are pushed away. No, not now. After break."[40] Agency workers, a group already considered to be 'lower status' (as noted in Chapter 3), thought access to masks and PPE was more limited for them compared to those directly employed by the factory.

It was not just in factories that there were issues around PPE. A Bulgarian 'bank' worker in a local hospital in Norfolk said:

---

[35] Focus group (Great Yarmouth, November 2021).
[36] Telephone conversation (April 2020).
[37] Telephone conversations (April 2020).
[38] Telephone conversation (April 2020).
[39] Telephone conversation (April 2020).
[40] Focus group (Great Yarmouth, November 2021).

'Really unhappy about lack of the proper PPE. We were working in the ward where one case of COVID-19 came and the whole ward got infected. Patients were vomiting and had diarrhoea, and we were expected to clean and help them with simple mask and gloves. We had to go and beg the core hospital staff to give us full PPE. They said yes, but then had to go and look for it with us, as it was somewhere in a closed box.'[41]

C. Issues in the GYROS dataset

Having looked at life in chicken factories, including during the Covid-19 pandemic, we turn now to consider the issues that EU migrant workers brought to GYROS. As we shall see, there is a striking dissonance between what is happening on the factory floor, as described by the residents in the House and focus groups participants, and what GYROS' clients sought help about.

Employment-related queries represent about 7 per cent of case notes in the GYROS database. Within the dataset, 50 per cent of clients were employed: 38 per cent were working full-time, 11 per cent were working part-time, 1.5 per cent were self-employed, 21 per cent were not employed and another 27 per cent were categorized 'not applicable', meaning either the individual was unable to work due to their immigration status or their employment status was deemed irrelevant to the issue they presented with. There were just under 250 different employers or agencies with which GYROS interacted. The majority of these were employment agencies recruiting to the local poultry factories.

The gender split for employment queries is in line with the gender split of the dataset as a whole, with 56 per cent of enquiries from women and 41 per cent from men. For those making employment-related queries, the median age was 45 and the median number of years in the UK was seven. Although just 7 per cent of enquiries were expressly related to employment, most of the welfare benefit enquiries (26 per cent) related to those applying for in-work benefits (see Chapter 6), showing that most of the migrant workers in the GYROS database were doing low-paid jobs. However, first they needed to find a job.

1. Help to find work

The database provides insight into the help required *before* people get into work. Almost half (48 per cent) of employment-related enquiries concerned

---

41   COVID-19 telephone conversation (2020).

finding work. The case notes show that GYROS is often the first port of call for help finding work, and clients were helped to create CVs or fill out application forms. For example:

> Client said that she is desperate to find some work, client has Food Hygiene Certificate and experience working in a restaurant setting. ... I called Birds Eye and was advised that client should just bring her CV and leave it at reception or contact GI-GROUP for vacancies at production.

She was advised to go to Birds Eye and take her CV around the local coffee shops.[42] A month later, the client returned, having received a job offer, and was given help to save her CV electronically. GYROS will keep copies of clients' CVs on file, and the database shows some clients coming back to seek assistance in updating their CV when looking for a new job. Given the poor levels of English language and low levels of digital literacy (60 per cent of GYROS' clients rate their IT skills as less than 5 out of 10, with 10 being excellent),[43] among clients, help with CV writing is a common request.

Support with CV preparation has value beyond assisting the client in obtaining work. As much work in Great Yarmouth, a coastal resort, is seasonal, periods of work are often combined with periods when people need to access benefits. Jobseekers applying for benefits, and now Universal Credit, must demonstrate that they are looking for work and an up-to-date CV must be uploaded to the Universal Credit journal.[44] For those with limited English and digital skills, this can be a significant hurdle, but not uploading a CV can lead to benefit sanctions, which, in turn, can lead to rent arrears and other debt issues. These administrative systems create pathways to legal problems which may arrive back at GYROS' door. So by keeping an electronic copy of clients' CVs, GYROS helps avoid problems down the line.

2. Commonly experienced work problems

What about the problems clients seek help with from GYROS once they are in work? The categories of enquiry are summarized in Figure 4.1.

The cases in the database, like the individual stories in Section B, paint a grim picture of working conditions, especially in poultry factories, with instances of bullying, poor management, refusal of toilet breaks and even some instances of exploitation and modern slavery. Yet the employment

---

[42]   Client ID 441.

[43]   Barnard et al (2022), n 29, 380.

[44]   For more, see Chapter 6, B.4.

Figure 4.1: Employment support enquiries on the GYROS database, 2015–2020

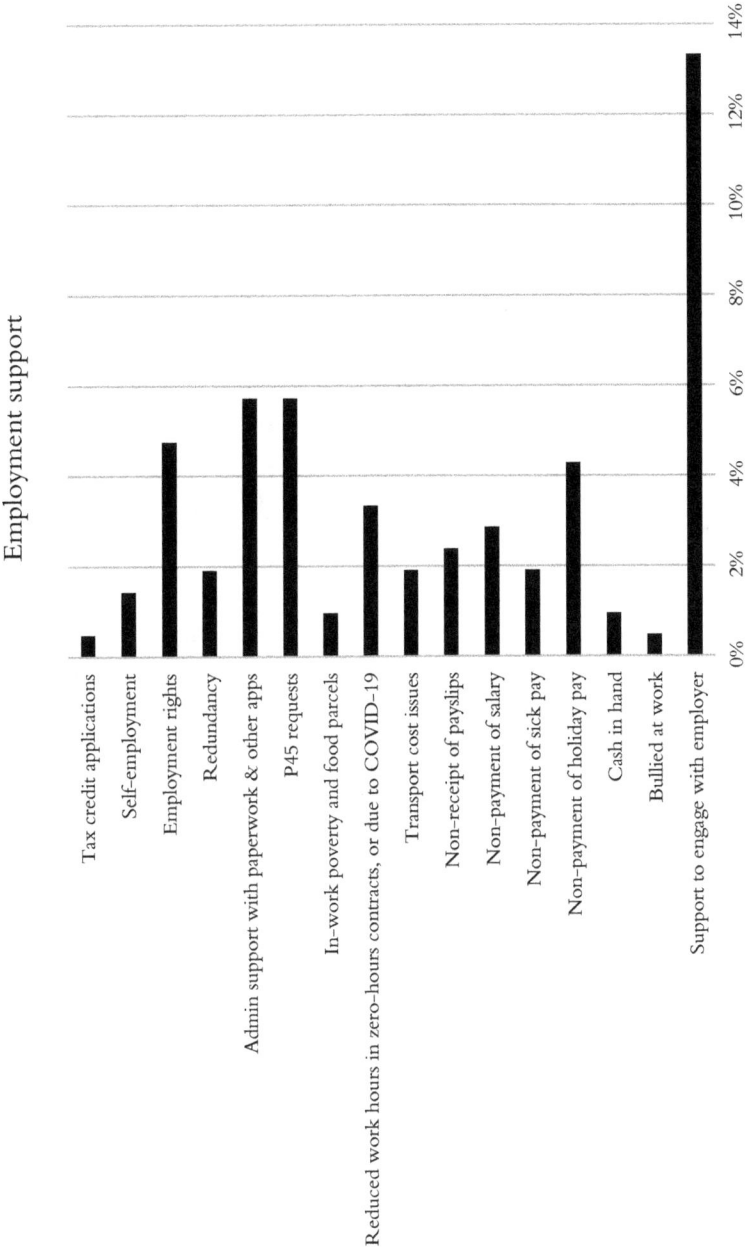

Employment support

Note: Based on an assessment of the case notes undertaken by the research authors

support requested from GYROS is often not linked to the substantive employment law issue itself, but associated issues: help to engage with employers; administrative support with paperwork; requests for P45s; concerns about reduced hours; and non-payment of wages, sick pay and holiday pay. There are also issues about loss of tied accommodation, which we address in Chapter 5, but here we shall look at these main employment issues in turn.

2.1 Support to engage with employers

A significant element of the help provided by GYROS is related to language, helping individuals to understand their employment contracts or to read health and safety materials provided by their employers, which they are required to sign. Clients also come to GYROS for help to request time off work on, for example, the grounds of ill-health or for trips 'home'. GYROS will usually write a letter on behalf of the client, which they can then present to their employer.

Occasionally, clients come in for help due to verbal abuse or other bullying at work. One client, a Lithuanian woman aged 66 and working full-time in a poultry factory, attended GYROS for help to write a complaint to Human Resources about bullying by the assistant manager in her workplace. Despite having been in the UK for 11 years, she rated her English language skills as 'very limited'. According to the GYROS case note: "As she cannot write English, I wrote it for her in her words."[45] A Polish national who had been in the UK for two years, came in on behalf of her partner because "his team leader has recently been promoted and since [then] she is verbally abusive towards him and other workers. Client approached manager above her; however, things haven't improved."[46]

The data also contains examples of refused toilet breaks, one client reporting that he was "told by his supervisor to wait until breaktime, [and] when the client asked again, he was told he can go, but doesn't need to come back".[47] The client was told by the agency's site manager to go home that day after he contacted them. GYROS called the agency and the client returned to work, switching to the night shift so he would not have to work with the same supervisor. The notes record that the client was advised by GYROS to return if he wanted assistance to contact his union; whether he did is not clear. It may be (as indicated in many of the case notes and through discussion with the

---

[45] Client ID 631.
[46] Client ID 481.
[47] Client ID 497.

caseworkers) that clients *choose* to continue to work rather than seek to have their rights enforced.[48] This is one of only two instances in the entire dataset[49] where trade union membership or help from a trade union is mentioned. However, no consideration is given to addressing issues more formally such as taking a case to an employment tribunal (see further Section E.2).

2.2 Reduced hours

The issue of reduced hours for those on zero-hours contracts is a repeated theme in the dataset. This was evident particularly where the worker had a period of sickness or was facing childcare issues. One client had to self-isolate due to a COVID-19 outbreak in the factory and found upon his return to work that he was being offered fewer hours. His previous shifts had been filled by someone else while he was away.[50] As we saw in Chapter 1, Darius contacted GYROS in April 2020 – the case note explained that 'he has no money to live', as his working hours had been reduced. He said his children receive a £15 voucher for food each week; he was advised to go to the foodbank'.[51] Darius had experienced the same situation four years previously too. The case note recorded that he had asked GYROS whether the employment agency had to offer minimum hours. The adviser noted: 'I explained to client that agency normally is 0 hours contract …. Client said that he hasn't been called in for work for last 2 weeks and when he calls his manager on site, he doesn't answer his phone.'[52] Darius was helped to register with a different agency.

2.3 Lack of payslips and nonpayment of wages, sick pay or holiday pay

A frequent issue is employers' failure to provide employees with payslips.[53] Take, for example, the case of Nikolai, for whom the lack of payslips was just one element of his problems:

---

[48] C. Barnard, A. Ludlow and S. Fraser Butlin, 'Beyond employment tribunals: enforcement of employment rights by EU-8 migrant workers' (2018) 47 *Industrial Law Journal* 226.

[49] The other instance involved a man in Suffolk who was working as a driver and had damaged the car in a car park. Notes record that he joined a union after this incident, but they were unable to provide him with the legal services he needed as his employer was taking him to court.

[50] C. Barnard and F. Costello, 'EU nationals, new barriers for Covid-19 support' *UK in a Changing Europe* (8 April 2021), available at: https://ukandeu.ac.uk/eu-nationals-new-barriers-for-covid-19-support/, accessed 25 January 2022.

[51] Client ID 18.

[52] Ibid.

[53] N. de la Silva, L. Granada and D. Modern, *The Unheard Workforce* (London: Latin American Women's Rights Service, 2019), available at: https://lawrs.org.uk/wp-content/uploads/2020/11/Unheard_Workforce_research_2019.pdf, accessed 25 January 2022; de la Silva

[Client had been] working for employer for three years without any payslips. He thinks if he approached his employer to ask for payslips, he will be fired. Client instead is seeking support to apply for a new job and would like help with a CV and to complete an application form. Children's services are involved with the family due to their current financial situation; family are in receipt of food parcels and have been unable to fully furnish their rented property. Client is struggling to apply for UC [Universal Credit] due to lack of paperwork.[54]

GYROS' response was not to seek to enforce his employment rights, but rather to help him write a CV, complete application forms and call potential employers. Nikolai was employed by a new factory the next day. He was then able to apply for Universal Credit again, with help. In time, children's services 'stepped down' their involvement, as the family's situation, and particularly their income, had become more regular.

The issue of non-receipt of payslips, rather than coming up as a direct employment enquiry, was more often part of client enquiries about benefits. The database shows that GYROS clients, like Nikolai, run into problems when trying to access certain benefits due to the lack of payslips. One case note recorded:

Client is pregnant and due in June. Client is not employed at the moment and wanted to know if she can get MA [Maternity Allowance]. I checked her test period (March 2017–June 2018) and her employment is in that period. She had two jobs: from one, only four payslips (August–Sept[ember] 2017) and no payslips from the other.[55]

The client was unable to prove entitlement to Maternity Allowance despite having worked throughout the relevant period.

Clients also access GYROS' help when payslips are incorrect. For example, a case note recorded that a client who was working at a pizzeria in Great Yarmouth said "that her wages are less than are in the payslips – even the hours are wrong. In the payslips, the wages are calculated as the minimum wages, but in reality she earns around £5 [per hour]."[56] In this instance, as the client was potentially being paid an hourly rate £2.20 less than the

---

et al reported that 20 per cent of their client group working in the cleaning, hospitality and domestic work sectors did not receive payslips.

[54] Client ID 163.

[55] Client ID 1242.

[56] Client ID 1275.

minimum wage,[57] GYROS referred the client to a free legal advice service located in the Town at the time (2016).[58]

As well as employers failing to pay minimum wage, GYROS case notes recorded failure to give holiday pay. For example, one client was

> advised at the CAB [Citizens Advice] to come to GYROS for us to help him write the letter to his employer requesting for wages to be paid. … Client was under a lot of stress and overwhelmed that he couldn't get the help he needs so far, and that his dishonest employer will get away with not paying him. I wrote a letter to the employer.[59]

Sometimes it was clear that significant perseverance had been required to obtain unpaid holiday pay. In one case, GYROS contacted a company repeatedly over a period of two months to claim £400 in holiday pay for a client.

3. Health issues

We turn now to some of the health-related issues noted in the GYROS database which are connected to repetitive tasks on the factory line, being required to lift heavy weights and the cold conditions in workplaces. A small number of GYROS' clients made claims for injury at work. One client was awarded £14,000 in compensation for a broken arm sustained at work. Another client had returned

> to work on part-time contract; however, she is unable to continue to work due to her health issues – frozen shoulder diagnosis. Client's doctors have suggested that client's illness is caused by her workplace. I helped client to contact a lawyer's firm to see if they would take the compensation case on.[60]

However, examples of clients making claims for injury are few and far between. As one GYROS worker said, "legal advice is a luxury for people who have money",[61] and in all her years at GYROS, she has never had anyone make a claim; she said they only came to GYROS[62] for help when

---

[57] For more, see 'National minimum wage and national living wage rates' *Gov.uk*, available at: www.gov.uk/national-minimum-wage-rates, accessed 10 February 2023.

[58] For more, see the website of Norfolk Community Law Service at: www.ncls.co.uk/, accessed 11 February 2023.

[59] Client ID 86.

[60] Client ID 171.

[61] Focus group with GYROS staff (online, March 2021).

[62] Ibid.

an accident at work caused other problems. For example, Beatriz[63] suffered a hand injury at work and had an operation. According to her case note, she had to stop working and "started to suffer from financial instability". She accumulated rent arears, because even though she was receiving housing benefit, she still had to pay a rent top-up, which she could not afford. She received Employment Support Allowance for a period, but after the medical assessment, that payment stopped. She then claimed Jobseeker's Allowance but that required her to be actively looking for work, which proved difficult with her health condition and poor English. She did approach the council (Housing Options) for help finding cheaper accommodation but was told that because she had such large arrears, if she became homeless, she would be considered 'intentionally homeless', and therefore not eligible for support. The case note reported that Beatriz was "really distressed and unhappy with the outcome of the visit to the council". She was subsequently taken to court by her landlord, and the court ordered her eviction. With help, Beatriz booked viewings for potential flats and found one in the centre of Town. The GYROS adviser observed: 'From a safeguarding point of view client's case is closed; however she will at times need service support.'

D. Employment tribunal cases with similar facts

So far we have looked at how the House residents and focus group participants described their working lives and at the employment issues seen in the GYROS database. We wanted to see if the experiences described were unique to Great Yarmouth or whether similar practices were happening elsewhere. So we looked at employment tribunal cases in the last three years where an EU national was involved and reasons for the case going to a tribunal. While the number of cases was very small (see Section E), we were struck by the fact that the few cases that did get to a tribunal revealed a pattern of experiences similar to what we had found in Great Yarmouth. So in the tribunal cases, individuals raised complaints about toilet breaks being refused at work,[64] managers shouting at staff for minor misdemeanours[65] and potential bribery over favours for shifts. Two cases referred to the same incident, in which two members of staff, partners, gave whisky to a supervisor to persuade him to change their shift pattern so that they could work coordinated shifts; the

---

[63] Client ID 783.

[64] For example, Case no 2205875/19 *Matijosaitene v Good Eating Co Ltd*; Case no 1601756/2019 *Toth v HR GO (Liverpool) Ltd*.

[65] On the facts the Claimants lost their race discrimination case because this happened to all staff, irrespective of nationality: Case no 2603660/2019 *Blaszczak v Quorn Country Foods Ltd*; Case no 2401670/2020 *Zolecka v Tavspackaging Ltd*.

internal disciplinary process of the employer had found that the supervisor was joking when he proposed this[66]). Wage deductions and poor-quality tied accommodation also featured in judgments.[67]

Problem clustering of the kind experienced by Nikolai (discussed earlier) was also evident in the employment tribunals. For example, in *Baran v Mario Lasi and Salvatore Lasi*, the claimant, who worked as a chef at an Italian restaurant, was dismissed while in hospital following a diagnosis of pancreatic cancer. Sometime later, he was taken back to the restaurant, where he also lived, and found that his belongings had been packed up.[68] His claims for disability discrimination, wrongful dismissal and failure to provide a written statement, payslips and written reasons for dismissal, as well as a wages claim relating to failure to pay him while off sick, were all upheld.[69]

There are a number of cases concerning abuse towards EU8 migrant workers and between different nationalities within the EU8 group. First, there was a subset of cases where the majority of the workforce was of one nationality and the claimant alleged that they had been harassed because they were of a different nationality – for example, Lithuanian workers harassing a Polish worker[70], a Czech worker experiencing difficulties in a 'Polish' factory,[71] isolation because other workers only spoke Polish,[72] and the preference of a Lithuanian supervisor to have Lithuanian workers.[73] There are also examples of allegations of abuse by non-EU migrant workers towards EU8 migrant workers, particularly following Brexit.[74] However, in one case, the tribunal rejected a claim of race discrimination when there had simply been questioning of an EU8 migrant worker about the situation post Brexit, a conversation they said would have been held up and down the country after the referendum vote.[75]

Finally, a number of cases address allegations relating to employers requiring staff to speak only in English or to speak in their native tongue only when away from other staff or clients. This was variously claimed, and in some

---

[66] Case no 2416777/2019 *Drofti v Deli Solutions Ltd*; Case no 2413708/2019 *Nagy v Balarz and Deli Solutions Ltd*.

[67] For example, Case no 1400430/2019 *Drimusch Holland*; Case no 1803731/2021 *Fryc v Petr Kolar Construction ltd*.

[68] In one judgment, it was noted that the claimant's belongings had been put in the corridor after he was dismissed (Case no 3304471/2018 *Szymaniak v Jason Hunt*).

[69] Case no 3306950/2018 *Baran v Mario Lasi and Salvatore Lasi*.

[70] Case no 3321500/2019 *Smagacz v Mercury Personnel Solutions Ltd*.

[71] Case no 2500072/2019 *Capandova v Biffa Polymers Ltd*.

[72] Case no 1404115/2019 *Kleinova v Higgidy Ltd*.

[73] Case no 4101671/2022 *Bartosik v PRL Realisations 1 Ltd (in administration)*.

[74] Case no 1307164/2019 *AB v XZ* and Case no 1600187/2019 *Davies v Tui UK*.

[75] Case no 2405428/2016 *Paczkowska v R-Com Consultancy Ltd*.

cases upheld, to be race discrimination (in different cases, it was claimed as direct discrimination, harassment and indirect discrimination).[76]

E. Interface with the law and enforcement

1. EU law requirements

Given the significant employment law issues raised in the previous sections, what is the legal position with regard to EU migrant workers and rights enforcement? Article 7(1) of Regulation 492/11 lays down the principle of equal treatment:

> A worker who is a national of a Member State may not, in the territory of another Member State, be treated differently from national workers by reason of his nationality in respect of any conditions of employment and work, in particular as regards remuneration, dismissal, and, should he become unemployed, reinstatement or re-employment.

The problem is that for those working in the factories in Great Yarmouth, there are often no UK nationals working alongside them with whom to compare. As Jolanta, a Polish national, said: "I mean find me an English person in the chicken factory – there are none."[77]

UK employment law does, of course, apply to the factories in Great Yarmouth, assuming the individuals fall within the personal scope of the rules (that is, they are an 'employee' for the purposes of, say, claiming unfair dismissal under Part X of the Employment Rights Act 1996, a 'worker' for the purposes of claiming rights under the Working Time Regulations 1998 or claiming harassment or discrimination under the Equality Act 2010). Formally, therefore, the UK complies with its obligations under Article 7(1).

However, enforcement of EU and UK employment rights is a major issue. Article 3 of the Enforcement Directive 2014/54 says that member states must ensure judicial procedures 'for the enforcement of obligations under Article 45 TFEU and under Articles 1 to 10 of Regulation (EU) No 492/2011' are available to all Union workers and members of their family who 'consider themselves wronged by a failure to apply the principle of equal treatment to them, even after the relationship in which the restriction and obstacle or discrimination is alleged to have occurred has ended'. Again, formally speaking, the UK has complied with its obligations under the

---

[76] Case no 2206362/2020 *Bukowska v Mizhan Euro Ltd*; Case no 4104949/2019 *Warlinski v MSG Laboratories Ltd*; Case no 1805886/2020 *Sokolova v Humdinger Ltd*; Case no 3313268/2019 *Wilk v Wackers*.

[77] Barnard et al (2022), n 28, 370.

Enforcement Directive. EU migrant workers had/have access to employment tribunals in the same way as nationals[78] and, as the cases in Section D show, some workers do manage to bring claims. Yet we estimate that claims brought by EU migrant workers account for only 0.199 per cent of total claims (265 claims)[79] – a tiny share of cases going to tribunals.[80]

So why is this? Our earlier research shows there are a number of reasons why it is rare for migrant workers to take their cases to employment tribunals[81] – not least worry about losing their job, language barriers and fear of becoming entangled with the 'state'. And if they do engage with the legal process, as some of the employment tribunal cases we looked at showed, it can be fraught with difficulty. In *Bocian*,[82] for example, the claimant received assistance from a (paid) representative to write letters to his employer during a disciplinary process, but then sought advice from solicitors, who did not advise him on time limits. Once he was dismissed, those solicitors did not reply to his emails, and the representative spoke to the Advisory, Conciliation and Arbitration Service (ACAS) and told the claimant that he had to await his appeal outcome before starting early conciliation. At a preliminary hearing, the tribunal had to consider whether his claim was out of time. The judge specifically noted that:

> The reasons for [the delay] are firstly that he is a Polish national whose command of English is at best limited. He required a translator for the disciplinary hearing and the appeal hearing, and the Respondents arranged that on each occasion. He had a translator for the present proceedings. He described his own command of English as '5 out of 10'. He was an operative working in a meat processing factory. His knowledge of what were for him foreign legal procedures was, I considered, very limited. Secondly, whilst he did seek advice from

---

[78] L. Merrett, 'New approaches to territoriality in employment law' (2015) 44 *Industrial Law Journal* 53.

[79] We identified 265 claims over the three years in which the judgment contained an express reference to nationality or reference to an interpreter. Seventy claims had both an express reference to nationality and an interpreter. It is much more difficult to compare this to the number of claims disposed overall, because we do not yet have the 2021/2022 Ministry of Justice dataset. But assuming that there were approximately the same number of disposals in 2021/2022 as there were in 2020/2021, that would give about 133,300 claims, so the 265 claims would represent 0.199 per cent of claims.

[80] Although it is more than double the number of tribunal cases compared to an earlier dataset analysed for the period 2010–2012: C. Barnard and A. Ludlow, 'Enforcement of employment rights by EU-8 workers in employment tribunals' (2016) 45 *Industrial Law Journal* 1.

[81] Barnard et al (2018), n 48.

[82] Case no 4118198/2018 *Bocian v Millers of Speyside Ltd*.

a Scottish solicitor, and had initial advice shortly after the dismissal, latterly his attempts to secure advice failed. The solicitor concerned did not reply to him. In any event he was not able to afford legal representation, and that probably explains the lack of response further from her.

Together with the erroneous advice from his representative, this formed the basis of the tribunal's judgment that it had not been reasonably practicable for this person to bring his claim within the time limits.

In the UK, the problem of lack of enforcement of employment rights is exacerbated by the absence of trade unions in many workplaces[83] and lack of a general system of labour inspectors. A number of agencies work in the field: the HMRC enforces the minimum wage;[84] the Employment Agency Standards Inspectorate (EASI)[85] was set up to protect the rights of agency workers by ensuring that employment agencies and businesses treat their workers fairly; the Gangmasters Licensing and Abuse Authority (GLAA),[86] which license gangmasters who provide workers in agriculture, horticulture, shellfish gathering and any associated processing and packaging, and investigate reports of worker exploitation and illegal activity, such as human trafficking, forced labour and illegal labour provision; and the Health and Safety Executive (HSE),[87] which has enforcement powers in respect of health and safety matters. However, as we have argued elsewhere,[88] their

---

[83] Cf Article 3(2) of Directive 2014/54: 'Member States shall ensure that associations, organisations, including the social partners, or other legal entities, which have, in accordance with the criteria laid down in their national law, practice or collective agreements, a legitimate interest in ensuring that this Directive is complied with, may engage, either on behalf of or in support of, Union workers and members of their family, with their approval, in any judicial and/or administrative procedure provided for the enforcement of the rights referred to in Article 1'.

[84] 'National minimum wage: policy on enforcement, prosecutions and naming employers who break national minimum wage law' *Gov.uk*, available at: www.gov.uk/governm ent/publications/enforcing-national-minimum-wage-law/national-minimum-wage-pol icy-on-enforcement-prosecutions-and-naming-employers-who-break-national-mini mum-wage-law, accessed 4 January 2023.

[85] For more, see 'About us | Employment Agency Standards Inspectorate' *Gov.uk*, available at: www.gov.uk/government/organisations/employment-agency-standards-inspectorate/ about, accessed 15 March 2023.

[86] For more, see 'What we do' *Gangmaster's & Labour Abuse Authority*, available at: www. gla.gov.uk/who-we-are/what-we-do/, accessed 15 March 2023.

[87] For more, see the HSE website at: www.hse.gov.uk/, accessed 15 March 2023.

[88] C. Barnard and S. Fraser Butlin, 'Where criminal law meets labour law: the effectiveness of criminal sanctions to enforce labour rights' in A. Bogg, J. Collins, M.R. Freedland and J. Herring (eds) *Criminality at Work* (Oxford: Oxford University Press, 2020), 70–94.

intervention in day-to-day matters in the workplace is limited, not least due to shortage of resources.

2. GYROS' role in addressing employment issues

We turn now to consider in more detail how GYROS respond to the employment (law) problems presented to it. What is striking is the paucity of mention that advisers or clients make to the employment tribunal system. Out of the 6,856 case notes in the GYROS dataset, 22 entries included the word 'tribunal', but none of those mentions were related to employment tribunals. In two cases, reference was made to ACAS. In the first, in 2014, a case note relating to a female Lithuanian recorded: 'client needed help to submit an early conciliation form on ACAS website as solicitor advised so at Legal Drop-in. I helped client to do that. ACAS will contact client within 2 days. I can't help in this matter any longer as it's legal issues.'[89] In the second, a male Lithuanian lorry driver had been dismissed, and the GYROS adviser wrote to his employer on topics including overtime payments and holiday pay. A subsequent entry in a case note shows that the client's employer had telephoned GYROS:

> as they received a phone call from CAB [Citizens Advice] and wanted to know if we are still dealing with his case or [if] it's only CAB. I explained that from our end his case is closed and as he wanted to take it further, we advised him to go to CAB and perhaps get ACAS involved.[90]

It is unclear why GYROS referred the client to Citizens Advice rather than assisting him with early conciliation as the first step towards an employment tribunal claim. It could be because if a client can receive support elsewhere (such as from Citizens Advice), then GYROS would seek to avoid duplication of effort entailed in them also working with the client on the same issue. GYROS position their service as being very much directed at those who cannot access mainstream (that is, English language) services or those who need specialist immigration advice.

In the dataset, there were no references to the HMRC or the HSE in case notes on enquiries related to employment issues, and no references to the EASI. There was just one reference to modern slavery – although none expressly to the GLAA. This was related to a factory worker who came to

---

[89] Client ID 1184.
[90] Client ID 86.

GYROS (Ipswich) to report suspected modern slavery at the factory where he was working. There was no further update on the case.

The lack of mentions in the case notes about tribunals may be explained by one adviser's view: "In all my [ten] years at GYROS, I have only had three people who made complaints to tribunals, but a lot who have made complaints to me! People don't follow it through."[91] This suggests that workers are hesitant to enforce their rights via formal legal pathways and advisers are hesitant to recommend going to tribunals. So what happens to the individuals? For those going to GYROS, they seek practical resolution of their problems, which GYROS tries to provide, often by ringing the employer to sort out the issues:

> Client thought he was no longer working for (Agency) and wanted to know why he did not receive P45. I called to main office to speak to the agency directly and administrator informed that client is still employed, and he still has outstanding holiday pay. Client did not know he was still employed as he hasn't been called for any shifts. Said he will then try to get some work with them; if not he will come back if he needs to in order to request P45.[92]

This accords with Genn's research, in which people were asked what they wanted from their advisers – 68 per cent of people wanted advice on how to resolve their problems, and 47 per cent wanted advice about their legal rights.[93] This pragmatism gets immediate results but does not address the systemic underlying issues. In fact, this caused significant concern for a representative from one local law centre.[94] She said that when someone comes in with an employment issue, there may be other issues at play – for example, discrimination – but non-legally trained advice workers may "miss great chunks of law out".[95] The advice will be partial and very much dependent on the knowledge of the adviser. Solicitors, she suggested, have a much broader knowledge, are regulated by the Solicitors Regulation Authority and have their case work audited. They may also see the systemic issues beyond the individual circumstances. For her, amateurism is a real problem in the advice sector, with "a lot of dabbling" and many people "noble in objectives, but [with] limited self-awareness of limitations".[96] Hodges, on the other hand,

---

[91] Focus group with GYROS staff (Great Yarmouth, March 2021).

[92] Client ID 485.

[93] H. Genn, *Paths to Justice, What People Do and Think about Going to Law* (Oxford: Hart Publishing, 1999), 95.

[94] Phone conversation with law centre lawyer (online, 28 March 2022).

[95] Ibid.

[96] Ibid.

is wary of eulogizing the legal system. He says that employment tribunals, while providing legal redress for individuals, often result in little systemic change and 'often fail to have a broader impact on employer behaviour and workplace relations'.[97] We return to the issue of risks and benefits of pragmatic law in Chapter 8.

F. Conclusion

The data from the interviews, the GYROS dataset and the tribunal judgments give an insight into the working lives of EU migrant workers and the difficulties faced by this group of precarious and vulnerable workers, especially those on zero-hours contracts with unpredictable shifts and uncertain hours and wages, who are beholden to the whims of managers. Some of the difficulties are inherent to the hard physical labour required in the factories – cold, wet, demanding work where the targets are simply too difficult. Alongside these difficulties, there are others specific to EU migrant workers. These relate to language barriers and language segregation, challenges in understanding what is required in the work and hurdles to raising issues and concerns due to lack of significant support. We also see in the data the clustering of problems – a loss of shifts leading to a loss of income and difficulties with paying rent, in turn resulting in housing problems.

Set against this factual matrix, we have identified very limited interaction with the legal routes to enforcement; few tribunal claims are brought and there are almost no referrals from GYROS either to enforcement bodies or to other legal support for enforcing employment rights. This accords with our earlier research showing that few EU8 migrant workers enforce their rights via tribunals, and resource constraints substantially restrict the ability and extent of the enforcement work by the GLAA, the HMRC, the HSE and the EASI.

Two observations arise from the data. First, GYROS case notes reveal a pragmatic approach to the problems faced by this group of workers: seeking a resolution by engaging with the employer directly or assisting the worker to move jobs rapidly. This theme leads us to our work on pragmatic law, which we explore further in Chapter 8. Second, we see individuals displaying 'individual acts of resistance' operating 'against the law'.[98] In Ewick and Silbey's work, these acts of resistance to the law are disproportionately the stories of women, persons of colour, the unemployed – those who hold

---

[97] C. Hodges, *Delivering Dispute Resolution: A Holistic Review of Models in England and Wales* (Oxford: Hart Publishing, 2019), Chapter 15 on employment disputes.

[98] P. Ewick and S. Silbey, *The Common Place of Law* (Chicago: University of Chicago Press, 1998), 28.

less 'power' to engage strategically with the law and who need other tactics to navigate its hard edges.[99] In our data, this can be seen in those who pay for guaranteed shifts and even in those women who acquiesce to sexual favours for more favourable shifts, to ensure continued income – this, too, is a deeply pragmatic response by those women.

Finally, this chapter has shown how the law's hard edges have had an impact on the experiences of our interviewees and people within the rest of the data, even when the law is there to protect them.[100] For example, in order to access benefits, there is a need for particular documentation – like a P45 – which should be provided by an employer. When that's not provided, the individual has limited ability to challenge the refusal. Yet the law is inflexible in requiring the bureaucratic requirements to be met. This inflexibility of the law can also be seen in the next chapter in relation to housing: in the legal requirements in respect of eviction, which, if satisfied, mean the individual loses their home; and in the strict legal requirements for access to social housing. All of this contrasts with the informal living arrangements experienced by those living in the House and those whose stories we find in the GYROS dataset.

---

[99]   Ibid, 235.

[100] Virginia Mantouvalou argues that certain laws create structures of injustice, increasing workers' vulnerability and contributing to a clustering of disadvantage; *Structural Injustice and Workers' Rights* (Oxford: Oxford University Press, 2023).

5

Housing

A. Introduction

In this chapter, we look at housing, an important strand of our research. Specifically, we focus on the House of the title of our book, an HMO just off St Peter's Road (the Street of our title), and the experiences of its residents to help understand the issues with housing for those EU migrants living in Great Yarmouth. To gain a fuller picture, we also look at the housing-related issues which arise in the GYROS dataset.

The chapter begins with a description of the general housing situation in Great Yarmouth, particularly in the Nelson ward, where our research takes place (Section B). We then turn to look at the experiences of residents in the House. We shall see that the residents had a complex relationship with the House, their landlord and each other. To the outsider, the House was in a poor state, like so many others in and around St Peter's Road. However, to its residents, it was a place of peace, calm and safety – certainly much better than the places they had stayed in when they first arrived in the UK (Section C.2). In Chapter 1, we saw how Darius initially lived in a seven-bedroom HMO with other families. He did not receive a tenancy agreement for his accommodation and he paid rent in cash. This informality made it difficult for him to provide a paper trail to prove entitlement to benefits. These issues were seen repeatedly in the GYROS dataset: problems with landlords, the quality of accommodation and paper trails (Section D).

The case notes in the GYROS dataset also reveal how advisers respond to those problems. We see the pragmatism which characterizes so much of GYROS' work. However, this chapter also shows a much more prominent role of the law, which, for non-qualified community advisers, means advising clients on issues related to this field is more challenging than advising on other matters. One senior adviser said she felt most out of her depth when challenging housing decisions made by the local authority housing team, due to the complexity of housing legislation. We also see GYROS referring to other frontline organizations, especially the housing charity Shelter

(Section E). Although affecting a small number of EU nationals in our research, this chapter also considers social housing and homelessness support among the EU migrant community, focusing on the issues they face with the rules around housing support eligibility and increasingly strict housing and homelessness legislation[1] (Section F).

However, we begin by considering the general housing situation in Great Yarmouth.

B. Housing stock in Great Yarmouth

The housing stock in Great Yarmouth[2] is generally poor. Housing ranges from the swiftly erected postwar 'prefabs' (prefabricated buildings), to the Victorian terraced houses that were badly affected by the flooding in the 1950s, to the fine large Victorian and Edwardian houses which once served as accommodation for holidaymakers. These have now largely been converted by private landlords into HMOs, and many of them are rented to EU nationals. The poor quality of the accommodation makes life difficult for residents. Those who can, move out, either to Gorleston, a somewhat more upmarket seaside resort a couple of miles away on the other side of the river, or to Norwich, a lively university city about 20 miles away. This means that it is the most disadvantaged who are left behind, living in poor housing in the central wards of the Town, such as Nelson.

According to the Great Yarmouth Borough Council Housing Strategy, there are 45,318 dwellings in Great Yarmouth, of which 62 per cent are owner-occupied, 20 per cent are private rented and 18 per cent are socially rented.[3] The council notes that there has been significant growth in the private rented sector in Great Yarmouth in recent years, rising from 8 per cent of the total stock in 2001 to 18 per cent in 2011 and 20 per cent in 2017 – the period which broadly spans the arrival of EU nationals. This is

[1] Public Interest Law Centre, *Still Here: Defending the Rights of EU Citizens after Brexit and Covid19* (Public Interest Law Centre, July 2021), available at: www.pilc.org.uk/wp-cont ent/uploads/2021/06/PILC_EEA_A4_ONLINE-1.pdf, accessed 19 October 2021.

[2] Some of this section draws on C. Barnard and F. Costello, 'The darker side of the EU internal market ideal: free movement of workers living in a coastal town' in J. Adams-Prassl, S. Bogojevic, A. Ezrachi and D. Leczyjiewicz (eds) *The Internal Market Ideal: Essays in Honour of Stephen Weatherill* (Oxford: Oxford University Press, 2023).

[3] Great Yarmouth Borough Council, *Housing Strategy, 2018–2023*, available at: www.great-yarmouth.gov.uk/policies, accessed 23 November 2023. Data drawn from 'Supporting evidence', available at: www.great-yarmouth.gov.uk/media/2712/Great-Yarmouth-Boro ugh-Council-Housing-Strategy-Evidence/pdf/Housing_Strategy_-_Evidence_Append ix_2018.pdf?m=637025933557470000, accessed 23 November 2023, 2.

compared to a 9 per cent increase for England as a whole.[4] While there has been significant growth in the private rented sector in the Town, the standard of accommodation has not improved.[5] A former community development worker said: 'They're paying the price now because the damp and mould issues and, again, I guess it's the council not getting to grips with a place like Nelson ward. There's no plan for ... the quality of housing stock across Nelson ward.'[6]

The position is not helped by the fact that the Town has a high number of 'absent' landlords – these are individuals who have bought up "5 or 6 properties" but have no real link to Great Yarmouth or understanding of the communities and economic realities of the Town – nor by the number of 'dodgy landlords' – described as "those who take anyone and everyone".[7] Some residents in Nelson speak of exploitative landlords who rent rooms to women and establish transactional sexual relationships in lieu of rent.[8] The police too recognize that the availability of cheap accommodation causes issues in the Town. One interviewee from the local police referred to the "vulnerability, criminality, and poor health and social issues" associated with housing.[9]

The Housing Act 2004 imposes a duty on each local housing authority to monitor the private sector housing conditions in its area; Great Yarmouth does this through its Housing Strategy, which sets out its aims to improve accommodation in the Town. This may be through using their powers under the Housing Act 2004 to 'enforce remedial action where housing conditions are below the accepted standard'.[10] The borough recognizes that many of the houses locally do not meet the necessary standard.[11] The Council Housing Strategy (2018–2023)[12] says that approximately 1,800 dwellings in the private rented sector (of a total of 9,000, equating to 20 per cent) have Category 1 Housing Health and Safety Rating System hazards[13] – that is, those where

---

[4] Ibid.

[5] Cf Department for Levelling Up, Housing and Communities, 'A fairer private rented sector' *Gov.uk* (16 June 2022), available at: www.gov.uk/government/publications/a-fairer-private-rented-sector, accessed 21 March 2023.

[6] Interview with former council community worker (online, October 2021).

[7] Interview with council housing team worker (Great Yarmouth, October 2021).

[8] 'Right to succeed: emerging themes', document on file with researchers.

[9] Interview with local police officer (Great Yarmouth, November 2021).

[10] S. Garner and A. Frith, *A Practical Approach to Landlord and Tenant* (8th edn, Oxford: Oxford University Press, 2017), 359.

[11] Great Yarmouth Borough Council, n 3, 8.

[12] Ibid, 'Supporting Evidence' n 3, 10.

[13] Office of the Deputy Prime Minister, *Housing Health and Safety Rating System: Operating Guidance* (London: Office of the Deputy Prime Minister, 2006), available at:

the most serious harm outcome is identified (for example, death, permanent paralysis, permanent loss of consciousness, loss of limb or serious fracture).

The Council Housing Strategy also identifies four strategic objectives to meet current and future housing requirements in Great Yarmouth: (1) 'new homes' (ensuring there are enough good-quality new homes); (2) 'our homes' (improving the quality and use of council housing stock); (3) 'decent homes' (providing a good mix of decent homes across all tenures); and (4) 'healthy homes' (meeting the needs of vulnerable households). Under the 'decent homes' strand, the council recognizes the borough has a 'high number of Houses in Multiple Occupation (HMOs). Whilst they do provide low-cost accessible accommodation, we would like to see the overall number of HMOs reduce over a managed period or become better managed.'[14] To this end, the council introduced a Selective Licensing Scheme for the most challenged parts of the Nelson ward, with effect from 7 January 2019 to run for five years.[15] The aim is to improve housing and social conditions for private sector tenants in these areas, specifically targeting unethical landlords. The scheme has required 'landlords of most private rented housing ... to be licensed and meet conditions around health and safety and standards'.[16]

Reactions to the scheme have been mixed, including among council staff. One council worker said the scheme has meant that some landlords – even some "good ones" – have left, as the cost of getting their accommodation

---

https://assets.publishing.service.gov.uk/government/uploads/system/uploads/attachment_data/file/15810/142631.pdf, accessed 23 November 2023.

[14] Great Yarmouth Borough Council, n 3, 8.

[15] 'What is covered by the Selective Licensing Scheme' *Great Yarmouth Borough Council*, available at: www.great-yarmouth.gov.uk/article/5261/What-area-is-covered-by-the-Selective-Licensing-Scheme, accessed 23 November 2023. This was adopted under Section 80 Housing Act 2004.

[16] 'What does Selective Licensing mean?' *Great Yarmouth Borough Council*, available at: www.great-yarmouth.gov.uk/article/5263/What-does-Selective-Licensing-mean#_content, accessed 21 February 2023. Great Yarmouth Borough Council, 'Public notice: designation of an area for selective licensing', available at: www.great-yarmouth.gov.uk/media/3406/Selective-Licensing-PublicNotice/pdf/Designation_of_an_Area_for_Selective_Licensing___Public_Notice.pdf?m=636773736749230000, accessed 23 November 2023; according to the council: 'There are a number of potential consequences for failing to licence a property. A person who operates a licensable property without a licence is liable to prosecution and unlimited fines. The operation of an unlicensed property could lead to the Council, or a tenant, making an application to the First Tier Tribunal to obtain a Rent Repayment Order in respect of up to 12 month's rent or housing benefit monies paid. As a last resort, the Council is also empowered to take control of unlicensed premises by making an Interim Management Order. Furthermore, in relation to shorthold tenancies, no section 21 notice may be served under the Housing Act 1988 in respect of an unlicensed property. The Council may also use other legal remedies as appropriate', 1.

to the standard required for the licence was too high. Among the "good" landlords was one who took in homeless people if they were in receipt of benefits and engaging with community support, which was rare for landlords. Landlords refusing to rent is common for more vulnerable groups.[17]

Properties already subject to mandatory HMO licensing, such as the HMO in our research, are exempt from the scheme. We now turn to look at the House and the experience of its residents, in both the House and other accommodation they had lived in after coming to the UK.

C. The House and its residents

1. The House

As described in Chapter 2, the House, an HMO, is a sprawling three-storey, Grade II listed building, built in 1860. At the time of our research, it had eight tenants in six 'units'. While each unit was referred to as self-contained (by the landlord and the tenants), residents shared toilet and laundry facilities, and they all used the main front door. Most residents had lived in the house for more than five years, and Rasa had been there for over ten years. Only three residents (Vida, Ivo and Adomas) had lived in the house for less than two years. Residents did not get tenancy agreements unless they asked for one, nor did they receive rent receipts. Moreover, they were not named on utility bills.

The tenants had to navigate and manage the poor-quality physical space of the House. Part of the house was a construction site; indeed the back stairway was blocked by a cardboard sign saying: 'Construction: do not enter'. Rasa used this space to grow her indoor plants (Figure 2.6).

Frank, the landlord, knew there was work to do on the house, but because he was ill, this never came about. Some improvements had been made when the House was shut down by environmental health inspectors. According to Edita:

'Environmental health evicted us all. ... So it was only a couple of months. I stayed at friends. And then as soon as it was ready, like, you

---

[17] For example, 'No DSS' is now ruled unlawful discrimination: York County Court (2020). Statement of reasons: F00YO154. The anonymized Order and Reasons are available at: https://nearlylegal.wpenginepowered.com/wp-content/uploads/2020/07/20.07.02-Redacted-Court-Order.pdf; 'No DSS: landmark court ruling declares housing benefit discrimination is unlawful' *Shelter* (July 2020), available at: https://england.shelter.org.uk/media/press_release/no_dss_landmark_court_ruling_confirms_housing_beneben_disc rimination_unlawful, accessed 23 November 2023. See also J. Meers, '"Professionals only please": discrimination against housing benefit recipients on online rental platforms' (2021) *Housing Studies* (online) 1.

know, the basics done for the council to issue a licence for HMO …
then I moved in back upstairs to the top flat.'[18]

Frank said:

'I turned it into really a non-profit-making house [laughs]. Ah, it
does make a little bit of profit, which is invested in the house. I don't
take a penny out of it. I don't take a penny. It's quite a lot of money
for new windows at the front. It is a Grade I listed building. No,
Grade II. No, Grade I listed building [it is in fact Grade II listed],
and I am going to put new windows all in the front. And keep it in
good order.'[19]

There was no central heating in the House. Each room, including the
bathroom, had a plug-in electric heater. Rasa said she had only asked for a
heater in the bathroom five years before, but it had made such a difference
to her life; the bathroom used to be so cold, especially when she was
showering at 3 am, before leaving for her factory shift. The electric heater
in the bathroom was connected to an extension lead that was channelled
under the door and plugged in in the adjacent room. The fire was on 24
hours a day during the winter.

The window in the bathroom did not open (it was cracked down the
middle) and there was a significant amount of green moss growing on the
inside of the window; there was also black mould on the ceiling (Figure 2.5).
The windows throughout the house were single-glazed. Rasa said her front
bay windows were falling apart. She said that because she had arthritis, she
would sit at the small table in her kitchen in the winter with the heater
beside her knees to keep warm.

Vida said her ceiling leaked each time it rained and her possessions got
wet. She said that because of the landlord's ill health and as he was such a
nice man, she did not want to bother him to fix the roof. When Vida spent
some months of lockdown in Lithuania, Frank did not charge her rent and
kept her room available for her. She appreciated this generosity, describing
him as a "very nice, kind person". Edita also spoke highly of her time in
the House, especially of her relationship with Frank:

'if we ever needed to organize a party or anything, we were always
able to use one of the rooms, like, will clear it, will organize it all, and
Frank would always come by. You [were] always given a Christmas

---

[18]   Interview with Edita (Great Yarmouth, September 2021).
[19]   Interview with Frank (Suffolk, September 2021).

week for free, of rent. And back in time, he [Frank] used to take us out for Christmas dinner somewhere like on King Street. First time, going somewhere like Yankee Traveller or something. And he would like to pay for it, which was really nice.'

There was general concern about Frank's ill health and what might happen if he were not able to keep the House on. Terese said:

'I have always lived in the house and fear of having to move sometime in future is scaring me. I love to have a sea view in the mornings. I know that our landlord has ill health, and I am worried about the future. House is so quiet and friendly.'

In Chapter 2, we saw how the residents had improved conditions in the House (Heath et al describe this as 'customising the space'[20]) by installing a toilet on the second floor and adding a guest room. As Edita said: "So if the tenants need a guest room for family, that's amazing idea, I think. Not many HMOs will offer that." The manager of GYROS also noted that tenants made improvements to their accommodation:

'they're in desperate situations, and they rent whatever is available. … But people live in places and people renovate those places where they live. How many of our clients actually do the renovations in the properties they rent …. They go in and they do all the painting, they change the flooring. They ask the landlord, and the landlord says, of course, do whatever you want. That's good for the landlord, obviously, and people do it.'[21]

2. First accommodation

Though the House was in poor condition and lacked heating and Wi-Fi, it was quiet, calm and safe. This was valued by the residents, because it was such a contrast to the accommodation they had lived in when they first came to the UK; they had 'moved up'. Many recalled their first night in the UK and the conditions of the housing they were first provided with; as noted earlier, Rasa (now the matriarch of the House) spent her first night in the UK (in 2004) in the living room of a caravan:

---

[20] S. Heath, K. Davies, G. Edwards and R. Scicluna, *Shared Housing, Shared Lives: Everyday Experiences across the Life Course* (London: Routledge, 2018), 90.

[21] Interview with GYROS manager (Great Yarmouth, September 2021).

'And we were seven people in the sitting room [of a caravan], and we are sleeping some on sofas, somebody on chairs. Three girls, no three boys and four girls. And we are sleeping how we come, nowhere to change, no nothing, because next morning you went to work and then [next] afternoon gave for us right room [shared room in caravan] ... I arrive at eight o'clock at night. And the next morning, four o'clock, I went to work.'

This overcrowded accommodation also lacked basic facilities. Rasa said that after her first night in the caravan, "they put us in a little hotel. A double room. Very little room. We washed our jeans in a toilet sink. The basin ... we washed our jeans there. And it was horrible."

Edita told a similar story. When she first arrived in the UK, she was placed in a shared room with other women. She had no control over whom she shared with, and that could change at any time.

'I still think it was wrong on so many levels that you don't even get asked if you want to be in a room or do you want to share or anything. You have no, you felt you had no say. You could go and rent elsewhere, but that meant you would need to pay [£10 per week not to live there], and you get deducted for it ... [I shared with] a Polish woman and then another Lithuanian woman and another Lithuanian woman. I mean there was one of them [who] was a proper hoarder, car boot [sales] was a big one, it was all about car boots, and [she] just kept buying stuff and she was just bringing so much .... And she had so much stuff. It was everywhere. ... And then after that there was another Lithuanian woman who, who was, like, she was a compulsive cleaner and organizer, and ... it got to the extent that she would reorganize my personal belongings and I couldn't find, like, for example, my shoes.'

These houses could be unsafe too, especially for women. Edita was physically assaulted in the first place she stayed in and no one intervened:

'And everyone knew about it, but no one even called the police out. Like I had to handle it. And because I was so new in the country, like, it would never cross my mind to go to police, like getting god forbid [the police] kind of thing.'

By contrast, when she was assaulted in the House (a tenant entered her room, pulled off her duvet and took pictures), Frank and her co-residents reacted very differently and got the police involved:

116

'I was interviewed [by the police] ... you know, like it was a proper, like, it was such a big, like, I've never expected that. Like someone would put so much effort to get things right for me. And then there was a proper investigation and I had to go to police [to] check the pictures. Thank God it was only my bum in underwear. Okay. And I recognized obviously the bedding and everything .... The victim support did send me loads of stuff, like, to read and booklets. I obviously disregarded them all. I guess other tenant and [Frank] were enough support.'

Others had struggled with landlords not complying with their legal responsibilities. For example, the residents talked about landlords who had refused to provide a tenancy agreement (Lina) or landlords who lied about Council Tax responsibilities (Camilla). Camilla said:

'First time when I come in England, I have a problem. I live in first my house two years and after I move, and after about four years I have paper from Council Tax, but I no pay Council Tax. Because this landlord, he says I no need to pay this. Just pay rent and everything is covered. It's included. And after two years, I have paper for £2,000.'

Camilla said she was called to the office of the chicken factory where she worked and told that the debt repayment would be deducted via an attachment on her earnings. She said it was humiliating to discuss a debt she was completely unaware of with her employers. She had to repay the full amount, after having already paid for Council Tax as part of her rent.

3. Interim conclusion

People sharing accommodation, of course, face various difficulties. As Heath et al note, compulsory sharing raises issues of inequality within contemporary British society:

It is one thing to have to share whilst saving for a mortgage deposit or until one is able to afford to rent a property on one's own, or to have to share in order to subsidise one's housing costs once already on the housing ladder. It is, however, quite another thing to face long term reliance on shared rentals in parts of the sector often owned and managed by unscrupulous landlords and with little prospects of being able to change one's circumstances in the foreseeable future'.[22]

---

[22]   Heath et al (2018), n 20, 130.

However, as we have seen, this is not how the residents of the House viewed it. We can see how they had moved through the (adapted) 'first house, any house, dream house' trajectory.[23] Having had poor experiences with previous landlords, the friendly affability and laissez-faire attitude of Frank lifted the House into 'dream house' category – or, at the least, it was the best option available.

Still, the residents did experience a lot of issues in the House – to do with paperwork, health and safety concerns and a dilapidated building – and these are also seen in the GYROS dataset, to which we turn in the next section. However, the residents liked the fact that they had the freedom to make changes to the House and could organize their own living arrangements. They also appreciated Frank's acts of kindness. For them, this outweighed the absence of formal paperwork and their concerns about the state of the accommodation. The informality of the landlord's approach to paperwork had not, in fact, caused them problems. This may be because they had all received settled status, or in Vida's case, pre-settled status. Apart from two tenants (Adomas, who had seasonal work, and Vida, who was just back from Lithuania), they had been in steady full-time employment for over five years. With most of them having settled status and with their relatively long periods of residence in the UK and established family networks in the UK, the residents in the House were in a stronger position than many other EU migrant workers. It is to those other migrants, who feature in the GYROS dataset, that we now turn.

D. Housing issues in the GYROS dataset

1. Introduction

Housing for EU migrant workers has always been a sensitive issue.[24] There were provisions on housing in the original Workers' Regulation 1612/68, now somewhat modified in the current Workers' Regulation 492/11. Article 9(1) of Regulation 492/11 provides that an EU migrant worker enjoys all the rights and benefits given to national workers in matters of housing, including ownership. Article 9(2) says that a worker 'may, with the same right as nationals, put his name down on the housing lists in the region in which he is employed, where such lists exist, and shall enjoy the resultant

---

[23] V. Parutis ' "Economic migrants" or "middling transnationals"? East European migrants' experiences of work in the UK' (2011) 52 *International Migration*, 36, 36.

[24] C. Barnard and S. Fraser Butlin, 'Free movement: a case study in state autonomy and EU control' in M. Dawson and M. Jachtenfuchs (eds) *Autonomy without Collapse* (Oxford: Oxford University Press, 2022).

Figure 5.1: Housing enquiries on the GYROS database, 2015–2020

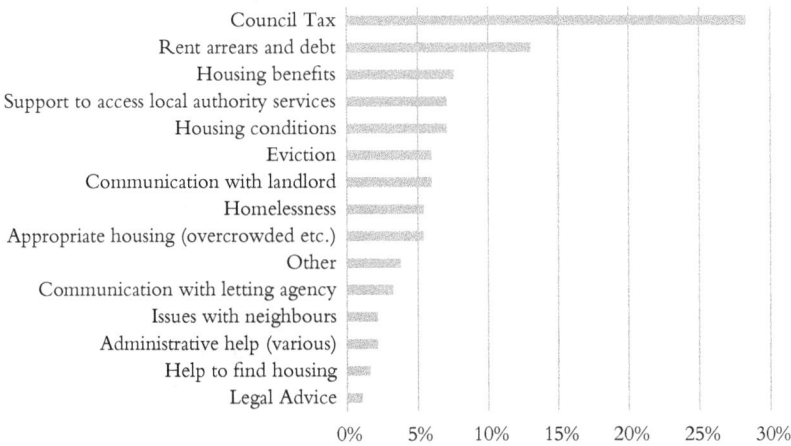

Note: Based on assessment of the case notes undertaken by the authors

benefits and priorities'. So what does this mean in practice in a town like Great Yarmouth, where the housing stock is so poor?

Approximately 7 per cent of enquiries in the GYROS dataset were related to housing. These included the poor quality of housing (53 per cent of clients in the dataset described the condition of their accommodation as 'average', 'poor' or 'very poor')[25] and the fact that their housing was tied to their employment, so if their employment ended, homelessness would follow. The largest number of enquiries concerned Council Tax; this was followed by issues with rent arrears and debt (Figure 5.1) – issues we return to in Chapter 7

In the GYROS data and the interviews we conducted with professionals in the Town who were working on housing issues (current and former borough council staff, Citizens Advice staff, debt advisers, staff at a specialist private advice agency, police, those working in foodbanks, library staff, homeless support workers and others – see appendix), five housing issues were recurring: the refusal by private landlords to rent to particular groups; the standard of accommodation; bureaucracy, systems and debt; tied accommodation; and eviction. We consider these in turn in the sections that follow. These sections also give an insight into how GYROS tackled the problems faced by clients.

---

[25] GYROS ask all clients about the type of housing they are in and the condition of their housing, as a triage question.

2. Refusal to rent to prospective tenants

The last decade has seen an increase in the growth of the private rented sector nationally, and this is evident in Great Yarmouth. At national level, the share of people in the private rented sector has grown from 17 per cent in 2010[26] to 19 per cent in 2020.[27] As noted in Section B, the figure is higher in Great Yarmouth (20 per cent of dwellings in 2017).[28] The majority of clients in the GYROS dataset are in private rented accommodation, renting directly from a landlord or via a letting agent. The Town has a number of multilingual letting agents, such as the Lithuanian letting agent on St Peter's Road. However, some private landlords refuse to rent to tenants in our cohort, as shown in this case note: 'Client said that he has been trying to find a property, but it is very hard as they do not accept him because he works for an agency with a zero-hour contract, even though he works 40 hours per week.'[29]

A Portuguese adviser who runs her own advice service in the Town also said some of her clients had been refused accommodation by landlords, due to being on zero-hours contracts. This meant they were pushed into temporary hotel accommodation or less regulated private accommodation with people who will take "anyone and everyone". She said "people become desperate, and they will take anything".[30] She had some clients paying £100 per week for a room in a run-down hotel that "is not in very good condition". The temporary nature of their accommodation prevented individuals from putting down roots in the Town:[31] they did not have a registered address, and they lacked somewhere to prepare meals or refrigerate food.

3. The standard of accommodation

The dataset revealed a range of problems associated with the standard of the accommodation clients were in. Some were mundane: 'Client came to say that although the landlord said that someone was going to repair the washing machine on Monday, no one came. I promised to let her landlord know.'[32] In another case, a client had to put up with plumbing not working for three months; GYROS called and then emailed the landlord to ask them to fix it.[33]

---

[26] 'English Housing Survey' *Gov.uk*, available at: www.gov.uk/government/collections/engl ish-housing-survey, accessed 5 January 2023.

[27] Ibid.

[28] Great Yarmouth Borough Council, n 3.

[29] Client ID 379.

[30] Portuguese speaking adviser (Great Yarmouth, November 2021).

[31] A. Grzymala-Kazlowska, 'From connecting to social anchoring: adaptation and "settlement" of Polish migrants in the UK' 44 Journal *of Ethnic and Migration Studies* 252.

[32] Client ID 178.

[33] Client ID 188.

Other problems were much more serious, including families living in overcrowded accommodation. This was particularly acute in cases where one family member arrived in Great Yarmouth and was then joined by the rest of the family:

> Client complained about her landlord, as he does not give her any tenancy agreement and now the landlord is complaining about the children, [saying] that she needs to keep them quiet, and she feels that he will ask her to leave. So, client is looking for another property. Client pays £230 p/w [per week] for 2 rooms in that house. One is for the children and the other is the living room that now is a room for client and her husband. Client started to fill [in] an application for a council house, but her English is not good enough to do it. I logged in and finished the application. With the consent of the client, I enclosed GYROS details for them to contact us if they need further information, as client does not speak English.[34]

There was no further update on the outcome of this case; the client did not return to GYROS until a year later, that time for help with her mobile telephone bill. The dataset contained little evidence of individuals complaining about overcrowding in HMOs, although GYROS was aware of this practice via anecdotal sources.

The dataset also showed clients coming in for help with the poor standard of accommodation:

> Client rented a property and according to client they went to view the property at night, and they thought that everything was ok, but when they moved to the property, they saw that it was not just clean up that it needed; it was a lot of things wrong with the property. [A]ccording to clients the heaters do not work, there are no doors in the rooms and the bathroom is next to the kitchen and the door does not close. When they talked with the landlord, he asked for the tenancy agreement and took it away from them and refuses to give them the £400 deposit and told them that if they are not happy with the things here, they should go back to Portugal.[35]

The GYROS adviser phoned the landlord, who said "he does not want to talk about it and that there was no problem with the property and [he] h[u]ng-up the phone". The adviser told the client that there was "no cooling

---

[34] Client ID 439.
[35] Client ID 494.

off period for a tenancy agreement" and once they signed the tenancy agreement they are bound by it. There were no other updates on this case.

This case was not an isolated example. Another case note referred to a client (Sara) who had asked her landlord to fix the ceiling after part of it had come down, hitting her and her son:

> According to client, her landlord came to the property last Friday late in the evening/night, with 2 other men and forced her to leave. Client was afraid and left the property and neighbour helped her moving the stuff away. I explained to client that she shouldn't have left the property as the landlord didn't present any eviction notice and that the council would consider that she made herself homeless. I advised client to go to the police and explain what happened.[36]

GYROS worked intensively with Sara on other issues in the six months that followed, including help with benefits, education for her child, debt (due to the NHS surcharge) and employment but there were no further developments in her housing case. We come back to this case later, when we discuss the interface between GYROS' advisers and the law (Section E). Sara's case (like Darius' and Lara's – see chapters 1 and 2, respectively) provides an example of the intensive support that clients need, often over several years. Their problems may cluster and are often multifaceted.

There were some examples in the dataset of children's services becoming involved where parents were not able to furnish their child's room or manage their accommodation appropriately to meet the needs of their children. This is often due to cycles of low-paid work and debt. We saw this with Nikolai's case in Chapter 4, when children's services became involved because the family was in receipt of food parcels and had been unable to fully furnish their rented property. We see this again in the following case note: 'Client said she received a health visitor last Thursday and that she noticed that her daughter's room was sparsely decorated. The health visitor called a company in order to get some donated furniture for the child.'[37]

4. Bureaucratic issues, paperwork and debt

The dataset shows issues tend to arise for GYROS' clients in the context of bureaucratic housing procedures and systems. Poor English language skills and IT skills, both pronounced among GYROS' clients, exacerbate these

---

[36] Client ID 1167.
[37] Client ID 63.

issues. Specifically, there is a lack of familiarity with UK systems. Some clients are not aware of the need to pay water or Council Tax bills, which do not exist in their home countries. Some are victims of unscrupulous landlords who tell them bills are included in the rent; they only find out later that this was not the case, as Camilla experienced. The digital march of systems too – such as the systems for Universal Credit and discretionary housing payments – means that administrative work which used to be done by the relevant professional is now pushed back to the customer.[38] And in many cases, the problems created by this ended up at GYROS' door.

In relation to housing enquiries, the GYROS dataset showed that clients struggle with Council Tax in particular – registering for it, not paying it and getting into debt to pay it and then facing court fines. The following case note shows just how complex navigating income thresholds can be, especially when income fluctuates:

> Client said that in Dec[ember] 2014 she received a CT [Council Tax] bill of over £500 and she could not afford to pay, and my colleague contacted GYBC [Great Yarmouth Borough Council] and made an agreement to pay £73 p/m [per month] for 3 months to cover her last CT bill as client's HB [Housing Benefit]/CT was awarded and she did not have to pay the full CT, but just £285. Then in January she received a letter for her to pay £202, but because she was paying by instalments, she thought that it was the same bill. … But what happened was that in January, client's HB/CT was cancelled as they did not qualify for HB/CT any more due to high income, so client was eligible to pay the full CT and that is why she received the bill, and it was overlooked. I explained to client that her CT bill from 2014 was £565.72, but she got some HB/CT which lowered her CT bill, but then she lost HB/CT and that her CT for 2014 go back to the full amount, she made some payments and some credit from CT benefit. Now client received a Court Summons to pay the full amount. I called CT and ask if we could make an arrangement so client could pay for it without them taking further action.[39]

The client agreed to pay £40 per month and to pay some money immediately, and she was advised to make a new Housing Benefit claim.

Unethical landlords also cause issues for clients, as shown in this case note:

---

[38] C. Østergaard Madsen, I. Lindgren and U. Melin, 'The accidental caseworker – how digital self-service influences citizens' administrative burden' (2022) 39(1) 101653, *Government Information Quarterly* 1.

[39] Client ID 46.

Apparently, client is paying his landlord by cash for water bill charges and has no receipts of these payments. According to client, his family and the other flats pay the landlord for water charges, but they have received a bill from water services with the same amount that they have paid to their landlord. Client is worried and said that [he] wanted GYROS to give him an update as well as client needs some of the documents given last time he was seen by GYROS.[40]

The debt issues resulting from these bureaucratic processes and systems is covered in more detail in Chapter 6.

While the dataset had many examples of bad practice, occasionally examples of genorosity did come to light:

Client called and said that her landlady sent a message asking for the rent. ... Client said that last month her landlady was very nice and did not charge for the rent, but she cannot keep going like this. ... I called the landlady and explained to her client's situation and that she is waiting for a reply from UC [Universal Credit] and that we are doing everything we can to help client as well. [Landlady] was very understanding and said that she will wait as she does not want to see client homeless with her children. She asked to be kept informed about client's situation and she will wait till client is able to make any payments. I told landlady that we will do.[41]

5. Tied accommodation

As we saw in Chapter 4, for some EU migrant workers, their accommodation comes with their jobs. If they are working on farms, their accommodation might be a caravan on site (see Figure 5.2). Given the remoteness of the farms, this helps with the early morning starts and long days. The caravans are normally ex-holiday caravans. Workers live six to a caravan (two in each room).

For those working in factories, it might be a room in (long vacant) tourist accommodation. We saw how Rasa was placed in the small 'hotel' room, where she would wash her jeans in the sink. We also saw in Chapter 2 how turkey producer Bernard Matthews hired a housing coordinator to support people they recruited in Lisbon. We also saw that both Edita and Darius had paid private individuals to arrange both their work and accommodation. The provision by recruitment agencies of accommodation to factory workers can

---

[40] Client ID 520.
[41] Client ID 19.

Figure 5.2: A caravan housing migrant workers in Cornwall

Source: image authors' own

lead to difficulties. As we saw in Chapter 2, the police said that community tensions arose when recruitment agencies placed large numbers of Romanian workers in a seafront hotel, since the absence of any communal space in the hotel had forced residents to socialize on the streets.

In the tourist industry, workers might be housed in a caravan park. This had been the case for Jorge[42] (Portuguese, 67, lived in UK since 2004). He lived and worked in one of the holiday parks near Great Yarmouth for 11 years. When the park closed, he moved into the Town. His case note says: 'client started working in [a local chicken factory] for a while when he became ill and was dismissed due to long absence, which also meant he lost his accommodation too, making him homeless.' Jorge approached GYROS for help to make a claim for Universal Credit. He received an advance payment, which he used to pay for two weeks' temporary accommodation. A fortnight later, he returned to GYROS for help with housing. His case notes show that he visited three different services: Housing Options at Great Yarmouth Borough Council, which referred him to the local charity supporting homeless people, which had no availability and referred him to the Job Centre, which referred him back to GYROS. GYROS called Great Yarmouth Borough Council to understand what their housing team had advised; due to language difficulties, Jorge had not understood his conversation with them. Language difficulties also meant he struggled to interact with other services, such as the Job Centre. Ultimately, GYROS

---

[42]   Client ID 383.

helped Jorge find private rented accommodation in the Town (a room in a house share).

Jorge's case highlights the problem of tied accommodation: when the work stops, so does the accommodation. The story of a Bulgarian Roma couple in their sixties is instructive. They moved to the UK in 2020 because they could not find work in Bulgaria, due to the discrimination they faced as Roma people. They could not speak English or read or write Bulgarian. They had been brought to the UK by an agency. They lived in one room, sharing bathroom and kitchen facilities with 15 others. They said alcohol and drug abuse was common in the accommodation. When the woman suffered serious ill health, making her unable to work, her husband took time off to look after her.[43] In December 2022, someone came to their door every day, telling them they had to leave. They had been to the police to complain about the harassment. They had been advised by GYROS, council staff and others that they did not need to leave unless they were issued with the correct court notices (see Section 6). However, a Bulgarian speaking work coordinator at the agency told them that they would never receive any paperwork and they would have to leave.

Historically, January is one of the busiest times of year for GYROS: seasonal poultry contracts come to an end and the accommodation tied to this also ends, meaning they see a large increase in homelessness applications. This happened to a younger Bulgarian couple who had lived with their children in the same agency-provided accommodation as the older couple. They were facing eviction since there was no longer any work available. Like the older couple, they could not speak English or read or write in Bulgarian. They did not know what they had signed at the employment agency, as the Bulgarian work coordinator told them that it was fine to sign, and they trusted him. He was now the one enforcing their eviction and refusing any paperwork. The combination of their work record and the fact they had children (in the case of the older couple, it was the fact that the woman had health difficulties) meant that they might be able to get help from the local housing team, but they would struggle to do so without paperwork, including evidence to show they were facing eviction.

6. Eviction

6.1 The GYROS dataset

As Sara's case shows (Section 3), complaints about the quality of accommodation can lead to landlords evicting tenants forcibly, thus breaching

---

[43] Bulgarian national focus group (Great Yarmouth, December 2022).

the relevant housing legislation.[44] Forcible evictions are not infrequent, especially when rent arrears are involved:

> Client said that letting agent has been around yesterday, demanding full payment of £1,700 rent arrears. She said that he was threatening her that if she doesn't pay then she will be on the street, her children will be taken into care and she will be deported to Lithuania. We advised client that if she feels threatened then she must call Police.[45]

Another client, Ramona, went to Cape Verde for her mother's funeral and returned a month later to discover she and her family were homeless. Ramona said the rent had been paid by her family while she was away, but her landlord had nevertheless turned off the electricity and put a padlock on the door, locking all of her belongings in the flat. She moved into temporary accommodation provided by the council. GYROS could not reach a Portuguese solicitor, so the adviser called the homeless charity Shelter, which advised GYROS to help the client write a letter to the landlord. GYROS also helped the client to complain to the police about her treatment. The police told the client that the landlord had presented court orders and an eviction notice under the Housing Act 1988, but given the poor treatment by the landlord, the client could make a complaint at the police station. Shelter followed up with the client.

The speed with which matters can accumulate and spiral out of control for individuals is seen in Clara's case (Box 5.1).

Box 5.1: Clara's story

Clara[46] was having difficulty paying her rent, as described in the following case note:

> Client said that her landlady came to her house to ask for the rent as she is 12 weeks in arrears. Client told the landlady that she is on SSP [statutory sick pay] and that her benefits have stopped and that as soon as she receives any money, she will pay the rent. Client said that landlady and her husband were rude and yelled at her and they changed the door lock. Also, client said that her 18 years

---

[44] Specifically, Housing Act 1988. See further, 'Private renting for tenants: evictions in England' *Gov.uk*, available at: www.gov.uk/private-renting-evictions, accessed 23 November 2023; 'Eviction notices from private landlords' *Shelter*, available at: https://england.shelter.org.uk/housing_advice/eviction/eviction_notices_from_private_landlords, accessed 23 November 2023.

[45] Client ID 186.

[46] Client ID 131.

old son was too nervous, and she asked him to leave the house as she was afraid that he would lose his temper, so he left and when he went to the front door he slammed the door and hit the glass and it broke. They [landlord] called the police and client's son was arrested and now he needs to go to court. Client understands that they will have to pay for the glass, but it was an accident. Client said that when the police came, they talked with the landlord and she does not know what [was said], because there was no translator, and the police asked for the property keys and client gave it to the police, although she does not understand why as they had changed the locks already.

The GYROS adviser sent an email to a contact at the police to get more information about the way her landlord acted, 'as it is not according to the eviction process'. The adviser also told the client to look for another property, as her Housing Benefit was being sorted out and she would have help with Housing Benefit and Council Tax.

Clara next presented to GYROS after having been to Great Yarmouth Borough Council:

Client said that she went to council and that the adviser called her landlady to advise her landlady to give the keys back to client. However, according to client all the calls went to voicemail and client is still living in friend's house. Council adviser gave client a Shelter card and advised her to call them.

I called Shelter but no one answered the phone. I also called council to get an update in client's claim. I tried several times and different numbers; the call went through several options and then it switched off after the options. I told client I would write an email to Council asking for an update regarding her HB [Housing Benefit] claim. Client was ok with this.

GYROS arranged for the Housing Benefit to be paid directly to the landlady, and Clara was able to return to her property. GYROS helped Clara report this incident to the police. The following case note reflects the advice from the police at the time:

The PC [police constable] told client that what the landlady did was not right, and client could take it forward if she wanted, but she needed to see what was best for her as she is now back at the property and her HB [Housing Benefit] has been paid to the landlady and it is up to client to decide. Client said that she does not want to do anything as she does not have any money to move out of the property. Once client is back to work, she will look for another property.

The case notes for both Ramona and Clara show that in these sorts of cases there is a need for multi-agency intervention. They also show that both the council housing team and GYROS rely on housing law experts at Shelter. Shelter holds the housing legal aid contract for Norfolk. The council advisers rely on GYROS' expertise when it comes to immigration status, especially around the EUSS and related eligibility and access rights. All agencies also rely on the police, but the police feel ill-equipped to deal with the complexity of housing law and eviction procedures. As a local police officer said:

> I think we probably don't get involved in as many landlord/tenant issues … because it sits within civil law, we're criminal law. I think there is a lack of knowledge for some police officers around actually some of it falls into our world. So, it's illegal to evict somebody, it is a criminal offence to evict somebody unlawfully.[47] But then falls into: are they doing it unlawfully, do you know what I mean? It is a really difficult area. … So, it's probably an area where we could expand on, it's an area where the neighbourhood policing teams are trying to improve on, but it's also around, we try to make sure they get directed to the right people. So, council housing officers, Citizens Advice, people like that.[48]

As we saw in the introduction, GYROS too feels that housing cases are where their advisers are most out of their depth. Yet the database case notes reveal staff adept at understanding the rules, especially concerning eviction and the right to seek help from the council. Take the case of a family in an overcrowded one-bedroom apartment:

> I told client that he still has some time as it will take some time for the judge to issue the order and that he will be given more 28 days. By then, client should be okay to go to the council and ask for help with a house and they will be able to offer him a temporary accommodation as they will not let him be on the streets with the children. I also explained he will need to pass 5 criteria, being homeless, having connection to the borough, having the right to public funds, have the right to reside and above all not to be found that he is in that situation by his own doing. … I could send an email to the council as well asking for his claim to be considered. Client was okay with that.[49]

---

[47] For more information on this, see 'How to deal with illegal eviction' *Shelter*, available at: https://england.shelter.org.uk/housing_advice/eviction/how_to_deal_with_illegal_eviction/what_is_an_illegal_eviction, accessed 21 February 2023.

[48] Interview with local police officer (Great Yarmouth, October 2021).

[49] Client ID 293.

The case notes also show staff are juggling other applications while managing the timelines associated with legal action. One case note recorded advice to the client not to leave the property despite receiving a notice requiring possession due to rent arrears; instead, they were advised to wait for a court order for possession, by which time their Housing Benefit application would have been addressed.[50]

Sometimes, the case becomes more complex because children's services are involved:

> Client has 3 children. His ex-partner left him on 10th May 2016 with their youngest child. The other two children are with client. Few months ago, his landlord decided to sell the house and client was evicted. GYBC [Great Yarmouth Borough Council] provided temporary accommodation and we helped him to claim UC [Universal Credit]. His UC payments started in November, but he paid only part of the rent initially. So, GYBC made a referral to children's services.

GYROS attended the appointment with the client, and an interpreter was also booked. The social worker explained that the client needed to make sure he did not become intentionally homeless. The adviser helped the client understand how much rent he had to pay. The client was helped into appropriate accommodation.

6.2 Possession hearings

Attendance at court is most likely for GYROS clients if they are being evicted. The possession list in Great Yarmouth is every other Monday and is a mixture of social landlords (Great Yarmouth Borough Council, Broadland Housing Association, Orbit Housing Association and Saffron Housing Association), private landlords and mortgage repossessions. Social landlords and mortgage repossessions are listed as four per 30 minutes, private landlords are two every 30 minutes. Generally, judges consider the appropriate time for social landlords is 5 minutes; for mortgagees, 10 minutes; and for private landlords, 15 minutes.[51]

We witnessed this 'conveyor belt justice'[52] in the possession hearings we attended in Norwich. The Shelter team (3.5 full-time equivalent posts) in Norfolk acts as 'duty solicitor' in Norwich every week and in King's Lynn

---

[50] Client ID 293.
[51] Information provided by the local judiciary on 13 February 2023.
[52] J. Robins and D. Newman, *Justice in a Time of Austerity: Stories from a System in Crisis* (Bristol: Bristol University Press, 2021), 9.

and Great Yarmouth every other week.[53] The Legal Aid Agency funds the Housing Possession Court Duty Schemes throughout England and Wales to provide on-the-day emergency advice and advocacy to anyone facing possession proceedings.[54] For many, seeing the duty solicitor just before their case is heard is the first opportunity they have had access to legal advice.

The Shelter duty solicitor said that the housing list is focused on landlords following the correct procedure; the court does not look at the broader circumstances leading to the eviction.[55] This, Shelter said, can be difficult for tenants to understand, especially if they feel they have been treated unfairly and would like this to be conveyed to the judge. However, most cases are resolved before the court hearing takes place. In many of the cases listed on the days we attended, a repayment plan had been negotiated (at a fee of £355, added to the debts already facing the individual) and so suspended possession orders were granted; the threat of legal action had in some cases galvanized the negotiation in the first place. The district judge in Norwich allowed time for tenants and landlords to ask questions and made sure they had understood the financial requirements, even if the wider process was bewildering. The judge also said that social landlords (the majority on the listing that day) had the resources to help their tenants manage arrears, arrange help with energy bills and provide food parcels. By contrast, with private landlords, the sense was that tenants were on their own.[56]

The perception of the local judiciary was that the distribution of work between mortgage possessions and possession claims by social and private landlords in Great Yarmouth was not particularly different to that in other courts in the area. A judge noted that:

'While there are a few more EU migrants in Great Yarmouth, that is reflective of the local demographic, but does not seem to be significantly different to other courts. If anything, it is King's Lynn [which] has the larger number of Eastern European litigants in possession cases compared to other local courts, and a correspondingly greater need for interpreters.'

The judge added:

'The significant difference with private landlords in Great Yarmouth is that they are more naive/amateurish, and they are more likely to be

---

[53] Due to the lottery of provision, there is no equivalent scheme in Suffolk, the neighbouring county.

[54] 'Housing Possession Court Duty Schemes (HPCDS)' *Gov.uk*, available at: www.gov.uk/government/publications/housing-possession-court-duty-schemes-hpcds, accessed 23 November 2023.

[55] Shadowing at Norwich Court: Possessions Listings (November 2022).

[56] Ibid.

self-represented. This may reflect the cheaper housing stock and that the landlords have less resources.'

The fact that the local judiciary had not noticed a significant number of EU migrants before them may support the view that many of the housing issues facing GYROS' clients do not make it as far as the court room. In part, this may be due to the help GYROS and Shelter are able to give before cases get to court, but it may also be due to the informality of some of the housing arrangements, meaning that the landlords simply throw the tenants out rather than going through the formal eviction process.

E. GYROS' response to these problems

In describing cases recorded in the GYROS dataset in Section D, we also gain an insight into the work of GYROS' advisers, who take a holistic person (and problem)-centred approach to helping their clients, translating paper work, undertaking case work such as contacting landlords, accompanying and supporting in meetings with the Housing Team or Children's Services, for example.[57] As we have seen, they are reliant on Shelter to help avoid evictions where possible. Where GYROS' clients have gone to court, it was as defendants in eviction processes. As we saw in relation to employment, in Chapter 4, they do not rely on the formal legal process to enforce their rights, let alone go to court. For example, harassment by a landlord, as in Sara's and Ramona's cases, is a criminal offence.[58] Yet the police were not called and, as the interview with the police officer shows, there is

---

[57] For more on the multifaceted role of advice givers see: I. Koch and D. James, 'The state of the welfare state: advice, governance and care in settings of austerity' (2022) 87 *Ethnos* 1, 7; A. Forbess and D. James, 'Acts of assistance: navigating the interstices of the British state with the help of non-profit legal advisers', (2014) 58(3) *Social Analysis Berghahn Journals* 73

[58] Section 1(3A) Protection from Eviction Act 1977: 'Subject to subsection (3B) below, the landlord of a residential occupier or an agent of the landlord shall be guilty of an offence if—

(a) he does acts likely to interfere with the peace or comfort of the residential occupier or members of his household, or

(b) he persistently withdraws or withholds services reasonably required for the occupation of the premises in question as a residence, and (in either case) he knows, or has reasonable cause to believe, that that conduct is likely to cause the residential occupier to give up the occupation of the whole or part of the premises or to refrain from exercising any right or pursuing any remedy in respect of the whole or part of the premises. See also 'How to deal with harassment from landlords or agents', *Shelter*, available from: https://england.shelter.org.uk/housing_advice/eviction/harassment_by_a_private_landlord, accessed 23 November 2023.

considerable confusion on the part of the police as to whether this is a civil or a criminal matter.

We have also seen the issues related to the poor quality of accommodation in the Town – the leaking roof in the House and the collapsed ceiling in Sara's flat. In *Walker v Hobbs*,[59] a breach of an implied term was found (in relation to fitness for habitation) after 'the ceilings were in a ruinous and dangerous condition and fell down and seriously injured the female plaintiff. ... [T]he ceilings were in a dangerous condition, and therefore that the rooms were not, speaking in a broad sense, fit for human habitation.'[60] Similarly, in *Summers v Salford Corporation*,[61] it was held that a window in a main room which could not be opened was a breach. This recalls the window in the bathroom in the House – the only form of ventilation in that room – which could not be opened due to the large crack in the glass and the considerable moss growing inside its wooden frame. More recently the Homes (Fitness for Human Habitation) Act 2018, said to 'represent the biggest advance in tenant's rights relating to housing conditions for a generation'[62] requires all houses (new tenancies from March 2019 and in due course all tenancies[63]) to be at a certain standard for human habitation, and that standard should be maintained. With the new Act, 'the court can make the landlord carry out repairs or put right health and safety problems. The court can also make the landlord pay compensation to the tenant'.[64] Yet there is no mention of the legislation or of legal remedies in the GYROS dataset. As we saw in the previous chapter, on employment, EU migrant workers mainly accept the issues they face or move on; GYROS can help with that process of moving on.

F. Social housing

The social rented sector represents about 17 per cent of households nationally and 18 per cent in Great Yarmouth,[65] making it smaller than the private rented sector.[66] About 15 per cent of EU nationals in the UK are in social

---

[59] *Walker v Hobbs & Co* (1889) QBD 458.
[60] Ibid, Lord Coleridge CJ.
[61] *Summers v Salford Corporation* [1943] AC 283, 1 All ER 68, HL.
[62] HHJ J. Luba, C. O'Donnell and G. Peaker, *Housing Conditions, Tenants' Rights* (6th edn, London: LAG Education and Service Trust Limited, 2019), 5.
[63] Ibid, 6.
[64] Department for Levelling Up, Housing and Communities, 'Guide for tenants: Homes (Fitness for Human Habitation) Act 2018', *Gov.uk* (6 March 2019), available at: www.gov.uk/government/publications/homes-fitness-for-human-habitation-act-2018/guide-for-tenants-homes-fitness-for-human-habitation-act-2018, accessed 15 March 2023.
[65] Great Yarmouth Borough Council, n 3, 8.
[66] 'English Housing Survey', n 26.

housing, slightly lower than for UK nationals (16 per cent) and non-EU nationals (19 per cent).[67] The GYROS dataset shows that only about 10 per cent of their clients live in council accommodation (a significantly lower share than the national figure). Therefore, most participants in our research were in the private rented sector and we have focused on this reality throughout the chapter. However, can those (low-paid) EU nationals have access to housing in the social rented sector?

When free movement of persons was first being discussed in the early 1950s, there were concerns among some EU member states that EU nationals and their joining family members might overwhelm social housing support in host countries. These concerns were not borne out in practice. Specifically, in the UK, '[e]vidence soon emerged revealing that relatively small numbers of foreign nationals, and virtually no migrant workers, were gaining access to and living within the social rented sector'.[68] Access to local authority housing support (social housing and homelessness support) is dependent on EU migrants satisfying a number of tests. EU nationals with settled status (more than five years of residence) are automatically eligible for support, because they have an automatic 'right to reside' (dependent on further housing eligibility tests, which are applicable to all, as outlined by the GYROS adviser to the family in overcrowded accommodation). By contrast, those who have pre-settled status (less than five years of residence) need a 'qualifying right'[69] to access housing support. This means they must satisfy the right to reside test and show they are habitually resident in the UK. To pass the right to reside test, the individual must show they are a qualified person[70] residing lawfully in the UK. Generally, jobseekers, students and self-sufficient people are not eligible for assistance.

To show they are habitually resident in the UK, individuals have to demonstrate when they moved to the UK and their residence in the UK, using documents such as tenancy agreements, rent payments and utility bills. This is where the lack of paperwork discussed in sections C and D becomes a major stumbling block. The effect of these rules would be that, as an example, an EU national who has lived in the UK for four years but has not been working for the last year and is now experiencing housing precarity

---

[67] For more, see 'Migrants and housing in the UK: experiences and impacts' *The Migration Observatory at the University of Oxford* (2 September 2022), available at: https://migration observatory.ox.ac.uk/resources/briefings/migrants-and-housing-in-the-uk/, accessed 23 November 2023.

[68] D. Robinson, 'New immigrants and migrants in social housing in Britain: discursive themes and lived realities' (2010) 38 *Policy and Politics* 57, 57.

[69] Immigration (European Economic Area) Regulations 2016 SI 2016/1052.

[70] A definition is provided in Chapter 3, n 31.

will struggle to access any housing support, as they have no 'qualifying' right. They will therefore be described as 'NRPF' (no recourse to public funds). This can be particularly acute for those facing homelessness or for victims of domestic abuse who may find they are unable to access any accommodation or refuge as they are unable to meet the requirements of the prescribed tests. We return to consider the application of these tests in more detail in Chapter 6 alongside recent cases challenging this position.

G. Conclusion

One of the themes of this book is precarity. This chapter has shown how precarity plays out in respect of housing: difficulty in getting access to accommodation for those on precarious zero-hours contracts, poor-quality and sometimes structurally unsound accommodation, rapid loss of accommodation if it is tied to a job which comes to an end or where the landlord decides to evict the tenant, and then the difficulties of getting local housing support due to earlier lack of paperwork (from informal tenancy arrangements and names not appearing on bills).

The other theme of the book is pragmatism, especially by GYROS' advisers in addressing clients' problems. The advice that GYROS advisers give on housing-related issues is more 'legal' than that for other areas we have explored. The advisers often learn the rules through experience with similar cases. However, we see no evidence of advisers recommending formal legal resolution pathways to address problems concerning, for example, unfit accommodation. The first response is to try to contact the landlord to get the problem addressed. Sometimes, as in the case of the House, it is the residents who fix the problems themselves. More often, tenants just live with the problems. That said, the council is trying to work to improve the housing. We leave the final word to a local police officer:

> 'I think locally there is a real drive to enhance standard of living, our accommodation … I think there's real opportunity on the back of COVID to springboard this town. Which sits outside the police's realm, but we have a part to play. The amount of money, which is coming into the new marketplace, the harbour, the third river crossing. And there's a real scope, you know what I mean, for the selective licensing to just bring up a standard of the accommodation. It is not about having this glorious expensive accommodation. It's about actually having a standard which is fit for purpose, safe and wholesome.'[71]

---

[71] Interview with local police officer (November 2021).

6

Welfare Benefits and Debt

A. Introduction

One of the most common reasons for clients approaching GYROS is to get advice on welfare benefits – just over 25 per cent of all enquiries were related to in-work benefits designed to 'top up' low-paid work. In this chapter, we look at how EU migrant workers in Great Yarmouth interact with the benefits system. EU law, and now the Withdrawal Agreement, gives migrant workers the right to claim benefits on the same terms as UK nationals. However, this chapter shows that many struggle to navigate the benefits system, not just because of language and digital literacy issues but also because of the strict entitlement criteria. Specifically, access to welfare benefits shows the complex bureaucratic bordering[1] experienced by migrant communities who may have to prove that they have been 'habitually resident' and have a 'right to reside', in order to claim certain means-tested welfare benefits, such as Universal Credit. We saw this with Darius in Chapter 1, as he had a 'further evidence interview' at the Job Centre, where he had to provide his tenancy agreement and proof of rent payments. He also had his Habitual Residence Test interview, where he had to produce documents showing residence in the UK (payslips, a P45, employment contracts, GP letters, a National Insurance number letter). Given the volume of documentation needed to prove entitlement, claims may be frustrated where, as shown in earlier chapters, workers have not received payslips, P45s or tenancy agreements.

Debt, the other issue we examine in this chapter, is also a common problem for GYROS' clients. Zero-hours contracts combined with low pay mean individuals are often living pay packet to pay packet, and there

---

[1]   P. Manolova, 'Inclusion through irregularisation? Exploring the politics and realities of internal bordering in managing post-crisis labour migration in the EU' (2021) *Journal of Ethnic and Migration Studies* 1, 1.

is often no money for unexpected bills. Further, if the individual had paid an intermediary to help them to find employment and accommodation in Great Yarmouth – either before departure or after arrival in the UK – that initial debt must be paid off (even when, as in the case of Darius, the employment never transpired).

Issues around benefits and debt are in fact interrelated. Delays in accessing benefits, particularly when individuals face additional eligibility checks, mean debts accrue quickly. This problem was exacerbated in 2015 when Great Yarmouth was selected as a pilot area for the introduction of Universal Credit, a process which turned out to be far from smooth, leading to significant delays in payments. Further, the digital application process, which foreshadowed the later digital-only nature of the EUSS application (Chapter 3), has increased the difficulties for GYROS' clients, many of whom struggle with technology. They are also affected by the 'poverty premium'[2] due to payment demands, cost of court summons and late payment fees, which aggravate their already precarious financial situation.

In this chapter, we focus less on the experiences of the residents in the House than we do in other chapters, as most were in full time employment, did not have dependent children and were not claiming any welfare benefits (although Adomas briefly received Universal Credit when he was in-between jobs – a common occurrence related to seasonal work in the area). The residents also do not seem to have had issues with debt, apart from Camilla's experience with her previous landlord and her Council Tax bill (Chapter 5). So the examples used in this chapter are drawn from the GYROS dataset. We begin by looking at problems EU migrant workers experienced when attempting to access benefits (Section B) and then we consider issues around debt (Section C). Having described the problems these migrants face, we then consider how GYROS helps its clients with these issues. As in other chapters, we see pragmatism in the advisers' approach and a desire to help clients sort out their problems so as to avoid further problems developing and the accrual of additional debt.

B. Welfare benefits

1. Introduction

Welfare benefits in the UK are a mix of contributory, means-tested and circumstance-specific benefits (for example, Disability Living Allowance or Personal Independent Payments for those with disabilities or managed

---

conditions[3]). For EU nationals, access to benefits in the UK has increasingly been restricted. By 2014, the growing catalogue of restrictions included:

> the introduction of a three-month prior residence rule for Jobseeker's Allowance, which has been extended to Child Benefit and Child Tax Credit; the scrapping of Housing Benefit for all EU jobseekers; the withdrawing of job centre language interpretation for EU jobseekers; the introduction of a six-month cut-off for Jobseeker's Allowance, now reduced to a three-month cut-off, coupled with a 'compelling evidence of genuine prospects of work' test; and the introduction of a 'minimum earnings threshold' to have work classified as 'work'.[4]

Further, in 2013, the Coalition government introduced Universal Credit, replacing Income Support, income-based Jobseeker's Allowance, income-related Employment Support Allowance, Housing Benefit, child tax credit and working tax credit.[5] This seismic change, introduced to 'simplify and streamline'[6] the welfare benefit process, reduce error and fraud, increase employment incentives (to 'make work pay'[7]) and reduce poverty,[8] affected all claimants. However, claimants with literacy issues, including many of GYROS' clients, were particularly affected. New claimants are required to create an online Universal Credit account to submit a claim. Creating an account requires an email address and mobile phone number, a point noted by the United Nations Special Rapporteur on extreme poverty and human rights, who said: 'The British welfare state is gradually disappearing behind a webpage and an algorithm, with significant implications for those living

---

[3]   C. O'Brien, *Unity in Adversity: EU Citizenship, Social Justice and the Cautionary Tale of the UK* (Oxford: Hart, 2017), 21–22.

[4]   C. O'Brien, 'The pillory, the precipice, and the slippery slope: the profound effects of the UK's legal reform programme targeting EU migrants' (2015) 37 *Journal of Social Welfare and Family Law* 111, 111.

[5]   P. Dwyer and S. Wright, 'Universal Credit, ubiquitous conditionality and its implications for social citizenship' (2014) 22(1) *Journal of Poverty and Social Justice* 27, 27.

[6]   S. Steele, *Universal Credit: A Reading List* House of Commons Briefing Paper (May 2021), available at: https://researchbriefings.files.parliament.uk/documents/CBP-9211/CBP-9211.pdf, accessed 14 February 2023.

[7]   Department for Work and Pensions, 'Welfare Reform White Paper: Universal Credit to make work pay: radical welfare reforms bring an end to complex system' (November 2020), available at: www.gov.uk/government/news/welfare-reform-white-paper-univer sal-credit-to-make-work-pay-radical-welfare-reforms-bring-an-end-to-complex-system, accessed 10 January 2023.

[8]   Steele, n 6.

in poverty.'[9] We consider the impact of the introduction of Universal Credit on those living in Great Yarmouth later in the chapter. First, we look at the requirements for EU nationals claiming benefits.

2. EU eligibility and systems

2.1 The requirements

Under EU law, EU migrant workers can claim social advantages under Regulation 492/11, and EU citizens can claim social assistance after the first three months of residence under the Citizens' Rights Directive 2004/38. The interplay between these provisions is complex. In essence, workers, including work-seekers, enjoy equal treatment in respect of social advantages under Article 7(2) of Regulation 492/11 from the first day of their arrival in the host state (albeit host states can impose proportionate, justified residence requirements for the migrant to establish a real link with the labour market of the host state,[10] which may delay the worker from receiving the social advantage until a genuine link with the host territory, via residence, has been realized[11]). In *Even*,[12] the court defined 'social advantages' broadly to include all benefits[13] which,

> whether or not linked to a contract of employment, are generally granted to national workers primarily because of their objective status as workers or by virtue of the mere fact of their residence on the national territory and the extension of which to workers who are nationals of other Member States therefore seems suitable to facilitate their mobility within the [Union].

Non-economically active citizens enjoy equal treatment under Article 24(1) CRD, including, in principle, access to social assistance. In *Brey*,[14] the court said that the phrase 'social assistance' meant

> all assistance introduced by the public authorities, whether at national, regional or local level, that can be claimed by an individual who does

---

[9] P. Alston, *Extreme Poverty and Human Rights* Note by the Secretary-General, United Nations General Assembly Report A/74/493 (2019) available at: https://documents-dds-ny.un.org/doc/UNDOC/GEN/G19/112/13/PDF/G1911213.pdf?OpenElement, accessed 23 November 2023, 13.

[10] Joined Cases C-22/08 and 23/08 *Vatsouras* [2009] ECR I-4585, para 40.

[11] Case C-138/02 *Collins v Secretary of State for Work and Pensions* [2004] ECR I-2703.

[12] Case 207/78 *Criminal Proceedings against Even* [1979] ECR 2019.

[13] Ibid, para 22.

[14] Case C-140/12 *Pensionsversicherungsanstalt v Brey*, EU:C:2013:565, para 61.

not have resources sufficient to meet his own basic needs and the needs of his family and who, by reason of that fact, may become a burden on the public finances of the host Member State during his period of residence which could have consequences for the overall level of assistance which may be granted by that State.

This definition suggests that social assistance benefits are those intended to protect against destitution, such as Universal Credit[15] or Housing Benefit.

However, non-economically active citizens (and workers) can be denied social assistance for the first three months under Article 24(2) CRD.[16] For those resident in another member state beyond three months of residence and up to five years of residence, the court in *Dano*[17] said, and it was confirmed in *CG*,[18] that the right of residence is subject to the conditions set out in Article 7(1)(b) CRD, which requires economically inactive citizens to have sufficient resources for themselves and the members of their family, because otherwise there was a risk of 'allowing economically inactive Union citizens to use the host Member State's welfare system to fund their means of subsistence'.[19]

Post Brexit, settled status gives entitlement to benefits on the same basis as British nationals. Their status means that they have the right to reside for benefit purposes, although they still need to show they are habitually resident. However, applicants with pre-settled status cannot rely solely on their status.[20] They must also demonstrate an independent qualifying right to reside for benefit purposes. This means they must have a qualifying right under what were the Immigration (European Economic Area) Regulations 2016, so they must show that they are a worker, self-employed or have retained worker/self-employed status, or are family member of an EEA citizen in one of those categories.[21]

---

[15] For a consideration of the classification of this benefit as a social assistance benefit, see Report by the Social Security Advisory Committee under Sections 174(1) of the Social Security Administration Act 1992 and statement by the Secretary of State for Work and Pensions in accordance with Section 174(2) of that Act (2012), para 16. However, in C-709/20 *CG v Department for Communities in Northern Ireland* EU:C:2021:602, para 71, it was classified as a social assistance benefit.

[16] Case C-67/14 *Alimanovic*, ECLI:EU:C:2015:597.

[17] Case C-333/13 *Elisabeta Dano and Florin Dano v Jobcenter Leipzig*, EU:C:2014:2358.

[18] C-709/20 *CG v Department for Communities in Northern Ireland* EU:C:2021:602.

[19] *CG*, para 77 and *Dano* paras 74, 76 and 77.

[20] The Social Security (Income-related Benefits) (Updating and Amendment) (EU Exit) Regulations 2019.

[21] This may also include other groups, such as students and *Teixeira* carers.

2.2 Current legal challenges to eligibility

This qualified right of access applying to pre-settled status holders has been tested in recent UK cases, some of which are still ongoing at the time of writing. In *Fratila*,[22] the claimants, Romanian nationals with pre-settled status, applied for Universal Credit in 2019. Their applications were refused on the basis that to access Universal Credit in the UK, they needed another qualifying right and could not rely solely on their pre-settled status to meet the requirements of the 'right to reside' test.[23] They argued that this contravened the prohibition on discrimination on the grounds of nationality under Article 18 TFEU, which still applied because the facts of the case arose during the transition period (ie before 31 December 2020). The High Court dismissed the respondent's claim, but the Court of Appeal[24] allowed their appeal, quashing the 2019 Regulations[25] and finding them directly discriminatory. The case was appealed to the Supreme Court, which delayed the case pending the outcome of the Court of Justice of the European Union in *CG*,[26] a case referred from the Northern Ireland Social Security Tribunal regarding another EU national with pre-settled status who had also applied for, and been refused, Universal Credit.

CG was a single mother of two who had been the victim of domestic abuse. She lived in a women's refuge after she left her abusive partner. She had never been economically active in the UK, having moved to the country in 2018 to join the father of her children. The Court of Justice of the European Union said she could not rely on the principle of non-discrimination (Article 18) to claim a right to equal treatment in respect of entitlement to Universal Credit.[27] This was because Article 18 TFEU applied independently only to situations governed by EU law with respect to which the TFEU did not lay down specific rules on non-discrimination; Article 24 CRD was the relevant, specific provision, and this applied instead. As we saw earlier, 'a Member State has the possibility, pursuant to Article 7 [CRD], of refusing to grant

---

[22] *Fratila and another (AP) v Secretary of State for Work and Pensions* [2021] UKSC 53.

[23] The Social Security (Income-related Benefits) (Updating and Amendment) (EU Exit) Regulations 2019. Available: The Social Security (Income-related Benefits) (Updating and Amendment) (EU Exit) Regulations 2019. See also The Immigration and Social Security Co-ordination (EU Withdrawal) Act 2020 (Consequential, Saving, Transitional and Transitory Provisions) (EU Exit) Regulations 2020, available at: www.legislation.gov.uk/uksi/2020/1309/contents/made, accessed 24 January 2023.

[24] [3] *Fratila v SSWP* [2020] EWCA Civ 1741.

[25] Ibid.

[26] C-709/20 *CG v Department for Communities in Northern Ireland* EU:C:2021:602.

[27] The Court of Justice of the European Union stated that the question of whether an EU national moving to or residing in a member state other than their own faced discrimination on grounds of nationality fell to be assessed by reference to Directive 2004/38 Article 24 and not Article 18 TFEU.

social benefits to economically inactive Union citizens who exercise their right to freedom of movement and who do not have sufficient resources to claim a right of residence under that directive'.[28] Following this judgment, the Supreme Court ruled in *Fratila* that the respondents also could not rely on Article 18 TFEU.[29] This means that 'until – and if – those 2.5 million holders of pre-settled status can upgrade to settled status, access to welfare benefits and housing support will remain largely contingent on demonstrating sufficient economic activity to meet the right to reside criteria'.[30]

However, in *CG*, the Court of Justice found that before refusing social assistance benefits, the relevant authority had to satisfy itself that the refusal would not expose the claimant to an actual and current risk of violation of their rights under the EU Charter of Fundamental Rights (before the end of the transition period). This would include rights such as respect for human dignity (Article 1), integrity (Article 3), respect for private and family life (Article 7), non-discrimination (Article 21) and primary consideration of the best interests of the child (Article 24). Charter rights had not been considered by the Supreme Court in *Fratila*, because they had not been raised in earlier proceedings.

The Charter was, however, at issue in *AT*.[31] AT was a Romanian national with pre-settled status but no other qualifying right to reside for the purposes of claiming Universal Credit. She was a single mother who had been the victim of domestic abuse. She first moved to the UK in 2016; her child was born in 2018. AT said she had endured domestic abuse from V, including while she was pregnant. In 2020, she was granted pre-settled status. In January 2021, the police were called to an incident at their home. V was arrested and AT and her child were placed in temporary accommodation and then in a women's refuge. A summary in the judgment outlines 'Her resources comprised £200 in a bank account, into which her Child Benefit had been paid, a £25 Tesco voucher and £15 from a fellow resident. Because her Child Benefit payments (£84.20 every four weeks) were not enough to cover her basic needs and those of her child, she applied for Universal Credit'.[32]

The First Tier Tribunal had said that without Universal Credit, AT and her child could not live in 'dignified conditions', therefore breaching their Charter rights. The Secretary of State for Work and Pensions appealed on the basis that *CG* referred to those with pre-settled status *before* the end of the transition period (December 2020) and that the Charter applied only to member states when they were implementing EU law and so did

---

[28] Para 78.

[29] *Fratila and another (AP) v Secretary of State for Work and Pensions* [2021] UKSC 53.

[30] A. Welsh, 'Permission to discriminate – EU nationals, pre-settled status and access to social assistance' (2022) 44 *Journal of Social Welfare and Family Law* 133, 134.

[31] *Secretary of State for Work and Pensions v AT* [2022] UKUT 330 (AAC), 2022 WL 17822237.

[32] Ibid [3].

not apply to the UK after the transition period. The Upper Tribunal said that AT could rely on the Charter after the end of the transition period and the Court of Appeal agreed.[33] It also held an individual assessment is required in all cases where a person (with rights under the Withdrawal Agreement) requiring universal credit would otherwise be refused on the grounds they do not have the right to reside. This case will have a significant impact on those who are more vulnerable – such as victims of domestic abuse – who previously have been described as 'no recourse to public funds (NRPF)', and therefore not entitled to any housing or social welfare support (chapters 3 and 5). Permission to appeal the case to the Supreme Court has been refused by the Court of Appeal. The Secretary of State for Work and Pensions did seek further permission to appeal from the Supreme Court in February 2024, which was ultimately also refused.[34]

Having looked at the complex legal landscape facing EU benefit claimants, we turn now to consider some of the issues seen in the GYROS dataset. In the next section, we focus on Universal Credit and the effect of the pilot on the Town, and the continued problems GYROS' clients have with Universal Credit, especially over its digital accessibility (Section 4) and overpayments (Section 5). We also look at how GYROS responds to the problems presented by its clients (Section 6).

3. Universal Credit and Great Yarmouth

The Universal Credit system was piloted in various areas, including Great Yarmouth, before being rolled out nationally. The scheme was marred with teething problems, including significant delays to payments. Councillors from all parties on Great Yarmouth Borough Council wrote to the then Secretary of State for Department for Work and Pensions, Damien Green, about their 'deep concerns' about the rollout of Universal Credit in the area,[35] not least because, as we saw in Chapter 2, Great Yarmouth had suffered considerably from austerity. They noted that foodbank use had

---

[33] [2023] EWCA Civ 1307.

[34] C. O'Brien, 'Court of Appeal decides the Secretary of State is wrong, wrong, wrong: The Charter applies to people with pre-settled status', (16 November 2023), published by the EU Rights and Brexit Hub Blog Series, available here: https://www.eurightshub.york.ac.uk/blog/court-of-appeal-decides-the-secretary-of-state-is-wrong-wrong-wrong-the-charter-applies-to-people-with-pre-settled-status, accessed 04 December 2023. See also: CPAG (2024), https://cpag.org.uk/news/supreme-court-rules-government-must-support-eu-migrants-risk-not-being-able-meet-most-basic-needs, accessed 08 Februaury 2024.

[35] T. Bristow, ' "We're being used as guinea pigs" – impact of Universal Credit welfare revolution felt hardest in Yarmouth' *Eastern Daily Press* (2 December 2016), available at: www.edp24.co.uk/news/20854721.were-used-guinea-pigs---impact-universal-credit-welfare-revolution-felt-hardest-yarmouth/, accessed 10 January 2023.

increased by over 200 per cent[36] as claimants waited, sometimes up to three months, for their first payment, and that Great Yarmouth Borough Council was owed £82,000 from 400 tenants who were in rent arrears due to Universal Credit payment delays. The councillors called for an 'urgent investigation' into the impact of the introduction of Universal Credit, saying it was causing 'unnecessary stress and anxiety for claimants' and asking 'why Yarmouth [had been] chosen as a pilot'.[37] The government also continued with its focus on a digital scheme, despite the evaluation of the Universal Credit pilot in May 2013 showing: 'Not all customer groups have access to the internet either with the right tools/equipment or internet access – some local authorities … report around 50–60%.'[38] As we have seen, many HMOs – including the House of this research – do not have internet access.

The GYROS dataset contains case notes dating back to the period of the introduction of Universal Credit. These show the serious problems faced by clients in terms of delayed payments. For example, Claudia had been the victim of a hit-and-run car accident, leaving her with a broken leg. She sought help to apply for Universal Credit when she could not get statutory sick pay, since her zero-hours contracts meant she did not meet the SSP threshold. She initially applied for contribution-based Employment Support Allowance, but this was refused:

> May 2016. Client received a letter from ESA [Employment Support Allowance] stating that she does not have enough contributions to claim ESA contribution based and that she needs to claim ESA income related; because we are on UC [Universal Credit] already, I told client that we need to claim UC and explained to her that it will take up to 6 weeks for the first payment and that her CTC [Child Tax Credit] will stop as well. Client said that it will be impossible to survive without any benefit; just CHB [Child Benefit] is not enough, and her HB [Housing Benefit] is suspended. I told client that I will send an email to HB. Client will come Friday to bring me a letter from school as evidence that her daughter is attending school.[39]

---

[36] Ibid.

[37] Ibid.

[38] Department for Work and Pensions, *Local Authority Led Pilots: A Summary of Early Learning from the Pilots* (July 2023), available at: https://assets.publishing.service.gov.uk/government/uploads/system/uploads/attachment_data/file/225068/rrep848.pdf, accessed 10 January 2023.

[39] Client ID 982.

Claudia's case was not an isolated example. In June 2016, Rita[40] approached GYROS as "she wanted to claim JSA [Jobseeker's Allowance] contribution", but the adviser explained 'that there is no more JSA because the postcode is now on UC [Universal Credit], and we should do UC instead'. As an EU national, she had to satisfy the Habitual Residence Test. Her appointment was booked for September, and the GYROS worker accompanied her to this appointment. In October the GYROS worker phoned the Department for Work and Pensions twice to check on the progress of the Habitual Residence Test assessment. Throughout this period, the client received no money. At the end of October, Rita was told that she did not pass the Habitual Residence Test; the GYROS worker advised her that she could request mandatory reconsideration of this decision and she did so in November, again with GYROS' help. In December, GYROS helped her to "contact UC [Universal Credit] to book an appoint for her husband to show his bank account details, which he already provides on his journal". The Universal Credit journal is an online record of all activities undertaken while claiming that benefit. Rita was struggling because the Job Centre needed to see her husband for him to show his bank details in person, but with his long antisocial work hours, this proved difficult. According to the case note: 'Client explained to them that he is working full time and doing overtime due to Christmas season, but the adviser said that anyway her husband needs to do it.'

This is the last enquiry for this client under the 'welfare benefits' label; a further enquiry on the client's record under 'debt' states that 'the client began receiving UC [Universal Credit] in February 2017', suggesting the mandatory reconsideration was successful. This means she received her first payment eight months after making the initial claim. Dores, another GYROS client, had similar experiences, including delays over establishing the Habitual Residence Test and payment delays due to system problems:

> 18/11/2016: Client said that she had not been paid yet. I accessed client's UC [Universal Credit] details and there was a note in her journal dated 16/11/2016 stating that they were aware that payments were missing due to a fault in the system but that they would try to issue a payment on that day. I called UC enquiry line and talked to agent. I explained the situation and agent said that the payments for 07 Sept[ember] to Oct[ober] and October to Nov[ember] were missing as well as August payment for the housing and child elements. Agent said that she would email the team responsible for the payment and speak with her manager so an urgent payment can be issued today.

---

[40] Client ID 1059.

I explained this to client and advised client to pay attention to her bank account and UC account.

The delays help to explain why clients like Claudia, Rita and Dores get themselves into debt.

Irrespective of these initial problems, Universal Credit is now a mainstay of the welfare landscape in the UK. For GYROS, Universal Credit enquiries were still the largest enquiry under the category of 'welfare benefit' in 2022 – particularly in relation to (in order) digital support, new applications and updating details. This shows that more than eight years after its introduction, clients still need help from GYROS to interact with the fully online system. This is relevant too for the EUSS, considered in Chapter 3, which has had a similar digital-first/digital-only rollout. For those with no digital skills, they will continue to need support. This has an impact on GYROS' strategic planning for future services (considered further in Chapter 8), especially in the context of funding this ongoing support.

4. Digital accessibility and English language skills

GYROS' clients need help to navigate the welfare benefits system due to both the online system(s) and digital barriers and English language barriers. As noted earlier, interpretation services were withdrawn for EU jobseekers;[41] the Coalition government maintained: 'Jobseekers whose lack of English is preventing them from getting a job, will be required to attend English language training or face losing their benefits as part of the government's radical shake-up of the welfare system.'[42] However, this assessment did not capture the multilingual world of work in and around Great Yarmouth (discussed in Chapter 4) and the poor English language skills of GYROS' client group, or how structural factors such as long working hours and working mainly with other non-English speakers can leave limited time for workers to improve their English language skills.[43]

GYROS' clients, therefore, need a lot of help navigating the online system, including basic help to set up email addresses so that they can make claims and help to create digital CVs:

---

[41] O'Brien (2015), n 4, 111.

[42] Department for Work and Pensions, 'Jobseekers on benefits who need help to speak English will have to take up free language training' press release (13 September 2011), available at: www.gov.uk/government/news/jobseekers-on-benefits-who-need-help-to-speak-english-will-have-to-take-up-free-language-training, accessed 15 February 2023.

[43] C. Barnard, S. Fraser Butlin and F. Costello, 'The changing status of European Union nationals in the United Kingdom following Brexit: the lived experience of the European Union Settlement Scheme' (2022) 31 *Social and Legal Studies* 365, 370.

Client has been in the UK since 2013, he was working at [local poultry factory] but this last month they did not call him back to work. Client wanted to claim JSA [Jobseeker's Allowance]; did JSA claim online, explained to client about the CV, that he needs to sign in every other week and needs to show that he is actively looking for a job. I also explained that he will need a UJM [Universal Jobmatch] account.[44] Client had no idea how to do it [as] he does not have an email account. I told client that I will create one for him.[45]

GYROS helped one client to maintain a digital Universal Credit journal for over three years,[46] and another brought her own laptop from home and asked GYROS staff to teach her how to log in and maintain her own digital journal.[47]

5. Benefit overpayments

Another common problem identified in the database is that of welfare benefit overpayments. Sometimes it is the system itself that causes the issue: the dataset records examples of clients being informed explicitly when they make an application that overpayment will occur and clawback is likely. Further, with the introduction of Universal Credit 'advance payments',[48] those loans needed to be paid back, causing clients yet more difficulty. This has affected GYROS' clients. Clients (often unknowingly) are paid benefits they are not entitled to; these then need to be repaid (see Section C). These overpayments can be due to clients' English language difficulties or simply because they do not understand how the UK system works. This issue is not unique to GYROS' clients.[49] Forbess and James, in their ethnographic study of welfare benefit claimants in both a Citizens Advice and a law centre setting, also found 'poor language skills and lack of basic system literacy'.[50]

---

[44] For more on the Universal Jobmatch, see Department for Work and Pensions 'Jobseekers required to use Universal Jobmatch' *Gov.uk*, available at: www.gov.uk/government/news/jobseekers-required-to-use-universal-jobmatch/, accessed 9 January 2023.

[45] Client ID 314.

[46] Client ID 725.

[47] Client ID 638.

[48] For more, see Department for Work and Pensions 'Universal Credit advances' *Gov.uk*, available at: www.gov.uk/guidance/universal-credit-advances, accessed 10 January 2023.

[49] M. Gray, 'Debt begets debt: public and private debt in austerity Britain' in J. Gardner, M. Gray and K. Moser (eds) *Debt and Austerity: Implications of the Financial Crisis* (Cheltenham: Edward Elgar Publishing Limited, 2020).

[50] A. Forbess and D. James, 'Acts of assistance: navigating the interstices of the British state with the help of non-profit legal advisers' (2014) 58 *Social Analysis* 73, 78.

They note that sometimes accessing welfare benefits can leave clients with problems 'as serious or, more serious'[51] than when they first accessed help. This can also be seen through the GYROS case notes.

In the case note that follows, overpayment of Housing Benefit was causing confusion.

> Client was working for [redacted] which went in liquidation. The client has an overpayment of HB [Housing Benefit] and cannot afford to pay. The client was claiming HB for one property and moved to another property and did not change the address and kept receiving HB. Client thought that because the amount was the same there was not a reason to inform HB team. I explained to client that she had to report it, as she was not living there anymore so she was not entitled to HB for that property even if she was entitled to HB to the new property [for which she had not applied], she had to do a new form reporting the change of address. I told client that I cannot argue with council as they are writing and asking for the money back. ... Because she is not working at the moment, we cannot make an offer to pay, I told client that I will speak with DIAL [a local debt advice charity] to see if we can do a DRO [debt relief order]. Client was happy with that.[52]

Some clients do not understand the system:

> Client has a TC [tax credit] overpayment, and he thinks that it was not his fault as TC was the one doing the calculations and they should not pay him if he was not entitled to [it]. I explained to client that TC based their calculations with the information provided in the claim form and for the year, and when there's changes like stop work, that entitlement changes as well and it is up to the client to inform TC about the changes to avoid overpayment.[53]

Sometimes clients can, with help, negotiate a long-term payment plan to pay back what was overpaid:

> 2017 – Client has an overpayment for tax year 2009–2010 of £2,668.15. Client wanted to call and arrange a payment plan and establish if he has any other overpayments. Called to TC [tax credit] adviser [who] confirmed that only overpayment is for 2009–2010, as

---

[51]   Ibid, 81.
[52]   Client ID 338.
[53]   Client ID 541.

he has paid for 2010–2011. However, there could be an overpayment for 2016–2017. But it's not possible to confirm until the renewal is made. Arranged a payment plan of £40 a month. April 2017 will be [the] first payment and … September 2022 will be last payment of £68.15. Payment plan is for 66 months, which will be taken on 26th of each month.[54]

However, sometimes sorting out a payment plan informally is not possible. The case study in Box 6.1 concerns a client, Johann, who was initially unaware the debt was even accruing.

Box 6.1: Johann's story

Johann first approached GYROS in early 2016:

> 26/01/16: Client received a letter from GYBC [Great Yarmouth Borough Council] regarding a £5,356 overpayment of HB/CT [Housing Benefit/Council Tax]. Client said that the figures are wrong and that he was not receiving HB/CT and that he informed them of all changes of circumstances. I asked client to bring me bank statements and payslips for the period of the overpayment so I can look into it. Client will bring it as soon as possible.[55]

The next case note outlines how the adviser worked with the client to understand his budget and negotiate a repayment plan with the council. Although not mentioned directly, the follow-up action suggests the client accepted he had received the overpayment, as outlined in the January note.

> 16/02/16: Client brought the information that I needed to do the personal budget and to contact GYBC [Great Yarmouth Borough Council] regarding his debt. I told client that now I need to write a letter to send to GYBC with the personal budget and evidence to see if they accept the £30 offer per month.[56]

By April, Great Yarmouth Borough Council had served the client with a notice demanding final payment.

> 06/04/16 – Client came with a sundry debt final notice regarding HB [Housing Benefit] overpayment (£5,356.56) and a letter stating that GYBC [Great

---

[54] Client ID 1299.
[55] Client ID 311.
[56] Ibid.

Yarmouth Borough Council] contacted client previously and their intention to request direct payments from client's employer. I told client that I did contact [debt collection agency] and that I was dealing with it through [name redacted] and that she told me that it was okay for me to send the information she requested like the financial statement and bank statements via email, which I did on the 26/02/16. I called [name redacted] and according to her they never received the email.

The GYROS adviser sent another email with the information. The council official said she would look into it to decide if she could accept the offer of £30 per month. Meanwhile, the GYROS adviser

told client that Council Tax will accept the £30 p/m [per month] till Jun[e] 2016 when client finishes paying part of his loan and then the same amount should be paid to CT [Council Tax] and then again in Dec[ember] 2016 when he finishes other loan, the same amount should pass to CT. ... I explained to client that [for] his CT for this year he needs to pay £44.72 as soon as possible, as it was to be paid on the 4/4/16 and then every week £27 for 43 weeks .... Client also has £17.79 to pay for his CT 2013 and ... he needs to pay that now to avoid further action which will increase the debt significantly. Client will pay it today.[57]

These notes show the difficulty of managing the repayments of a debt spanning an unknown number of years and the attempts to agree payment terms. However, the client returned later that month, this time with a direct earnings attachment. It appears from the case note that the council applied to the Magistrates Court for a liability order for non-payment.[58] A liability order gives the council greater powers of debt recovery if needed. The costs of this recovery action are added to Johann's debts. Great Yarmouth Borough Council's response (below) speaks to the role of Lipsky's 'street-level bureaucrats'[59] and the power individual local administrators can hold in the operation of state law at a street level.

27/04/16 Client called and told me that he received a copy of Direct Attachment of Earnings Order that GYBC [Great Yarmouth Borough Council] sent to his employer. I told client that I would call GYBC and will contact him as soon as possible. ... But anyway she said that they would not accept client's offer

---

[57] Client ID 311.

[58] For more on liability orders, see 'What is a liability order?' *StepChange*, available at: www.stepchange.org/debt-info/liability-order.aspx, accessed 15 February 2023.

[59] M. Lipsky, *Street-Level Bureaucracy: Dilemmas of the Individual in Public Services* (New York: Russel Sage Foundation, 1980).

as he tends to not keep the arrangements and due to the high amount of the overpayment, they have to recover it through his wages and client does not need to worry about it. I called client back and told him about it and client was okay with that. I remind him that he needs to keep his payments for the current CT [Council Tax] and the £30 every month for the debt with previous CT. Client was fine with that.[60]

There is no appeal tribunal to contest an order to reclaim benefit overpayments, so 'one must negotiate directly with HMRC',[61] a difficult task for those with poor language skills and system knowledge. This is not just a matter for EU migrant communities. In their 2022 report *Hardship by Design*,[62] StepChange (the UK's leading debt advice charity) said that the government can reclaim up to '25 per cent of the Universal Credit standard allowance (deducted automatically), or 15 per cent for claimants with earned income less than £60 per month'.[63] In 2022, around a million people – 42 per cent of all claimants – have deductions taken from their Universal Credit payments to deal with overpayments.[64] Given that Universal Credit overpayment is considered a 'priority debt' (see Section C), its repayment is prioritized over other debts a person might have. Usually, the repayments are automatically deducted from payments or earnings, as seen in Johann's case (Box 6.1).

In 2020, The Trussell Trust found that 47 per cent of people visiting foodbanks listed the Department for Work and Pensions as their main creditor.[65] This speaks also to Mia Gray's work on the role of the state as both debt creator and debt collector:[66] 'the UK's welfare system, the state safety net, has become implicated in exacerbating precarity and creating debt, particularly in low-income communities'.[67] She and others have

---

[60] Client ID 311.
[61] Forbess and James (2014) n 50, 8 (online version).
[62] StepChange, *Hardship by Design: How to End Unaffordable Debt Deductions* (June 2022), available at: www.hardship-by-design-unaffordable-benefit-deductions-briefing-june-22-stepchange.pdf, accessed 15 February 2023.
[63] Ibid, 1.
[64] Ibid, 3.
[65] G. Bramley, M. Treanor, F. Sosenko and M. Littlewood, *State of Hunger: Building the Evidence on Poverty, Destitution, and Food Insecurity in the UK* Year Two main report (The Trussel Trust, May 2021), available at: www.trusselltrust.org/wp-content/uploads/sites/2/2021/05/State-of-Hunger-2021-Report-Final.pdf, accessed 23 November 2023, 25.
[66] Gray (2020), n 49.
[67] Ibid, 57.

also criticized the automation of the benefit systems, when debt recovery 'decisions are increasingly occurring without human oversight'.[68]

6. Interim conclusions

We have seen that 'the UK welfare system is convoluted and complex'.[69] For EU nationals in the UK, the complexity is exacerbated by lack of language and digital skills as well as having to show eligibility. Clients experience what Susan Bibler Coutin calls 'hyper documentation'[70] when having to prove their legal status and entitlements. The following case note illustrates the multiple hurdles facing one EU national's claim for Child Benefit:

> Client received a letter regarding her reconsideration, the letter stated that CHB [Child Benefit] maintained their decision that client is not entitled to CHB as she does not have the right to reside. I explained to client that at the time she made the claim she was not exercising her treaty rights. I explained to client that in order to be eligible to receive benefits in the UK we need to be a qualified person and for that, we need to be a worker, jobseeker, self-employed, self-sufficient or a student and when client made the CHB [claim] she was not working or exercising her treaty rights.[71]

This case note also tells us something about how GYROS advisers work: explaining the rules but also identifying with the clients ('we need to be a qualified person and for that, we need to be …'). In the final part of this section, we pull together what we have seen and learned from the case notes as to how GYROS works.

7. GYROS' response

What Sections 3–6 have shown is how GYROS staff interpret and navigate complex UK and EU law around eligibility of EU nationals to welfare benefits. GYROS advisers are not legally trained, but as we noted for housing (Chapter 5), welfare benefits is an area where the 'law' is more explicit in the advice the advisers give. The rules and entitlements attached to welfare

---

[68] Ibid, 57. See also N. Timmins, *Universal Credit, Getting it to Work Better* (Institute for Government, 2020), available at: www.instituteforgovernment.org.uk/sites/default/files/ publications/universal-credit-getting-it-to-work-better_1.pdf, accessed 15 February 2023.

[69] O'Brien (2017), n 3, 21.

[70] S. Bibler Coutin, 'Immigration, law and resistance' in M. Valverde, K.M. Clarke, E. Darian-Smith and P. Kotiswaran (eds) *The Routledge Handbook of Law and Society* (1st ed, London: Routledge, 2021), 260–261.

[71] Client ID 938.

benefits are 'everyday' issues for the advisers, with welfare benefits being the most common category of enquiries. GYROS staff learn by doing, increasing their knowledge incrementally with each case (Chapter 8). Advisers must have a working knowledge of rights to be able to give advice. However, as sections 4 and 5 of this chapter show, GYROS' role goes beyond mere advising. They explain (and translate) the rules (relating to, for example, the R2R test/ habitual residency or how Housing Benefit works when the client changes address), help to assemble the paperwork (for example, bank statements), assess what is practical (for example, in relation to a repayment plan and its terms) and negotiate repayment plans, set up individuals on online systems (for example, by providing an email account), follow up on correspondence with, for example, the council, and work with other more specialist agencies, such as DIAL. This is pragmatic law in operation.

C. Debt

1. Introduction

On the GYROS database, 10 per cent of cases accessed help for issues related to debt and money advice. However, this does not present the whole picture. For example, for those making a housing-related enquiry (7 per cent), the majority of enquiries concern Council Tax and, more specifically, issues around Council Tax arrears; the second most common enquiry in this category concerns rent arrears. Those claiming help with welfare benefits (25 per cent) are also routinely experiencing debt issues (as reflected in the case notes in Section B), as they are navigating either getting access to income or 'topping up' their low income. In this way, the GYROS database shows evidence of the situation recognized in the literature as 'problem clustering'[72] – that is, they are experiencing multiple issues at once and, with a domino-like effect, one problem leads to another. The case notes from the GYROS database show that debt is often not the 'presenting' issue, but it underpins (more usual) presenting issues, such as housing or welfare benefits. Sometimes clients are also simply unaware debt has been accrued until they receive a letter from, say, the Council Tax officer. This is especially the case

---

[72] H. Genn, *Paths to Justice: What People Do and Think about Going to Law* (Oxford: Hart Publishing, 1999); A. Buck, N. Balmer and P. Pleasence, 'Social exclusion and civil law: experience of civil justice problems among vulnerable groups' (2005) 39(3) *Social Policy and Administration* 302; A. Buck, P. Pleasence and N. Balmer, 'Do citizens know how to deal with legal issues? Some empirical insights' (2008) 37 *Journal of Social Policy* 661; P. Pleasence, N.J. Balmer, A. Buck, A. O'Grady and H. Genn, 'Multiple justiciable problems: common clusters and their social and demographic indicators' (2004) 1 *Journal of Empirical Legal Studies* 301; L. Clements *Clustered Injustice and the Level Green* (London: Legal Action Group, 2020), 3.

if they are unfamiliar with UK systems and do not realize they have to pay Council Tax or other bills, such as for water.

In the next sections, we consider some of the causes of debt and the consequences of debt, before looking in more detail at what the GYROS case notes tell us about how they help their clients.

2. Why are clients in debt?

2.1 Causes of debt

The causes of debt are many, but for GYROS' clients it has much to do with low pay, unpredictable working hours for those on zero-hours contracts (as described in Chapter 4) and unexpected bills. It may also be due to ill health, which causes the problem or aggravates existing problems (Chapter 7). Take the case of Irina (a case we return to in Chapter 8):

> Client came in with both of her children to ask me to help her understand letters that she has received. There was a full bag with unopened envelopes from various utility companies, debt collectors, Council, GP, DVLA, [Driver and Vehicle Licensing Agency] TV licence. I asked client why she has ignored the letters previously, she said that she doesn't understand and was wrongly advised [to] ignore letters as she already pays the rent and does not need to pay any utilities. Client also mentioned that [it's] due [to] low mood and lack of motivation following bereavement of her husband 2 years ago.[73]

In the case of Mia, it was her employer's difficulties that caused her problems:

> 10/12/18- walk-in. Client's work was suspended for 1 month due to her employer's personal matters. Client's landlord insisted that client makes UC [Universal Credit] claim. I advised client that in future she should not take landlord's advice re benefits. I helped client to contact UC as she has failed HRT [Habitual Residence Test]. I asked for mandatory reconsideration on basis that client was temporarily unemployed for 1 month and is back in employment. ... Client had 5 weeks off work in total and was back in work on 1/12/18. Client has provided all the requested evidence to the Job Centre.[74]

This case provides a good example of how a short period (here, five weeks) without work can put a client into rent arrears (and other arrears), which

---

[73] Client ID 1111.
[74] Client ID 674.

can be hard to overcome. Delays with Universal Credit (which continued into the next year) exacerbated the situation for this client, who still had no news on her mandatory reconsideration more than three months after she applied. The notes said:

> 18/3/19 walk-in. Client hasn't had any update on her UC [Universal Credit] mand[atory] rec[onsideration] following the call on 18/2/19. I called UC and was advised that DWP [Department for Work and Pensions] are experiencing a large backlog of mand[atory] rec[onsideration;] however client's rec[onsideration] will be escalated one more time and her account noted accordingly.

The notes also said: 'I explained that client is a single parent of two young children and also she is carer for her elderly mother, her rent is in arrears since November last year and she has received eviction threats from her landlord.' There are no other updates on this client's case.

Clients may also be in debt because of a failure to understand how systems work in the UK. The following case note covers Magdalena's case, based on her not knowing she needed to 'top up' her rent payments:

> 22/05/18 walk-in – client received a letter from her housing association regarding a £1,456.59 rent arrears. According to client her rent is being covered by HB [Housing Benefit]. I told client that she has a top-up that she needs to do, and client said that she did not know about it. I told client that according to the letter she has a £19.56 top-up p[er] week and now they increased £5 on top of the £19.56, which leaves £24.56 p/w [per week] top-up.[75]

For some, English language difficulties have caused serious problems. Magda ended up in court on the accusation of not having a TV licence, even though she did have one and had been paying for it (although some payments had been returned); her English was not clear enough to explain this to the person on her doorstep:

> 24/03/2020 Client called to ask [for] help as she is worried about her TV Licence. She had a few payments that have been returned and for 2 months she couldn't pay. ... Someone went to her house about TV licence and when they asked her, she said she didn't have TV Licence instead of explaining the situation due to her English [language]. Client will be having to go to court. I told the client to bring her

---

[75] Client ID 462.

bank statement [as] proof that she did try to make the payments ....
Client requested a translator to go to court with her so this should
be provided; however I told the client to take her daughter with her
just in case.[76]

And sometimes debt is due to the unscrupulous behaviour of private
landlords. We saw in Chapter 4 how one of the residents of the House,
Camilla, got into financial trouble for nonpayment of Council Tax at a
previous tenancy, having been assured by the landlord that he was paying
it – her case is not an isolated one:

> Client's husband came and said that he wanted an update regarding
> the water situation. Apparently, client is paying his landlord by cash for
> water bill charges and has no receipts of these payments. According to
> client, his family and the other flats pay the landlord for water charges,
> but they have received a bill from water services with the same amount
> that they have paid to their landlord.[77]

Once GYROS' clients get into debt, there is often a 'poverty premium' to
pay, which only serves to make the debt worse.

2.2 Cost of debt: the poverty premium

The dataset shows examples of what has been referred to as the 'poverty
premium'[78] – in other words, it is expensive to be poor. GYROS clients
experience this poverty premium in the form of payment demands, costs
for court summons and late payment fees. This issue affects many low-
income families in deprived areas: research has shown 'one quarter of British
households (24 per cent) are estimated to experience at least one type of
poverty premium',[79] including 'pay as you go' electricity meters, high interest
rates on credit cards and loans, and any non-standard billing methods.[80] Take
Jan's case, for example; she was already in arrears on his energy bill:

> 23/07/18 walk-in Client came to us with a letter from E.ON [utility
> company] asking to pay £1,370.93 until 31 of July. Called E.ON

---

[76] Client ID 407.

[77] Client ID 520.

[78] *Mapping the Poverty Premium in Britain* Personal Finance Research Centre, University of
Bristol (Fair By Design, 2022), available at: https://www.bristol.ac.uk/geography/resea
rch/pfrc/themes/financial-exclusion-poverty/local-poverty-premium/

[79] Ibid, 1.

[80] Ibid, 2.

and they said that the client had an agreement with them but only made one payment in March. To keep the agreement, he has to pay £150.00 a month plus what he spends every month. E.ON said the best option for him is to have a prepaid meter and [pay] the debt from the new meter. Client doesn't know where the meters are in the house. Advised client to ask the landlord where the meters are and give the company the reading.[81]

These debts have long-term consequences. The following case note shows how addressing a debt can in fact compound it:

Client brought a form from County Court regarding a claim made by [redacted] Solicitors on behalf of BT PLC due to failure in keeping payment arrangement. Debt with BT PLC is £524.59 + £60 court fee +£70 solicitor/professional fee. Total amount £672.59 to pay. I called solicitors. We filled [in] the form over the phone with client's information and also with the income and expenditure info[rmation] that was given by client. Solicitor explained that as client has a minus income of £600, she could contact an independent debt adviser .... Client has 2 options. Option 1 – pay the full [amount] in 6 months, £112 per month, and no county court admission will be added to her credit file, which will affect her credit for 6 years. Option 2 – choose to pay an affordable amount for her but will have her credit affected for the next 6 years. Client said that she cannot afford to pay in 6 months, so she offered to pay £20 per month on the 19th.[82]

So, the additional costs (court fees and solicitors' fees) were added onto an original debt – the debt the client could not pay in the first instance – equating to an almost 25 per cent increase on the original debt. The client then renegotiated a cash repayment plan, even though her expenditure exceeded her income by £600 per month.

Others face penalties in addition to the original fine:

29/3/16 Client has received CT [Council Tax] Cancellation Notice of £166. Client told me that she only gets to work 1 day per week and her partner about 3 days per week, therefore they are behind with their CT payments. Client is unable to clear full amount of £166. I contacted council to find out if client could agree to repayment plan. Client will incur £65 Summons fine; this is unavoidable unless client

---

[81] Client ID 418.
[82] Client ID 458.

make full payment today. Client can make an offer once Summons letter received, which total owed would be £231. Client agreed to pay £20 every week from 1/4/16 and must contact council when Summons letter received for this offer to be accepted, client aware, will come back to GYROS.[83]

In this example, the £65 summons fee is 40 per cent of the cost of the original debt, avoidable only if the client could have cleared the debt on the same day. She was unable to do so due to the limited hours she and her husband worked.

2.3 COVID-19 and debt issues

The COVID-19 lockdowns were another reason why migrant workers got into debt. As Chapter 4 shows, the majority of migrant workers in Great Yarmouth work in food processing – largely in poultry factories, as there are three factories operating in rural areas surrounding the Town.[84] COVID-19 outbreaks in these factories briefly focused attention on the fact that migrants make up a significant number of staff on the factory floor. Take, for example, Banham Poultry. Operating in Norfolk for over 50 years, it supplies chicken products to supermarkets and accounts for 7 per cent of chicken processing in the UK. It employs about 1,100 people, many of them European migrants.[85] In early September 2020, there was a COVID-19 outbreak in the factory, with more than 120 people testing positive, almost all working on the cutting room floor. At the time, all workers and their households had to isolate for 14 days if they had not tested positive or had not been tested, and for 10 days if they had a positive test result; their households, including children, had to isolate for 14 days.[86]

Many workers did not receive the £94.25 per week statutory sick pay because they earned less than the £118 per week needed for eligibility; others who were forced to isolate but were not sick, such as family members, did not receive statutory sick pay at all. And some who were entitled to statutory sick pay still wanted to work: 'workers told the BBC that in the

---

[83] Client ID 1319.

[84] See Bernard Matthews website at: www.bernardmatthews.com/; the 2 Sisters Food Group website at: www.2sfg.com/; the Banham Poultry website at: www.banhampoultry.co.uk

[85] 'Coronavirus: Banham Poultry factory Covid 19 outbreak "contained"' BBC News (7 September 2020), available at: www.bbc.co.uk/news/uk-england-norfolk-54056299, accessed 15 February 2023.

[86] Informal work contracts made contacting workers for test and trace difficult and English language barriers made public health and isolation guidance messages (which were often updated) difficult to communicate.

early stages of the [Banham Poultry] outbreak, employees had turned up to work despite presenting with COVID-19 symptoms, because "they were afraid to take sick leave, because sick pay is so low.'"[87] A government grant – a Test and Trace Support Payment of £500 – was introduced on 28 September 2020[88] to ensure that those on low incomes were able to self-isolate without worrying about their finances. However, for those isolating before 28 September (including the 120 workers and their extended family members at Banham Poultry), no such payment existed, and the new payments were not backdated. Further, for many, the bureaucracy of support put it either out of reach or, at a minimum, difficult to access. The availability of the Norfolk Assistance Scheme,[89] with its more flexible eligibility requirements, in fact proved more effective in meeting workers' basic needs (for food and heating).

More generally, working in low-paid positions, often without formal contracts, meant that many migrant workers were not reached by the support measures put in place by the government, either because they earned too little or because of their insecure, temporary and part-time work.[90] They inevitably got into debt. A debt adviser in Norfolk said that many debts accrued, unchecked, during the pandemic, because agencies like Great Yarmouth Borough Council were not going out and proactively chasing debt repayments as they might have been doing otherwise. He said "because nobody chased these debts, people just ignored them a bit".[91] He said his service had been much busier since all lockdown restrictions had been lifted and "chasing" and enforcement of payments had restarted.

Finally, it is not just the loss of income caused by the pandemic that has created problems; lockdown and self-isolation also aggravated other problems such as mental health issues. Take Ana[92] (who we met in Chapter 4).

---

[87] M. Precey, 'Coronavirus: Banham Poultry workers "turned up for work sick"', *BBC News* (10 September 2020), available at: www.bbc.co.uk/news/uk-england-norfolk-54091419, accessed 23 November 2023.

[88] Prime Minister's Office, 'New package to support and enforce self-isolation' *Gov.uk* (20 September 2020), available at: www.gov.uk/government/news/new-package-to-support-and-enforce-self-isolation, accessed 15 February 2023.

[89] For more, see 'Norfolk Assistance Scheme (NAS)' *Norfolk County Council*, available at: www.norfolk.gov.uk/care-support-and-health/support-for-living-independently/money-and-benefits/norfolk-assistance-scheme, accessed 15 February 2023.

[90] For more, see C. Barnard and F. Costello, 'Migrant women unable to access Covid-19 support' *UK in a Changing Europe* (21 April 2020), available at: https://ukandeu.ac.uk/migrant-women-unable-to-access-covid-19-support/, accessed 15 February 2023.

[91] Interview with debt adviser (online, June 2022).

[92] This case study was developed by GYROS for their *Seldom Heard Voices* report (Norfolk Community Foundation, 2023), available at: www.norfolkfoundation.com/our-work/publications/, accessed 4 October 2023.

Six months after starting work in a factory, Ana had her first 'breakdown'. She described accessing mental health services as: "Hard. Very Hard". Her GP prescribed medication, which she took briefly before finding a new job. Shortly afterwards, she and her family caught COVID-19. Ana found the isolation overwhelming. Her husband was unable to start a new job, because he had tested positive, and this caused money issues. "It was horrible. We were all so unwell. It was so isolating. We had no one. Everything fell apart." Ana's story is a reminder of problem clustering, with mental health issues being exacerbated by testing positive for COVID-19, leading to an inability to secure income, leading in turn to debt. This shows the impact debt and financial issues (as well as other compounding factors) can have on mental health.[93]

3. How GYROS responds to the issues

The previous sections have shown how GYROS' clients get into debt and how trying to get themselves out of debt may exacerbate their problems. They also showed, indirectly, how GYROS helped some of their clients with, for example, contacting the relevant claimant (such as the council) to see if a repayment plan could be arranged and supporting them with practical advice and translation services. In this section, we look in more detail at the different ways GYROS help their clients. As we have seen in other chapters, the advisers' approach is pragmatic and focused on resolving problems.

3.1 Advisory work

For GYROS' clients, debt tends to be experienced in clusters. As has been shown, sometimes the main creditor to which clients owe money is the state (for example, due to benefit overpayments). However, some owe money to utility companies and private landlords. As we saw in Irina's case, clients sometimes arrive at a GYROS drop-in with a carrier bag of letters they have been unable to read because of language difficulties or because they were unable to face up to the issue. GYROS advisers then go through each letter, sorting them by urgency. GYROS is accredited to give debt advice by the Financial Conduct Authority, the regulator for financial services in the UK. However, GYROS advisers also refer clients to specialist debt advisers, such as DIAL,[94] a Great Yarmouth debt advice charity. They usually accompany the client to meetings with DIAL to provide language support.

---

[93] For more, see 'The Facts' *Money and Mental Health Policy Institute*, available at: www.money andmentalhealth.org/money-and-mental-health-facts/, accessed 21 February 2023.

[94] See the DIAL website at: www.dial-greatyarmouth.org.uk/, accessed 23 November 2023.

Debts are separated into 'priority' and 'non-priority' categories.

> 'Priority debts are those that must be repaid or the claimant will face unacceptable negative consequences, such as eviction for nonpayment of rent arrears. Non-priority debts are those such as unsecured credit (loans and credit cards), where statutory protections mean that the consequences for the individual in the event of nonpayment will not be as severe as those for priority debts.'[95]

In the case of Irina, the GYROS adviser said:

> 'I assured her that I will help her to resolve debt issues. I also advised her to come to walk-ins when unsure about the letters, most important not to ignore. As it is Sat[urday], I was unable to contact debt collection companies, advised client to come back on Wed[nesday]. I gave client a folder and helped organize her bills.'[96]

Sometimes, as with benefit overpayments, GYROS' role is to try to find a way forward, first by working out how much the client can afford to pay:

> 20/06/17 walk-in – the client has £2,318.42 rent arrears; the client was off sick for 6 weeks [and] she was being paid SSP [statutory sick pay] but that was not enough to cover her rent. The client started to work last week, and she wants to make a payment plan to cover the arrears. [A]lso, the client told me that she has utility bill outstanding as well. I asked the client to bring me the letters from creditors and last month's bank statement so I can do a financial statement to see how much the client has at the end of the month to offer to pay her debts.[97]

GYROS may be able to talk to the relevant creditor to negotiate a repayment plan:

> 04/02/2019 Walk-in. The client has a bill from Anglia Water which asked him to pay £4,005 for the water he used. I've contacted Anglia Water on behalf of the client, and I asked them to explain … why the bill is that high, they asked the client if he has any leaking in his property. He said that he had leaking at the boiler but now it is repaired. They asked him about his financial situation, family members, how they use the water. They decided to make a discount for him and to put them under the

---

⁹⁵ StepChange, n 62, 4.
⁹⁶ Client ID 1111.
⁹⁷ Client ID 1289.

lite tariff. They ask him to pay only £900 from £4,005. Anglian water asked him to pay £35 each month until he covers his debt of £900.[98]

There are also examples in the GYROS database of advisers making a debt relief order on behalf of a client.[99] To apply for a debt relief order (DRO), the person's total debts must be less than £30,000. In practice, it means that clients do not pay anything towards their debts for 12 months, and after that the debts are written off. However, a DRO has a negative impact on an individual's credit score. For many of GYROS' clients, a debt relief order is their only option, as this case note shows:

Multiple debts – speeding fines which cannot be included in DRO [debt relief order]. The client got a distress warrant in meantime and the court attended. Grant of time to pay for £140 has been awarded, £20 every month. After the initial assessment the client has no income and debts in the region of £10k, he is likely to be eligible for DRO.[100]

30/03/17 – client made an application for UC [Universal Credit] in January 2017 but till today she has no payments. [B]ecause of that client acquired some debts. [C]lient has a bank loan around £7,000, utility bills, rent arrears and CT [Council Tax]. [C]lient did not bring any creditor letters, I booked to see client next week to do a financial statement and asked her to bring bank statements and creditor letters so I can see if we can do DRO [debt relief order].[101]

In some instances, GYROS advisers must act quickly to help clients. In the following case note, the client kept missing the payment days, paying a day or two late, and the GYROS adviser worked with DIAL to prevent bailiffs from entering the client's house to seize her goods:

DIAL called the enforcement agent and asked them to accept client's offer of £100 per month. The agent refused, DIAL mentioned that without a court order they cannot actually enter her house and she is not going to let them in. The agent was particularly difficult, and DIAL ended the conversation and called the office. He managed to stop the seizure of the goods, but client (as offered by her) will pay

---

[98] Client ID 846.
[99] For more, see The Insolvency Service, 'How to get a debt relief order (DRO)' *Gov.uk*, available at: www.gov.uk/government/publications/getting-a-debt-relief-order/getting-a-debt-relief-order, accessed 15 February 2023.
[100] Client ID 1222.
[101] Client ID 55.

£100 next Friday (12th August) and as much as she can after that by the end of the month. We stressed again how important it is for her to make the payments on time. If she fails, there is not much that we or DIAL can do anymore.[102]

Finally, the advice GYROS advisers give may not be what the client wants to hear, especially where the consequences are serious. Take Maria's case. She claimed Income Support and Maternity Allowance. The GYROS adviser explained that

> she will not be entitled to get income support as she has only been in the UK for less than 3 years. Also explained that if she signs the forms and sends them over, when her claim is refused, she will lose her right to reside in this country and lose all the benefits.

> Client seemed reluctant to accept our advice because that was a Job Centre [adviser] telling her to do so. I explained it is her choice to send the declaration to Job Centre.[103]

3.2 Basic needs

At times, GYROS' involvement is proactive, helping clients to set up, manage, amend and cancel their utility bills, especially when changing address, to avoid problems down the line:

> Electric. Registered client and client will receive 2 separate letters, one with the payment card and the other with the bill to pay monthly and a budget plan. Next bill will be on 7th May. Client understood … Anglia Water (sewerage). Registered client. Client will receive a booklet and £15 payment will be made on 22nd of every month – 1st payment will be on 22nd April.[104]

More usually, the GYROS advisers react to problems which have arisen. Often it is working out a repayment plan, but it can be more immediate help – for instance, where the client needs food parcels and help with payments for gas or electricity. So in Darius' case (Chapter 1), GYROS ensured he and his children got help from the local foodbank when they were experiencing difficulties. The Town has various foodbanks and there

---

[102] Client ID 1266.
[103] Client ID 331.
[104] Client ID 346.

is provision of hot meals for those who need them throughout the week. These foodbanks are mostly church led, though The Trussell Trust also provides this service. As we have seen, foodbank usage increased 200 per cent when Universal Credit was introduced to the Town. For GYROS clients considered NRPF (see Chapter 3), directing them to foodbanks may be the only help GYROS can offer.

> 02/08/2016 (Walk-in) Client came to Walk-in to seek help. She was referred from another client and came with her brother with whom she is living with and who is supporting her financially and emotionally. Client came to the UK, has never worked and is pregnant. Baby is due on 08/08/2016. Client wanted to know what benefits she can apply [for] and what she can do. I explained that client is not entitled to MA [Maternity Allowance] as she never worked here but that we could help with items for the baby and that we could refer her to other organisations.[105]

For others, GYROS steps in with financial payments:

> 11/8/14 (Walk-in) Client came to me today as she has not [received] any payments from JCP (Job Centre Plus) or Council and does not know what to do. She is behind with her rent. I called Council and found out that they are waiting for bank statements. Client requested them on 7th Aug[ust] and Lloyds said that it will take 5–7 days to reach her. I talked to GYROS Manager and agreed that we can pay for her electricity for this week and her rent, she can also come to our cafe and have food whenever she needs. I [explained to] her that I will talk to her landlord and let him know that we will pay for one week, but we are working on her case, and she will be paid in near future. She was very grateful and said that from her earnings she will pay for her electricity and food.[106]

As we saw in Chapter 2, GYROS runs a community cafe as part of their community outreach programme. They use the cafe to help people access volunteering opportunities, learn English, gain a UK-based reference (based on their volunteer work) and share (and celebrate) their food and culture. The cafe also acts as a meeting point in a central community hub. The cafe opened in 2012 and was initially supported through National Lottery funding. Reserves from the cafe are 'unrestricted funds' which GYROS

---

[105] Client ID 782.
[106] Client ID 1134.

can use if they have a client in need of emergency funding. GYROS has also used the income from the cafe to keep the charity afloat in times when other sources of funding dropped off or came to an end. Advisers use the cafe as a meeting place too and can direct clients there when they need food during opening hours (if the foodbank or other provision is closed). GYROS lost this extra resource during the COVID-19 pandemic. The cafe was relaunched in the Time and Tide Museum in August 2023.

D. Conclusion

This chapter has outlined the issues GYROS' clients have faced with welfare benefit claims and debt. Cumulatively, these two enquiry labels account for 35 per cent of GYROS' work. We see a cohort of people facing great precarity due to low-paid work and zero-hours contracts, and coming up against a system which itself is causing problems: hurdles to prove eligibility, delays and errors in payments. Equally, we see issues of debt, also driven in some instances by systems (the poverty premium) and structural factors (such as low pay and zero-hours contracts), but driven too by a lack of knowledge of UK systems (such as the need to pay water bills and Council Tax, and the fact that there are different providers for gas and electricity).

As other research has shown, these are not issues unique to migrant communities. Debt is pervasive across the UK, especially in areas of high deprivation like Great Yarmouth. But as one debt adviser said, migrant communities are more likely to have issues involving "priority debts" (see Section C.3), especially those newer to the UK:

'It takes time to learn, you know, to learn how the whole system works. Mostly this first debt will come if you [are in] some trouble, if you lose the job or something like that. And this first debt will come as priority ... so you're late with your rent, late with your Council Tax .... Only later on come[s] more sophisticated ones, like credit cards and stuff like that .... They [the migrant community] are not often seeing debts as a result of overspending or stuff like that. Usually, they get into some trouble and couldn't pay [for] their necessities.'[107]

He also said that migrant communities do not come to the UK to claim benefits (and as we have demonstrated, access is qualified). Instead, he said, people come to the UK to work (Chapter 4): "It takes some creativity to just to leave your country to go to another country to find a job. You need to have ... you know, you can't be very, like, a laid-back person. You need

---

[107] Interview with debt adviser (online, June 2022).

to have some drive to do something like that."[108] However, if this work is low-paid, it will be topped up by in-work benefits,[109] which are also given to low-paid UK nationals. However, often, even these payments are not enough, and people get into debt.

Finally, this chapter has shown how COVID-19 has exacerbated the already precarious situation of migrant workers. Others too[110] have noted that the effect of the crisis was felt most keenly by those from lower socioeconomic groups[111] and those from minority ethnic backgrounds,[112] and by migrant workers[113] in low-paid ('key worker'[114]) positions. Those seeking help from GYROS fit into a number of these categories. And, as Ana's case showed, for some mental health issues were aggravated by the COVID-19 lockdowns and lead to debt, and debt can also cause mental health problems. We have also seen how health issues have been caused by the work EU migrant workers undertake in the UK, such as in chicken factories (Chapter 4), and by the poor quality of their housing (Chapter 5). It is to these health issues and to EU migrant community access to healthcare in the UK that we turn next.

---

[108] Interview with debt adviser (online, June 2022).

[109] 'The fiscal impact of immigration in the UK' *The Migration Observatory at the University of Oxford* (30 March 2022), available at: https://migrationobservatory.ox.ac.uk/resources/briefings/the-fiscal-impact-of-immigration-in-the-uk/, accessed 16 February 2023.

[110] R. Shretta, 'The economic impact of COVID-19' *University of Oxford* (7 April 2020), available at: www.research.ox.ac.uk/article/2020-04-07-the-economic-impact-of-covid-19, accessed 15 February 2023.

[111] F. Ryan, 'Britain has a hidden coronavirus crisis – and it's shaped by inequality' *The Guardian* (15 April 2020), available at: www.theguardian.com/commentisfree/2020/apr/15/britain-coronavirus-crisis-inequality-hungry-domestic-violence, accessed 15 February 2023.

[112] P. Campbell, 'Coronavirus is hitting BAME communities hard on every front' *The Conversation* (15 April 2020), available at: https://theconversation.com/coronavirus-is-hitting-bame-communities-hard-on-every-front-136327#:~:text=Emerging%20evidence%20suggests%20that%20black,only%2014%25%20of%20the%20population, accessed 15 February 2023.

[113] C. Barnard and F. Costello 'Working conditions of migrant "key workers" in the Covid-19 crisis', *UK in a Changing Europe* (8 April 2020), available at: https://ukandeu.ac.uk/working-conditions-of-migrant-key-workers-in-the-covid-19-crisis/, accessed 15 February 2023.

[114] C. Barnard and F. Costello, 'Migrant workers and Covid-19', *UK in a Changing Europe* (28 March 2020), available at: https://ukandeu.ac.uk/migrant-workers-and-covid-19/, accessed 15 February 2023.

7

Access to Healthcare

A. Introduction

Poor health is a recurrent theme in this book. Many GYROS clients attribute the health problems they experience to the conditions of their work and housing. As we saw in Chapter 4, the chicken factories where many work are cold, and they describe the working conditions as poor. The production line is fast, workers are often denied toilet breaks and the loads they lift can be heavy. We saw Regina's issues with her back and knees due to heavy lifting and Edita's fingers swollen from the cold. The workers and their families also live in poor housing, as we saw in Chapter 5, with damp and mould common problems.[1] We saw how the leaking roof and the absence of central heating caused ongoing problems in the House, with Rasa's arthritis triggered by the cold and Camilla was injured from tripping up on the stairs.

Some of these health issues could have been avoided if employment and housing law had been enforced, an issue that Genn has examined in her pioneering work on health justice. Genn's research has highlighted just how many of the health issues experienced by patients result 'from unenforced laws or incorrect denial of critical services, leading to preventable poor health outcomes'.[2] She says this raises issues of health justice and highlights

---

[1] A recent tragic example highlighting the significance of the bidirectional link between enforcing/realizing rights and health was the death of two-year-old Awaab Ishak following prolonged exposure to mould in social housing in Rochdale. The senior coroner said that this 'should be a defining moment for the housing sector'; quoted in M. Brown and R. Booth, 'Death of two-year-old from mould in flat a "defining moment", says coroner', *The Guardian* (15 November 2022), available at: www.theguardian.com/uk-news/2022/nov/15/death-of-two-year-old-awaab-ishak-chronic-mould-in-flat-a-defining-moment-says-coroner, accessed 17 February 2023.

[2] H. Genn, 'When law is good for your health: mitigating the social determinants of health through access to justice' (2019) 72 *Current Legal Problems* 159, 163. See also: S. Beardon and H. Genn, *'The Health Justice Landscape in England and Wales: Mapping Social Welfare Advice legal services in Health Settings'*, (UCL Centre For Access to Justice and The Legal

the health-harming impacts of lack of access to justice pathways, especially in the context of work and housing. In England and Wales, there are more than 380 advice services 'providing social welfare legal advice and assistance in healthcare settings',[3] commonly referred to as 'health justice partnerships'. Genn says that the most common matters dealt with by these partnerships are welfare benefits, debt, housing, employment, and health and community care – issues which, as we have seen, also come to GYROS' door.[4]

As shown in chapters 4 and 5, much employment and housing law is not enforced by the EU migrants we interviewed or those in the GYROS dataset. State agencies – such as the Gangmasters and Labour Abuse Authority, the Health and Safety Executive and the Employment Agency Standards Inspectorate do very little by way of everyday enforcement. GYROS help mitigate some of the worst effects, but their response is mainly to try to help clients find other jobs or to ask landlords to do repairs; they do not use formal legal pathways to help clients enforce their rights. The World Justice Project has found that one in three people with justiciable problems became physically or mentally ill as a result.[5] We saw in chapters 5 and 6 that GYROS clients who are facing debt risk losing their homes and, unsurprisingly, their mental and physical health suffers.

In some jurisdictions, there is discussion of preventative law. According to Zuckerman et al, 'as with preventative medicine, new generations of lawyers are practising a form of preventative law which allows for the identification of legal needs before they turn into legal- and health-emergencies'.[6] GYROS' pragmatic work also has a preventative element. For example, advisers make sure clients are registered with a GP. This helps avoid difficulties with social services (as it can demonstrate care for children's health needs) and immigration law (as it can show residence for the purposes of EUSS applications). This can also help prevent the emergence of further health issues, or at least it means the individual is already in the healthcare system if they become ill. During the COVID-19 pandemic, as we see later in the

---

Education Foundation, 2018), available at: https://www.ucl.ac.uk/access-to-justice/sites/access-to-justice/files/lef030_mapping_report_web.pdf, accessed 23 November 2023, 7.

[3] H. Genn, 'When law is good for your health: mitigating the social determinants of health through access to justice' (2019) 72 *Current Legal Problems* 159, 188.

[4] Ibid, 185.

[5] World Justice Project, *Global Insights on Access to Justice* (World Justice Project, 2018), available at: https://worldjusticeproject.org/sites/default/files/documents/WJP_Access-Justice_April_2018_Online.pdf, accessed 16 January 2023, 6. In this study, 46,000 people across 45 different countries were asked about everyday experiences of legal problems.

[6] B. Zuckerman, M. Sandel, E. Lawton and S. Morton, 'Medical-legal partnerships: transforming health care' (2008) 372 *The Lancet* 1615, 1616.

chapter, GYROS' preventive work included accompanying NHS staff on vaccine buses and going out to local farms to provide information about vaccines in the workers' own languages.

Given the healthcare issues experienced by migrant workers that we saw in chapters 4, 5 and 6, this chapter focuses on the ability of EU migrant workers and their families to gain *access* to healthcare in the UK. We begin by examining the legal entitlement of EU migrants to healthcare in the UK (Section B), and then we examine whether they take up the available healthcare. It is well known that migrant communities encounter language and cultural barriers when trying to access healthcare.[7] To gain a better understanding of their clients' needs, GYROS conducted a survey in 2015 and again in 2022 to identify 'whether there are cultural and/or practical barriers experienced by Norfolk's migrant worker communities when accessing GP and acute health services in Norfolk'.[8] This survey shows that 'barriers do exist, but that they are complex; arising from differences in cultural norms and practices around accessing such services in country of origin, as well as in cultural and practical barriers that exist within the UK system'.[9] We look at the results of this survey in Section C.

Against this backcloth, in Section D we look at the healthcare issues which appear in case notes in the GYROS database. Given the prevalence of health-related issues, it might be expected that this would have been a dominant issue. Yet health enquires equate to just 4 per cent of all enquiries in the database. This low share is explained in part by the fact that healthcare issues often arise in the context of other enquiries, such as those to do with employment, housing and debt (as discussed in chapters 4, 5 and 6). In this chapter, we focus on those enquiries labelled as being in the 'health' category in the database. We see how already precarious lives are easily knocked off course by ill health and consider the personal and practical issues this generates for individuals. We also, as in other chapters, see the very practical, or pragmatic, ways that GYROS responds to those problems.

---

[7] H. Jayaweera, 'Access to healthcare for vulnerable migrant women in England: a human security approach' (2018) 66 *Current Sociology* 273; S. Germain and S. Yong, 'COVID-19 highlighting inequalities in access to healthcare in England: a case study of ethnic minority and migrant women' (2020) 28 *Feminist Legal Studies* 301.

[8] L. Humphries, Great Yarmouth Refugee and Outreach Support, with King's Lynn Area Resettlement Support and Mobile Europeans Taking Action, *Migrant Workers Accessing Healthcare in Norfolk* (Healthwatch Norfolk and Community Relations and Equality Board, 2015), available at: https://healthwatchnorfolk.co.uk/wp-content/uploads/2015/11/15-07-Migrant-Workers-Accessing-Healthcare-in-Norfolk.pdf, 6.

[9] Ibid, 4.

B. EU nationals' access to healthcare in the UK

1. Access to healthcare

The right to health is identified as a human right in the Universal Declaration of Human Rights[10] and the International Covenant on Economic, Social and Cultural Rights.[11] Nevertheless, the rights of EU migrants to access healthcare in the UK is complicated. Access to healthcare is not expressly provided for in either the Workers' Regulation 492/11 (although healthcare might be considered a social advantage under Article 7(2)) or the CRD (Citizen's Rights Directive 2004/38). On the contrary, Article 7 CRD requires that those who migrate and are not economically active (students and persons of independent means) have comprehensive sickness insurance so as not to be a burden on the host state's national healthcare provisions.

In respect of those moving temporarily, the Court of Justice of the European Union has developed complex and sophisticated case law interpreting Article 56 TFEU and the Social Security Regulation 883/2004 on the right to travel to another member state to receive treatment there, case law which is largely reproduced in the Patients' Mobility Directive 2011/24.[12] Regulation 883/2004 also makes provision for emergency treatment in the host state. However, none of this covers migrant workers living in the host state seeking to gain access to primary (first point of contact with the system – for instance, via a GP), secondary (hospital and community care) and tertiary (highly specialized treatment) healthcare provision.[13]

It appears that the UK government considered access to healthcare to be a social advantage and so provided free access to all.[14] Indeed, there is no evidence of the UK ever trying to enforce the comprehensive sickness

---

[10] 'Universal Declaration of Human Rights', *United Nations*, available at: www.un.org/en/about-us/universal-declaration-of-human-rights, accessed 17 February 2023. Article 25 (1) states: 'Everyone has the right to a standard of living adequate for the health and well-being of himself and of his family.'

[11] 'International Covenant on Economic, Social and Cultural Rights', *United Nations Office of the High Commissioner for Human Rights*, available at: www.ohchr.org/en/instruments-mechanisms/instruments/international-covenant-economic-social-and-cultural-rights. Article 12 states: 'The States Parties to the present Covenant recognize the right of everyone to the enjoyment of the highest attainable standard of physical and mental health.'

[12] OJ [2011] L88/45. For details, see: C. Barnard, *The Substantive Law of the European Union* 7th edn (Oxford: Oxford University Press, 2022), Chapter 8; T. Hervey and J. McHale, *European Union Health Law* (Cambridge: Cambridge University Press, 2015).

[13] NHS Providers, 'The NHS provider sector', available at: https://nhsproviders.org/topics/delivery-and-performance/the-nhs-provider-sector, accessed 16 January 2023.

[14] Department of Health and Social Care, 'Healthcare for EU citizens living in or moving to the UK', *Gov.uk* (19 March 2019), available at: www.gov.uk/guidance/healthcare-for-eu-and-efta-nationals-living-in-the-uk, accessed 23 November 2023.

insurance provision on students or PIMs (persons of independent means). In 2022, the Court of Justice of the European Union ruled that eligibility for NHS treatment counted as comprehensive sickness insurance.[15] The NHS operates residence-based eligibility for its services, so a patient must be 'ordinarily resident' in the UK – that is, their residence 'lawful.[16] Once ordinarily resident in the UK, a person can access NHS care free of charge, with secondary care and tertiary care available via referral from a GP (primary care). Access to a GP is the usual first route through which most people access NHS care.[17]

Consequently, EU nationals in the UK pre Brexit enjoyed full access to the NHS, and this remains the case for those with settled and pre-settled status provided the individual is ordinarily resident in the UK.[18] Those who have not applied under the EUSS may lose their right to free healthcare. This is considered in the next section. EU nationals arriving post Brexit under a visa scheme must pay the NHS surcharge (£624 per person per year as of 2022, to increase to £1,035).

2. The position of those under the European Union Settlement Scheme

EU and European Free Trade Association/Swiss citizens, and their non-EU and non-European Free Trade Association/Swiss family members, lawfully residing in the UK by 31 December 2020 retain their entitlement to healthcare where they meet the ordinarily resident test. From 1 July 2021 (the EUSS deadline), they must pass the test and hold either settled or pre-settled status under the EUSS.

> 'Those who are awaiting the outcome of an application submitted on or before 30 June 2021 will remain entitled to free healthcare, subject to the ordinarily resident test, until a final decision on their application is made, at which point their treatment will either become chargeable

---

[15] C-247/20 *VI v Her Majesty's Revenue and Customs* EU:C:2022:177, paras 68–69, noted by G. More (2022) 59 *Common Market Law Review* 1915; C. O'Brien, 'UK wrongly insisted on comprehensive sickness insurance for years, EU court finds' (15 March 2022) *Free Movement*, available at: https://freemovement.org.uk/uk-wrongly-insisted-on-compre hensive-sickness-insurance-for-years-eu-court-finds/, accessed 1 March 2023.

[16] Department of Health and Social Care, 'NHS cost recovery - overseas visitors Guidance for NHS service providers on charging overseas visitors in England' (22 September 2023), available at: https://assets.publishing.service.gov.uk/government/uploads/system/uplo ads/attachment_data/file/1186860/nhs-cost-recovery-overseas-visitors_september2023. pdf, 5.

[17] Ibid.

[18] Department of Health and Social Care, 'Healthcare for EU citizens living in or moving to the UK' (19 March 2019) *Gov.uk*, available at: www.gov.uk/guidance/healthcare-for-eu-and-efta-nationals-living-in-the-uk, accessed 17 February 2023.

if they are refused status or remain free if they are awarded settled or pre-settled status.'[19]

If a person submits a late application (after 1 July 2021), they are chargeable from the deadline (30 June 2021) until they submit their late application. They are then non-chargeable while their late application is being considered by the Home Office and then they become chargeable (if the application is refused) or remain non-chargeable (subject to the ordinarily resident test) when a decision is made. If the application is refused, they become chargeable from the day of refusal. If the application is granted, then the treatment would only be chargeable for the period over which the application was late.[20] Those who have not applied to the EUSS are not considered ordinarily resident and will incur a 150 per cent charge. The 'cliff edge' deadline of 30 June 2021 meant that some groups – especially those more vulnerable – particularly the old and the young (see Chapter 3) – missed the deadline.

In response to freedom of information requests sent to the six local hospitals in East Anglia, undertaken in October 2021 with a follow-up in June 2022, we found that attitudes to charging varied widely. It was clear that not all of the NHS trusts maintained comprehensive records of those being charged. One hospital reported: 'The Trust does not record the immigration status of overseas visitors who are charged for NHS services.' This makes it difficult to understand if charging impacts some groups more than others. According to a response from one hospital in the area, since 2018, 24 per cent of people charged (40 out of 164) were EU nationals, and numbers have been rising each year. This response indicated that the main reason people were charged was 'no documents', which we return to later. Another trust reported that since 2018 they had referred 276 of their 'debtors' to the Home Office, 'for outstanding debts over 2 months old and over £500', the threshold to share this information with the Home Office.[21] These debts are also referred to debt collection agencies, with evidence in the GYROS database of some clients (pre EUSS) incurring a 43 per cent cost penalty on top of their

[19] See guidance on implementing the overseas visitor charging regulations, n 16, 78.

[20] 'Joining family members' who enter the UK with an EUSS Family Permit are non-chargeable for the first three months of their residence in the UK. They must apply for status under the EUSS within three months of entry to the UK. If they are late in doing so, they become chargeable for the period between their individual deadline (three months after entry to the UK) and the date of submitting a valid application to the EUSS. They are non-chargeable while their application is decided, at which point they either become chargeable if refused or remain non-chargeable if granted status.

[21] Doctors of the World, *Access to NHS Services for EU Citizens after 1 July 2021 (England, Scotland, and Wales)* (May 2021), available at: www.doctorsoftheworld.org.uk/wp-content/uploads/2021/06/DOTW-Briefing_Access-to-NHS-Services-for-EU-Citizens-after-1-July-2021.pdf, accessed 23 November 2023, 4.

NHS charge (see Chapter 6 on debt): '15/07/2016: Client received a letter from NHS regarding a penalty charge for dental treatment. NHS charges £233.70/Penalty £100/Total £333.70.'[22]

Having looked at the legal position of migrant workers, we turn now to consider if EU migrant workers in and around Great Yarmouth use the local healthcare services and, if so, what their experiences have been. We draw on the health survey conducted by GYROS in 2015 and 2022, which help us to understand the health conditions that EU migrants experienced (compared with the local population; Section C). This provides the background against which we see EU migrants coming to GYROS for help (Section D).

C. GYROS health survey, 2015 and 2022

1. Introduction

As we saw in Chapter 4, the poor working conditions in factories have short-, medium- and probably long-term effects on workers' health. The question then is: what help do EU migrant workers and their families seek from the NHS? Much multidisciplinary literature has demonstrated barriers in migrant access to healthcare.[23] These have been described as:[24]

(i) *system- and provider-level barriers*, such as legal entitlement to access services, quality of care received, discriminatory practices and negative attitudes of frontline staff; and

(ii) *patient-level barriers*, such as knowledge of systems and how to use them, language barriers and issues adapting to a new healthcare system.

We looked at some of the system level barriers, especially legal entitlement, in the previous section. But what about patient level barriers? In 2015, GYROS ran a survey to identify 'whether there are cultural and or practical barriers experienced by Norfolk's migrant worker communities when accessing GP and acute health services in Norfolk'.[25] Clients accessing GYROS' Tuesday drop-in services were asked to complete the questionnaire. In 2021–2022,

---

[22] Client ID 295.

[23] See, for example, A. Gil-Salmerón, K. Katsas, E. Riza, P. Karnaki and A. Linos, 'Access to healthcare for migrant patients in Europe: healthcare discrimination and translation services' (2021) 18 *International Journal of Environmental Research and Public Health* 7901; Jayaweera (2018), n 7.

[24] S. Hargreaves and J.S. Friedland, 'Impact on and use of health services by new migrants in Europe' in F. Thomas and J. Gideon (eds) *Migration, Health and Inequality* (London: Zed Books Ltd, 2013) 27, 32.

[25] Humphries (2015), n 8, 4.

Figure 7.1: Age range of respondents in the GYROS health survey, 2015 and 2022

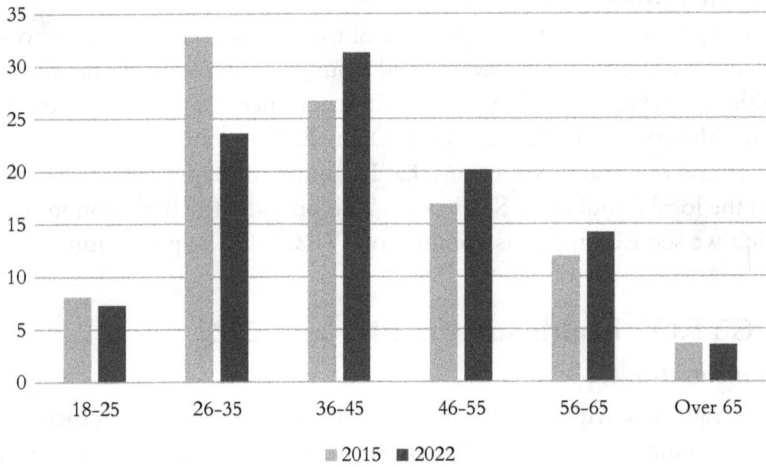

GYROS ran the survey again.[26] In the next section we provide an overview of the demographic data collected in both years of the survey (Section 2). We then look at specific issues arising from the data: access to healthcare; health conditions; and COVID-19 vaccination rates (Section 3).

2. Demographic data

In 2015, 368 people responded to the health survey, and in 2022, 292 people took part. The demographic data for both years were similar. The respondents were primarily women: 65 per cent in 2015 and 67 per cent in 2022. As might be expected following Brexit, with the ending of free movement and the establishment of the EUSS, the 2022 data saw an increase in age, with 70 per cent of respondents aged over 35 compared to 60 per cent in 2015 (Figure 7.1).

The 2022 data on 'year of arrival' show that EU migration to Norfolk increased substantially in 2004–2010 (EU8 migration) and remained relatively

---

[26] The 2022 survey was funded by GYROS through the National Lottery Community Pathways Project. For more on this, see 'Community Pathways Partnership: Connecting people across East Anglia', *GYROS*, available at: www.gyros.org.uk/cpp, accessed 23 November 2023. The project is in partnership with Access (formerly King's Lynn Asylum and Refugee Support) and Keystone Development Trust (formerly Mobile Europeans Taking Action). These organizations were also partners in the 2015 health survey.

Figure 7.2: Year of arrival to the UK for GYROS health survey respondents, 2022

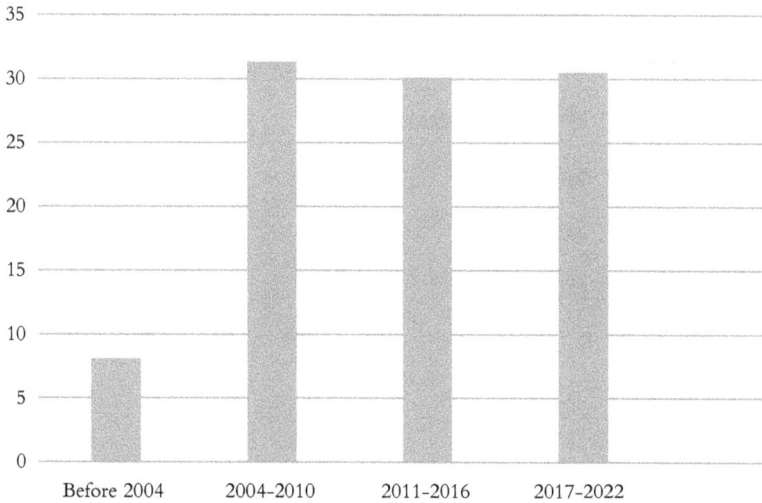

stable after this point Figure 7.2). This is in line with the migration 'phases' explained in Chapter 2.

In terms of the nationality of respondents, Figure 7.3 shows a notable growth in the share of Romanian nationals in the 2015–2022 period and a significant drop in the share of Polish nationals and some drop-off for both Lithuanian and Latvian nationals as well as other nationalities. The share for Portuguese nationals remained relatively steady (see Chapter 2).

3. Survey results

3.1 Access to healthcare

Some 94 per cent of respondents were registered with a GP in 2022 compared to 95 per cent in 2015. This high figure is unsurprising given the emphasis GYROS places on ensuring clients are registered with a GP (see Chapter 3). A closer look (noting very small numbers not registered) shows that men were less likely than women to be registered with a GP, and that Romanians and Lithuanians had lower rates of registration than other nationality groups. Those who self-described their English language skills as 'little/very little' were the group least likely to be registered with a GP. In general, self-reported English language skills were lower in 2022 than in 2015. This could be due to the increase in more recent arrivals in the 2022 data (Figure 7.2). Another finding, which has relevance for this lack of English language skills, was that just under 20 per cent of respondents in

Figure 7.3: Nationality of GYROS health survey respondents, 2015 and 2022

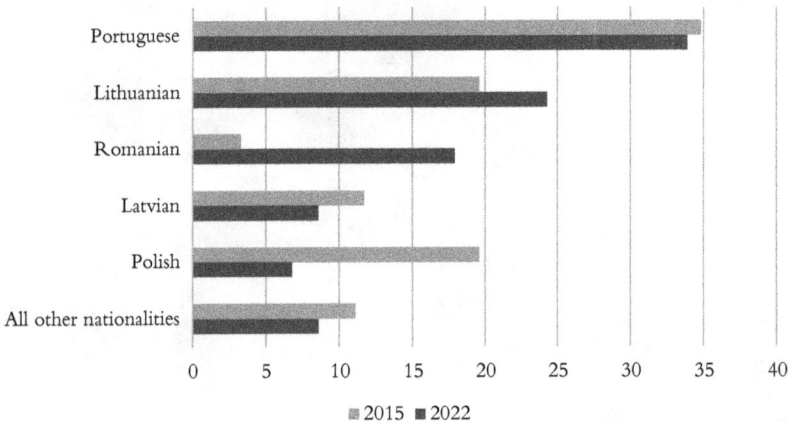

the 2022 survey, compared to 10 per cent in 2015, reported not being able to access an interpreter when they needed one.

Language barriers are therefore a significant issue for migrant communities when accessing healthcare. We return to this issue in Section D.2. In the Norfolk-based *Seldom Heard Voices* research (in which GYROS was a partner), it was noted: 'Among healthcare providers, it was felt that there is an expectation that friends and family will be happy to help translate. This is seen as very unprofessional and unhelpful by clients, who expect to have a translator.'[27] The report also says: 'GYROS raised the point that Portuguese interpreters are often not appropriate for their clients, as they [the NHS] will book a Brazilian speaker who cannot communicate with the client at all. They also criticised the quality of interpretation, especially when it came to conveying specific information around symptoms'.[28] GYROS clients reported that different vocabulary for some words and the different pronunciation of a Brazilian Portuguese speaker and a Portuguese speaker from Portugal can lead to confusion and stress when navigating a health appointment. As we noted in Chapter 6, interpretation services for EU jobseekers at Job Centres was withdrawn in 2014, with the Coalition government at the time emphasizing the need for users to have English language skills or training. This change

---

[27] Norfolk Community Foundation, *Seldom Heard Voices* (Norfolk Community Foundation, 2023), available at www.norfolkfoundation.com/our-work/publications/, accessed 4 October 2023, 16.

[28] Ibid, 13.

Figure 7.4: English language skills of GYROS health survey respondents, 2015 and 2022

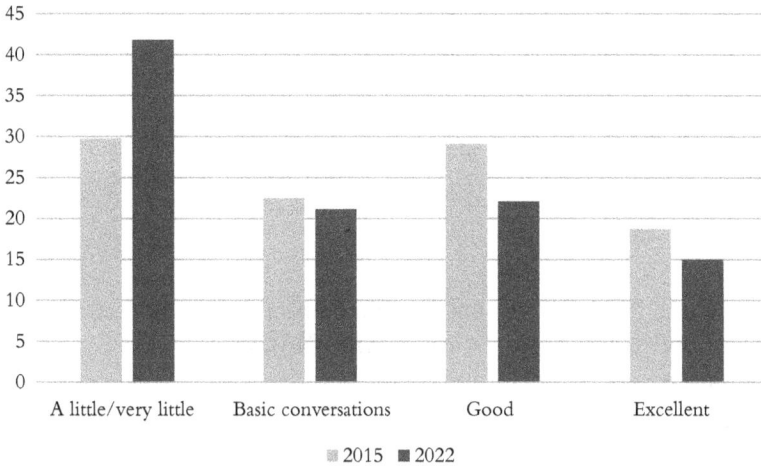

in policy had a knock-on effect for those accessing health services, as GYROS reported in 2015:

> In one of the focus groups, some described how they are reluctant to ask for an interpreter at the GP as they hear these scary stories about migrants who cannot speak English not being able to access benefits- so feel that asking for an interpreter would expose them. One Polish woman felt this very acutely and said she feels like everyone wants to 'kick out the Polish- like we are the biggest evil in the country- it feels like we are being pushed out'.[29]

As the GYROS survey data shows, the increase in lack of availability of interpreters has coincided with a decline in reported English language skills among users (Figure 7.4). That said, some GP surgeries do try to adapt: in the case of one Great Yarmouth surgery participating in our research, they put a marker on a patient's file to notify staff that an interpreter is needed. If an interpreter is needed, then the usual 10-minute appointment is extended to 20 minutes.[30]

Given the high level of GP registration, it is also unsurprising that primary health care (specifically GPs) was the health service most used by those in

---

[29] Humphries (2015), n 8, 24.
[30] Interview with employee at a local GP surgery (online, October 2021).

Table 7.1: Perception of care received compared with care for UK nationals

Response	2015		2022	
	Number	Percentage	Number	Percentage
Same	159	66.0	194	74.0
Better	4	1.5	21	8.0
Worse	79	32.5	48	18.0
Total	242	100.0	263	100.0

the survey. In 2022, 78 per cent of respondents had used GP services in the past 12 months (down from 86 per cent in 2015), with 88 per cent reporting that they were able to get an appointment with their GP when they needed one (up from 70 per cent in 2015). By contrast, use of dentists was low, with 57 per cent of respondents in 2022 saying they had never used a dentist in the UK (an increase from 40 per cent in 2015). This might be compounded by lack of availability of local dentistry services – Norfolk and Waveney are listed in the top five 'dental deserts' in the country.[31] In 2022, 53 per cent had never accessed Accident & Emergency; up from 46 per cent in 2015.

When asked about experiences at the GP, responses varied. Respondents were asked whether they felt listened to by the GP and could understand what was being said to them. These responses were similar for 2015 and 2022: in 2022, 41 per cent of respondents said they 'sometimes or never' felt listened to (38 per cent in 2015) and 59 per cent said they 'always' felt listened to (62 per cent in 2015), and perhaps unsurprisingly this was in line with the finding that 59 per cent in 2022 (60 per cent in 2015) could understand what was being said to them in appointments, and 41 per cent in 2022 (40 per cent in 2015) understand what is being said only 'sometimes/ never'. This indicates no improvement across the seven-year period, with at least 40 per cent of people being unable to understand what is being said to them in their GP appointment, compounded by lack of availability of interpretation.

Notwithstanding language barriers, when respondents were asked whether they felt they received the same level of care as UK nationals, the response was more positive in 2022 than in 2015 (Table 7.1). However, when GYROS undertook face-to-face interviews and focus groups with individuals about accessing health services, the responses were much less

---

[31] L. Coates, 'Norfolk and Waveney among top 5 "dental deserts" in England' *Eastern Daily Press* (8 May 2022), available at: www.edp24.co.uk/news/health/20625246.norfolk-wave ney-among-top-5-dental-deserts-england/, accessed 23 November 2023.

Table 7.2: Services accessed in the UK, 2015

Service	Percentage accessing care
GP	84
Accident and emergency	17
Maternity	17
Referral to a specialist	32
Dentist	49

positive.[32] This is part of a general pattern the charity has witnessed: clients are more reluctant to commit negative comments to paper (such as in surveys), especially in the context of access to services (such as healthcare), where they fear that this written record could have an impact on future services they might receive.[33] By contrast, in face-to-face conversations, interviewees feel more free to say what they think. Similarly, we found disparities when we asked if people had experienced discrimination, with very low levels of reporting in surveys compared to focus groups, where almost every attendee reported some form of (usually verbal) discriminatory comment, especially 'go home' rhetoric.[34] This finding has important implications for research with vulnerable and marginalized groups, suggesting surveys alone are insufficient to gain a true picture of the reality on the ground.

3.2 Health conditions

In the 2022 survey, 28 per cent of respondents reported having a long-term health condition – this question was not asked in 2015; however, respondents in 2015 were asked what health services they had accessed since arrival in the UK, thus providing some insight into health conditions experienced by this group. Table 7.2 shows the percentage of respondents accessing specific services. The GYROS database records that approximately 17 per cent of clients who answered a question on disability[35] had reported that they

---

[32] Norfolk Community Foundation, n 27.

[33] Ibid, 14.

[34] C. Barnard, S. Fraser Butlin and F. Costello, 'The changing status of European Union nationals in the United Kingdom following Brexit: the lived experience of the European Union Settlement Scheme' (2022) 31 *Social and Legal Studies* 365, 369.

[35] In GYROS data for 2019–2020, only 37 per cent of clients answered this question. The majority of responses were marked as 'unknown'.

did have a disability, compared to 21 per cent in general population statistics.[36]

These findings could indicate that migrant workers are in better general health than the local population, a phenomenon known as the 'healthy migrant effect'.[37] Migrants tend to be those with the resources, both material and physical, to be able to cross borders to take up work elsewhere.[38] In Great Yarmouth, migrant workers (usually young when they arrive) come to a place where the population suffers from significant poor health. As we saw in Chapter 2, life expectancy in the Town is lower than the average for England and this is particularly pronounced even within the Town itself, with people in the central wards having a life expectancy more than ten years lower than those in some of the outer villages. The mortality rate for all causes under 75 is higher than the average for England (397 per 100,000 population aged under 75 compared to 330 per 100,000 in England),[39] with the mortality rate for both cancer and cardiovascular disease higher in Great Yarmouth.[40] Levels of diabetes and dementia are also higher in Great Yarmouth than in the region or in England.[41] These figures now include EU migrant workers who have been in the UK since 2004 and are, by definition, ageing (the median age of those in the GYROS dataset was 45). They are no longer all examples of the 'healthy migrant': the 2022 survey shows 28 per cent have long-term health conditions.

Turning to health behaviours, the smoking rate is high in Great Yarmouth, at 20.6 per cent compared to 14.0 per cent for the region and 14.4 per cent for England.[42] However, the rate of smoking in our EU migrant worker cohort is higher again: 33 per cent in 2022 and 41 per cent in 2015 (this is reflected in the picture on the front cover of this book). The level of tuberculosis (TB) is also much higher in Great Yarmouth than in the region or England as a whole, with an incidence rate of 12.8 per cent compared to 5.6 per cent in the region and 9.2 per cent in England.[43] This issue was

---

[36] E. Kirk Wade, House of Commons Library, 'UK disability statistics: prevalence and life experiences' (29 July 2022), available at: https://commonslibrary.parliament.uk/resea rch-briefings/cbp-9602/, accessed 17 February 2023.

[37] M. Haour-Knipe, 'Context and perspectives: who migrates and what are the risks?' in F. Thomas and J. Gideon (eds) *Migration, Health and Inequality* (London: Zed Books, 2013), 13.

[38] Ibid.

[39] Public Health England, 'Great Yarmouth: local authority health profile 2019', available at: https://fingertips.phe.org.uk/static-reports/health-profiles/2019/e07000145. html?area-name=great%20yarmouth, accessed 17 February 2023.

[40] Ibid.

[41] Ibid.

[42] Ibid.

[43] Ibid.

raised in an interview with a member of staff at a GP surgery in the Town;[44] she said there was a time when TB became a very serious local public health issue and recalled an outbreak among migrant workers in the local chicken factory in 2014.[45] TB specialists were brought in to work with the local factories to prevent further spread of the disease. A community adviser recalled her husband (and others) getting TB when he was working in a factory: "and he had to stop, and he didn't want to go back to the factory again". She said: "People think it was something from the air conditioner or whatever from the air. But they never, they never did any investigation."[46] This example, together with the example in Chapter 4 where we saw that EU migrant 'key workers' who were on the frontline of food processing faced increased risk of COVID-19, shows how migrant workers can be exposed to more health risks than the local community.

3.3 COVID-19 vaccination rates

In the 2022 health survey, respondents were asked about uptake of the COVID-19 vaccine. The finding was that 45 per cent had not had any vaccine (by the time of the survey, three rounds of vaccinations, including the booster, had been available for everyone). Of those who had taken the vaccine, 89 per cent had taken more than one dose. Of those who had not had the vaccine, the largest nationality groups were (in order) Lithuanian, Romanian and Portuguese. While our analysis shows that year of arrival to the UK did not seem to have any impact on whether an individual had the vaccine, English language skills did seem to play a part. Of those who did not take up the vaccine, 49 per cent described their English language skills as 'little/very little'.

Most messaging around the vaccine was in English, and communication from GPs was usually also in English; GYROS did translate health information related to the vaccination for its clients. In Autumn 2021, GYROS advisers accompanied NHS health workers on the COVID-19 bus that was taking the vaccine 'out' to farm workers; their role was to help with translation. There were practical concerns, especially for those on seasonal employment contracts: if they received one vaccine in the UK and then needed to return to their home country (in 2021, the seasonal workers visited were largely from Kazakhstan), would they be able to get a second vaccine in their home

---

[44] Interview with employee at a local GP surgery (online, 29 October 2021).
[45] See 'Norfolk: chicken factory worker diagnosed with tuberculosis', *East Anglia Times* (24 March 2014), available at: www.eadt.co.uk/news/norfolk-chicken-factory-worker-diagnosed-with-tuberculosis-2133900, accessed 17 February 2023.
[46] Interview with local community adviser (Great Yarmouth, November 2021).

country and would that be recognized by the UK authorities so that they could return for the next season?

3.4 Interim conclusions

The survey data show system, provider and patient level barriers to EU migrant worker access to healthcare in the Town. The data also show that the higher the level of English, the more likely it was that the individual would access healthcare services and visit and meaningfully engage with a GP. Use of other healthcare services was found to be low, particularly for dental care. This low level of take-up may be explained on other grounds. In answer to the question 'Do you use medical services in your home country?', 40 per cent of respondents in 2015 said they travelled home for specific procedures and prescriptions or that they would travel home if they needed medical care; in 2022, the share was 42 per cent.

Finally, the data also shows that the level of long-term health conditions among the EU migrant workers in our cohort is converging with the national average, suggesting migrant workers, are increasingly an unwell population. This would support the suggestion made at the outset of this chapter that problems with work and housing may be taking their toll and, over time, diminishing any 'healthy migrant' effect. But it also reflects the reality that first- and second-phase EU migrants have been in the UK for 20 years. They are ageing and, as a result, experiencing more health issues.

We turn now to see if and how some of the issues that came out in the health survey appeared in the GYROS database.

D. Healthcare issues in the GYROS database

1. Introduction

In this section, we consider the enquiries categorized as 'health' in the GYROS dataset, 4 per cent of all enquiries. This percentage seems low given the prevalence of health issues identified in previous chapters. It is explained in part by the fact that sometimes health matters came up as part of other categories of enquiry, such as 'employment'. When looking only at 'health' enquiries, the case note analysis shows that clients sought help for (in order):

(i) administrative issues: help to make appointments or to communicate with the GP or hospital; help responding to a letter from the hospital asking the client to prove their eligibility for free services; and help where the client has received a bill for NHS services;

(ii) access to fit notes or other communication with the employer;

(iii) application for benefits when the client is not eligible for statutory sick pay or no longer able to work due to illness; and

(iv) substantive healthcare issues: GYROS has relatively frequent enquiries around cancer and cancer treatment, mental health and wellbeing, and more recently COVID-19.

As in previous chapters, we are interested not only in the issues which arise but also how GYROS' advisers respond to the issues presented.

2. Administrative issues

A lot of GYROS' clients come for help with navigating the health system: registering for a GP, making appointments and follow-up appointments, and understanding information they have been given by the NHS. Due to poor English, some clients need considerable help over several months. This is evident in the following case notes for one client:

> 12/08/2014: Client rec'd [received] a letter from surgery saying that she needs to book an app[ointment] for ECG [electrocardiogram] [and] to check her cholesterol levels again. I called surgery and booked appt [appointment].

> 04/11/2014: Translated and explained to client letter about eye care.

> 17/03/2015: Client received letter from Hospital, with results from her mammography, stating that there is no evidence of cancer.

> 05/05/2015: Client has received letter from Tuberculosis specialist service regarding her recent check-up. She had attached X-ray form that she needs to take to Hospital herself to X-ray department. Client is aware where it is and how to get there.

> 05/04/2016: Client had an appt. [appointment] at James Paget Hospital. She did not require it anymore, therefore, I called and cancelled the appt [appointment].[47]

This is a good example of GYROS acting not only as administrator but also as translator. The NHS England *Guidance for Commissioners: Interpreting and Translation Services in Primary Care* says that NHS England 'must have regard to the need to reduce inequalities between patients' with respect to: [t]heir ability to access health services; and [t]he outcomes achieved for

---

[47] Client ID 188.

them by the provision of health services'.[48] It also says: 'Interpretation and translation should be provided free at the point of delivery, be of a high quality, accessible and responsive to a patient's linguistic needs.'[49] However, the GYROS data (and indeed the health survey data discussed in Section C) show that translators were often not available or that the translation services that were available were not adequate:

> 7/7/17: ... Client went to see her new GP on Wed 5/7. Unfortunately, the doctor hasn't received any health records from old GP or Hospital, therefore, have booked to see client on Wed 26/7/17 at 14.40. Client told me that it was very difficult for her and doctor to communicate with interpreter over the phone and doctor asked client if she could bring friend or relative with her for next appt [appointment]. The doctor also said that she will contact hospital and GP (old) to get medical records. I called surgery to see if they are able to change appt so that I [am] able to accompany client. Appt changed – Fri 28/7 at 10 am.[50]

In some instances, the GP asked GYROS if they can help to provide language support:

> 15/1/16: Doctor called and was very concerned about home visit to client as of language barrier, she asked me if visit is still needed, which I explained to her that I can only tell her what the symptoms client has, as [his] mom told me yesterday and that client cannot walk. Doctor seemed rude on the phone. Mom told me that when doctor arrives, she will call her other son in Latvia to interpret over the phone, which doctor was not happy with, so I offered to come to interpret.[51]

GYROS helped this client to attend his hospital appointments for a fractured hip by booking transport and helping him to claim back the cost for transport, and by booking interpreters for his appointments. The notes also say that the client was helped with food parcel vouchers while he was unable to work.

[48] NHS England, *Guidance for Commissioners: Interpreting and Translation Services in Primary Care* (September 2018), available at: www.england.nhs.uk/wp-content/uploads/2018/09/guidance-for-commissioners-interpreting-and-translation-services-in-primary-care.pdf, accessed 23 November 2023, 14. (See also Section 13G of the National Health Service Act 2006.)
[49] Ibid, 6.
[50] Client ID 1191.
[51] Client ID 190.

Another administrative issue which arises in the GYROS database concerns eligibility to healthcare services. As we saw in Section B, some EU migrants are eligible for free access if they have settled status and are ordinarily resident in the UK; others pay a health surcharge; still others incur charges as overseas visitors accessing the NHS. The GYROS database shows examples of where EU clients have needed help providing evidence of eligibility:

09/10/2018: Client received a letter from Hospital asking for evidence that she is entitled to free healthcare. They asked for her passport and proof of address. I advised to send her payslips as well. She will send the[m] by email, although the deadline was 8th September. It is better to send it now even though it is a month late.[52]

Among those who had access to NHS services, some reported that they had received letters to say they were going to be charged. In one example:

09/02/2017: Client's wife received a letter from NHS regarding NHS charges. I wrote a letter to the Overseas visitor [office] and sent copies of documents to prove client is a family member of a qualified person.[53] I sent copies of ID cards for client, partner and daughter, tenancy agreement, partner's P60 and 2 payslips, [C]ouncil [T]ax letter, birth certificate and bank statement to prove relationship, residence and income.[54]

As we have seen in chapters 3 and 6, the administrative burden on migrant communities to prove their eligibility for services is significant, as clients need help to understand what is required and struggle to gather the evidence needed. Paper trails also impose a significant burden on the healthcare system itself. Take, for example, GP registration. Retrieving health records from abroad can be a problem, especially for small local surgeries.[55] Accessing medical records and translating documents from patients' doctors in their home country can be difficult, a fact also noted in focus groups research carried out by GYROS in 2015: 'There was a mixed experience of how GPs then used the information brought back from overseas – some GPs used it and continued treatment as directed by overseas doctors, others refused to look at it or consider it. This latter point caused huge frustrations with patients.'[56]

---

[52] Client ID 704.
[53] A definition is provided in Chapter 3, n 31.
[54] Client ID 63.
[55] Interview with employee at a local GP surgery (online, October 2021).
[56] Humphries (2015) n 8, 26.

In our interview with a representative from a local GP surgery, they made the point that the EUSS itself had put an additional burden on GPs because patients needed documentary evidence from the GP surgery to prove their registration to support their application to the Home Office. Some GP surgeries charged for this letter, although this particular interviewee's surgery did not. More generally, the interviewee said that language was the greatest barrier they faced in supporting patients who do not speak English.[57]

3. Arranging access to fit notes or communication with employers

As we saw in Chapter 4, a large part of GYROS' role is to communicate with clients' employers. This is shown in the following case note:

> The client needed assistance to contact her employer and to know the reason SSP [statutory sick pay] is not paid as she has been sick for 14 days and present[ed] her sick notes in time. I have just contacted her employer and obtain[ed] an information that SSP payment will be made 28/06/2016. They regret for the delay.[58]

It may take perseverance by the adviser to get the issues with statutory sick pay sorted out:

> 02/12/2016 Client said he sent his sick note to [Agency] but was not paid yet. Client has been working for them for 1 year now. ... First sick note was on 03/11 to 15/11/2016 and last one 22/12/2016 to 16/01/2017. I called [Agency] on mobile that client provided. [Agency] told me that he had called before and that at the time she explained that she did not have any info there but that she would try to get more info from the office. ... Client needs to wait a little bit more and [Agency] will try to contact the office again. As soon as she has info, she will contact client. Client understood.[59]

The client returned four days later, still not having heard anything from the agency. The adviser called the agency three times, but each time the calls went to voicemail. The client returned to GYROS five weeks later, this time for help to return to work after his illness.

---

[57]   Interview with employee at a local GP surgery (online, October 2021).
[58]   Client ID 753.
[59]   Client ID 1293.

15/01/2017 He said that his fit note was finishing, and he didn't want to ask for a new one as the situation with his landlord was getting worse. When resident was talking to me, he received a phone call from [Agency] asking him to go to work on Saturday. The resident told me that he was happy and said thank you to all GYROS team for the support that we offer him during the months that he was ill.[60]

In this example, the client returned to work despite his fit note, due to issues with his landlord.

4. Applying for benefits

Those who are sick often need to apply for benefits (see Antonio's story in Box 7.1). Once again, this raises issues of eligibility. Under EU law, worker status can be retained if a worker is temporarily unable to work due to illness. Proving worker status is retained might be crucial to passing the Habitual Residence Test, considered in Chapter 6.

01/10/16 client made a claim for UC [Universal Credit], but it was refused on the basis that as a European Jobseeker she is not entitled to UC. [C]lient has till the 15/10/16 to ask for a reconsideration. I asked client for her work history to see if she retained her worker status and she did. [C]lient has been working since 2012, not continuously, but for the majority of the time. [S]he got pregnant last year and since November 2015 she does not work. [C]lient is receiving MA [Maternity Allowance] and that will be until January 2017. [C]lient gave birth in July and she has mental [health] problems related to the pregnancy and cannot work. I asked client to bring all the evidence related to her illness and to ask her doctor for a sick note and that we need to establish that she can pass the HRT [Habitual Residence Test] and go for UC as a worker unable to work temporarily. [A]nd as soon as she brings me all the evidence I need I will write a letter to UC.[61]

The mandatory reconsideration of this client's Universal Credit application upheld the initial decision that she did not pass the Habitual Residence Test. The GYROS adviser told the client:

She can make a complaint and go to tribunal and that here is a form that she needs to fill in and send it to the tribunal so her case can be

---

[60] Ibid.
[61] Client ID 938.

heard by a judge, client said that she wanted to do that. I printed out the form and client will post it.

This was one of the rare cases where a GYROS client went to a court or tribunal on GYROS' advice. The client returned two years later. She had then made a successful application and was awarded the Personal Independence Payment. She had had a reassessment for this payment but had been awarded only standard living allowance, which she disputed. Her GP had written a supporting letter, and that had been taken into consideration when the decision was made. The notes say: 'Client told us that her conditions have worsened since, therefore, she has been referred back to a mental health clinic. We advised client to gather new evidence and do a change of circumstances rather than appeal the decision.' There are no further updates on this case.

In another case, GYROS received a call from a Cambridgeshire hospital enquiring what welfare benefits a Latvian patient with a brain tumour (and his family) were eligible for:

[Caller] from [redacted] Hospital called today, and I informed her that as far as we know, the clients are getting CHB [child benefit], CTC [Council Tax credits], DLA [Disability Living Allowance] and CA [Carer's Allowance] for both children and client is getting JSA [Jobseekers Allowance]. She wanted to know if they can get IS [Income Support] and HB/CTB [Housing Benefit/Council Tax benefit]. I said that they won't be eligible to IS but can get HB/CTB as he is a "retained worker" jobseeker. [Caller] asked if we could check it, I promised to follow this up and let [caller] know. I asked colleague to call client and give the client appt [appointment] with me to find out if client is getting HB.[62]

This is an example of the GYROS adviser acting as a support worker for this client as well as providing advice.

Box 7.1: Antonio's story

Antonio's[63] case shows just how difficult it can be for those with little support in the UK when they fall seriously ill. He came to GYROS' attention when he attended one of GYROS' sessions in the local library. His case also shows how sickness can quickly lead to debt and potential homelessness.

---

[62] Client ID 678.
[63] Client ID 891.

26/11/16 Appt [appointment] – [Redacted] called and said this resident went to the cafe worried about his health and income. He has lived permanently in Great Yarmouth for the last two years. [He] has been working for [Agency X] but he changed to [Agency Y] in the August 2016. This last month he discovered he has cancer and is not being able to work anymore. He has a debt for one month arrear and is depending on friends support with food. [Cafe Staff] suggested to him to go to [GYROS Office] and talk to a Service Connector. He presented at [office] accompanied by a friend, she left when we started our conversation. He has been in the UK since April 2014. He was working full time for [Agency] until October 2016. He was very upset and said felt very vulnerable, as a couple of weeks ago he was diagnosed with lung cancer. The resident reported that he does not have family in the UK. He explained that he has two sisters and mother back in Portugal, but the resident does not have contact with his family, he said that he has personal issues with family. He has 2 months' rent arrears. The resident hasn't had an income since October 2016. He said that his landlord allowed him to live in the house, but asked as he can't work that he will need to have support with benefits. I spoke with resident, made a support plan with him and we decided to do two first initial steps: 1) Call his landlord and explain to him that GYROS was going to help him to apply for benefits, but that was going to take some time. 2) Apply for UC [Universal Credit] ... I made one appointment for him next Friday 02/12/16 for apply to Universal Credit.

The next note shows how Antonio's problems began to cluster:

14/12/16 Resident came to office after his last appointment in the hospital and said he will have to have surgery on 22/12/16. He said he was unhappy about this decision, as he will spend Christmas in Hospital. The client also said he requested at the hospital a DS1500 form to ask for PIP [Personal Independence Payment], but they refused to give him DS1500 as he is not terminally ill. The resident said he feels very sad and in need of emotional support. I offered him a coffee from the office, which he had. I suggested to him about looking for psychological support, he did not want to go to psychological group support or individual counselling, as he does not feel as he can openly talk to people, also he feels that the language is a barrier. The resident said he was glad about the support we were giving to him, as he sometimes goes to the Cafe to talk with [staff there], as [this] makes him feel more relaxed. He said he was very worried about his operation and did not know if he was going to survive, as the operation would be high risk. The resident said one of his biggest worries was not being able to pay his debts and give back the help to all the people who have been supporting him. I said to the resident that at the moment it was important to be focused on his health and try to not think about other problems, I explained to the resident that the team at GYROS were supporting him with UC [Universal Credit].

The advisers helped Antonio apply for Universal Credit, the Personal Independence Payment and a medication exemption card. His first surgery went well, but soon afterwards he needed to have further surgery when another tumour was found, this time in his stomach. GYROS also liaised with his landlord and accompanied Antonio to his GP appointments and welfare benefit appointments.

Antonio was refused the Personal Independence Payment when he made his first application, because he was short of his two-year residence in the UK by four months and therefore ineligible to apply. He was advised to reapply in four months. Later, he missed a Universal Credit appointment because he was in hospital for surgery. The notes say that Antonio

> showed me a letter from his UC [Universal Credit] that he printed, and it said that he will be penalised for the appointment that he missed in February. He will need to pay [£]10.40 for each day that he didn't justify why he didn't attend to his appointment. [Antonio] said that he was surprised about this letter being sent now as he already justifies about the missed appointment in February.

He then asked GYROS for help making an appointment with the job centre via his online journal. The notes record that Antonio received a £250 fine for missing this appointment. However, he was in hospital having his lung removed. He was helped again to submit a Personal Independence Payment claim. He was advised by his work coach to attend English classes so that his employability is improved once he recovers. GYROS staff help to get him into English classes held in the library. The last case note records his Personal Independence Payment application was submitted via the local debt advice charity DIAL (with GYROS translating).

5. Substantive healthcare issues

As Antonio's case shows, clients are prepared to confide in GYROS about their healthcare conditions, which they may be reluctant to do with others. Other instances in the database show clients coming in with sensitive health letters which they needed help to read, translate and respond to – such as in relation to cervical smear tests or taking a stool sample.

> 22/06/2016: Client said her consultant told her he would make a referral for a lymph specialist as the arm operated was getting swollen and painful and that she should receive a referral. I called the Hospital and talked to admin who informed me that there was no referral made that showed on client's record. Client has an appoint[ment] for a Respiratory specialist next week ... but nothing regarding this. Admin said that we should call ... on Monday and ask about this ...

I explained this to client and told her I will call hospital next week and let her know. Client understood.

25/07/2017: Client brought a letter that stated that she needed to book an appointment at her surgery for repeat blood test at request of her GP. I called surgery and booked appointment.[64]

For some, GYROS' help with health issues is immediate and practical. The following case notes for one client illustrate this:

15/6/16 Client called me to ask to call out ambulance to her address. Client told me that [child] has been vomiting constantly all day. Client has tried to call ambulance but could not communicate due to language barrier.

15/6/16 I called 111 number and gave all details to client gave me about son's health condition. I was advised that ambulance will contact client to get more details and will use language line. At 15.36pm client called me to ask to interpret for her at the A&E [Accident & Emergency]. Doctor wanted to know about [her son's] past medical history, allergies, curr[e]nt medications, pains and diet. Client told doctors that [her son] was born [full] term and had never had serious illness, he complained about Tummy ache 5 days ago, he had high temperature and, therefore client took him to be seen by GP, who prescribed some medications. Today [her son] hasn't had any medication, he hasn't eaten anything [a]part from he drunk some energy drink. I also gave name and telephone number of health visitor that is working with family.[65]

In these sorts of cases, the role of GYROS advisers as translator is obvious. But what else do the case notes tell us?

6. GYROS' role

The survey data and the case notes in the database tell us quite a lot about the health of the EU migrant community in Great Yarmouth. They also tell us, indirectly, about GYROS' role advising, acting as intermediary/communicator and supporter/friend as the advisers accompany clients to appointments – appointments the advisers made for the clients. Yet health is rarely a presenting problem and very few clients come to GYROS solely

---

[64] Client ID 2.
[65] Client ID 186.

about a health issue – in the GYROS case notes we analysed, only three clients presented solely for a health-related enquiry, with no other help required. Normally, clients came to GYROS because they were experiencing other problems, such as employment issues, and mentioned health as part of those meetings; also, GYROS sometimes generated a 'health' enquiry by asking about GP registration. This is different therefore from the Health Justice Partnership service model where legal advice and health advice are co-located. Nevertheless, the clustering of issues individuals experience is similar. In the GYROS data, health was most clustered with enquiries around (in order) welfare benefits, debt, and immigration. As in Antonio's case, problems can quickly spiral out of control.

GYROS' intervention is multifaceted and always pragmatic. Take the case of Paola,[66] a Portuguese single mother with two children, who was from Guinea-Bissau. She had been living in the UK since 2008. She self-reported her English language skills as 'very limited'. She experienced multiple issues for which she needed help. Over the course of two years, she had 12 interactions with GYROS. She received help for: health issues, welfare benefits (Personal Independence Payment and Disability Living Allowance, due to her health issues) and housing (the client saw a rat in her kitchen and asked GYROS to call the council or Environmental Health). The GYROS worker helped the client navigate both hospital and GP appointments for cancer treatment – appointments which the client was unable to organize on her own. The case notes show she subsequently died from cancer. GYROS then began to help the wider family, including accompanying them to the Registrar's office to register the death and helping them to phone the HMRC to stop benefit payments. GYROS' advisers went to the bank with the client's family, bringing copies of the death certificate, and arranged for the bank's bereavement team to call the family. The family asked GYROS for advice on how to arrange the funeral in Portugal and for Paola's body to be transported there. The notes record that the GYROS adviser promised to do some research on how to manage this. The case note from a month later said: 'client will be buried in Portugal and family is travelling there so they can close this chapter.' GYROS continued to help the family sort out issues in relation to housing: a GYROS worker accompanied the family, including two children, to the council and were told that 'as the housing was temporary and client passed away, family needs to move out of the property'. With the help of other statutory providers, alternative accommodation was found for the family and GYROS then helped the family to respond to questions about the future care of the children.

---

[66] Client ID 2.

This example shows the broad range of support GYROS advisers offer their clients. They see clients facing multiple problems which need to be addressed pragmatically and holistically. In this way, their role is different to, say, lawyers with traditional legal specialisms, who will focus mainly on the relevant (legal) aspect of the problem. We return to this issue in Chapter 8.

E. Conclusion

This chapter has shown some of the health issues faced by the EU migrant population in Great Yarmouth, likely the consequence of the poor housing and working conditions they experience. With 28 per cent of those surveyed reporting long-term health conditions, the question of access to healthcare is particularly important. However, as the survey findings have shown, there are still those who do not access healthcare due to language barriers and other issues. Bureaucratic bordering – paperwork requirements – can also prevent meaningful access or timely access to help alleviate or prevent health issues.

For the people in our study, legal needs became health needs and vice versa. As Beardon et al note, 'the relationship between legal problems and health is bidirectional, with illness being one of the major factors leading to the development of social welfare legal problems such as issues with employment and eligibility for income support',[67] and vice versa employment, debt, housing issues and so on causing ill health, with stress and mental health issues. This bidirectional link is clear in the GYROS data, most prevalent in the problem clustering which occurs in cases such as Antonio's or Paola's.

The clustering of problems around health is clearly identified in the data and from interviews with GYROS staff. It appears that generally migrant workers move to the UK young(er), fitter and healthier than the local population (the 'healthy migrant effect'). However, their health is more severely impacted, and over a shorter period, especially in the context of the low-paid physical work they do, often in cold, wet conditions. Health-harming factors are compounded by social deprivation – poor-quality housing, damp and mouldy rooms with poor ventilation, low pay and debt issues with corresponding stress and anxiety. GYROS' work is therefore focused on addressing the day-to-day consequences of those (legal) problems (what we term 'pragmatic law'), not the causes. In Chapter 8, we consider the advantages and disadvantages of this pragmatic approach.

---

[67] S. Beardon, C. Woodhead, S. Cooper, R. Raine and H. Genn, 'Health-justice partnerships: innovation in service delivery to support mental health' (2020) 19 *Journal of Public Mental Health* 327, 327.

8

Drawing the Threads Together

A. Introduction

Through our work in Great Yarmouth, we have sought to understand, first, the lives of EU migrant workers living and working there and, second, the daily problems they face and how they handle them. For the EU migrant worker population in Great Yarmouth, that may involve engagement with GYROS, the frontline advice charity we have been working with. This has enabled us, third, to analyse the relationship between EU migrant workers and the advisers at GYROS, giving us insights into not only the approaches that the workers and advisers take to resolving problems, but also the role of the law and of law enforcement. What has become clear is that the 'law', as recognized and understood by lawyers, plays a limited role in the resolution of most problem situations EU migrant workers are facing. The response by GYROS advisers is pragmatic and focused on finding solutions, rather than on enforcing legal rights via traditional legal resolution pathways; we term this 'pragmatic law'. This approach, therefore, differs from the traditional literature addressing legal consciousness or access to justice.

As we have seen, the lives of low-paid EU migrant workers are characterized by precarity in the form of lack of regular employment and secure housing as well as the experience of debt and ill health. These problems often cluster together.[1] They are exacerbated by the need to produce paperwork for proof of residence – 'bureaucratic bordering' in the jargon[2] – to obtain access to rights. The problems are often legal in

---

[1] H. Genn, *Paths to Justice: What People Do and Think about Going to Law* (Oxford: Hart Publishing, 1999), 31.

[2] P. Manolova, 'Inclusion through irregularisation? Exploring the politics and realities of internal bordering in managing post-crisis labour migration in the EU' (2022) 48 *Journal of Ethnic and Migration Studies* 3687.

nature but they are not perceived as such by either the migrant workers or the advisers. The response by those workers to problems is often strikingly pragmatic: seeking to resolve the immediate issue rather than dealing with it through express recourse to legal rights or processes. Our earlier work showed that EU migrant workers were largely not taking cases to employment tribunals.[3] We suspected this was partly because there were barriers to doing so: language difficulties, unfamiliarity with UK systems and rights, fear of retribution, and cost. Our research in Great Yarmouth has revealed another dimension: that people are in fact accessing help for their problems, but they are seeking resolution 'at source'.[4] Further, their advisers, GYROS in this instance, are responding in the same vein: calling employers to sort out problems or helping clients find new jobs or new housing; or helping clients resolve debt issues. This approach is pragmatic; using interventions that are often effective for the individual and a relatively 'quick fix', but rarely go near formal dispute resolution pathways. Pragmatism, at least as we see it among GYROS' staff, is the response to the (legal) problems that are generated in part by the precarious lives lived by EU migrant workers. We explore these themes further in Section B.

The question, then, is how to think about what we see in our data. As noted in Chapter 1, while there are notable literature and expertise in law, legal studies, anthropology, sociology, critical legal studies and socio-legal studies that touch on the themes we have identified – and from which we have very much benefitted – ultimately, we have not been able to find a suitable framing within the existing literature on which to 'hang' our study. We explore that literature and identify its limitations in relation to our data (Section C), then set out our pitch for a fresh theoretical framing, based on the idea of pragmatic law, to describe and analyse the pragmatic solutions to legal issues seen at street level in Great Yarmouth (Section D). We find this framing useful not merely because it helps to describe what we see but also as it offers a prism through which to analyse the benefits and the risks of this approach to resolving legal problems.

---

[3] C. Barnard, A. Ludlow and S. Fraser Butlin, 'Beyond employment tribunals: enforcement of employment rights by EU-8 migrant workers' (2018) 47 *Industrial Law Journal* 226.

[4] C. Hodges, *Delivering Dispute Resolution: A Holistic Review of Models in England and Wales* (Oxford: Hart Publishing, 2019), Chapter 15.

B. Overarching themes

1. Precarity

1.1 Precarity and precariousness

The experiences of EU migrant workers described in this book highlight the reality of precarity 'and its companion precariousness'.[5] Standing identifies a new 'class-in-the-making' in society – the 'precariat' – defined as those for whom

> [it] is not just a matter of having insecure employment, of being in jobs of limited duration and with minimal labour protection, although all this is widespread. It is being in a status that offers no sense of career, no sense of secure occupational identity and few, if any, entitlements to the state and enterprise benefits.[6]

He recognizes migrants as one group within this emerging class. Vosko says that for migrant workers, this precarity is 'characterised by uncertainty, low income, and limited social benefits and statutory entitlement'.[7] Low-skilled work sectors[8] and the use of work agencies to find work[9] have been found to increase precarity.

These issues are echoed in our research: many of GYROS' clients and our interviewees found themselves in insecure work, uncertain accommodation and with limited access to welfare benefits. Those employed by temporary work agencies found themselves in a worse position compared to those directly employed by the factories they worked in, whether due to inferior equipment (Edita wanting her own (non-communal) wellies,[10] agency workers in our focus group wanting better PPE) or clients of GYROS not receiving payslips and having difficulties getting regular shifts.[11]

We would add that immigration status operates as an additional feature of precarity. As we have seen, having pre-settled or settled status acts as a gateway to employment, housing and welfare benefits; conversely not having either of these operates as a further factor in precarity. Moreover, we identified

---

[5]   C. Han, 'Precarity, precariousness, and vulnerability' (2018) 47 *Annual Review of Anthropology* 331, 335.

[6]   G. Standing, *The Precariat the New Dangerous Class* (London: I.B. Taurus, 2014), 41.

[7]   L.F. Vosko, *Managing the Margins: Gender, Citizenship and the International Regulation of Precarious Employment* (New York: Oxford University Press, 2010), 2.

[8]   H. Zhang, L. Nardon and G.J. Sears, 'Migrant workers in precarious employment' (2022) 41 *Equality, Diversity and Inclusion: An International Journal* 254, 260.

[9]   S. McKay and E. Markova, 'The operation and management of agency workers in conditions of vulnerability' (2010) 41 *Industrial Relations Journal* 446, 458.

[10] See Chapter 4.

[11] Ibid.

different levels of precarity – those with pre-settled status face much greater precarity than those with settled status. We look at this in more detail in the next section through the lens of bureaucratic bordering.

1.2 Bureaucratic bordering

Bureaucratic bordering[12] – that is, the requirement for paperwork to access rights – is most starkly seen in data relating to the EUSS. We have seen how those in insecure work and informal rental arrangements find it difficult to prove their residence in the UK because they do not have a paper trail of payslips or tenancy agreements. Manolova says: 'The concept of "bureaucratic bordering" demonstrates precisely these mundane, non-spectacular, non-noticeable ways in which the techniques of migration management encapsulate migrants' existence.'[13] And it is not just about obtaining migration status; having pre-settled or settled status affects GYROS' clients' ability to apply for Universal Credit.

Sometimes the work of GYROS' advisers is anticipatory, aiming to avoid these very 'bureaucratic' problems. For example, as we saw in Chapter 7, GYROS advisers ask each client if they are registered with a GP, irrespective of the nature of the initial enquiry. For those who are not registered, help to find a GP is given straightaway or through a follow-up appointment. This not only addresses the client's healthcare needs, but also acts as evidence of residence for EUSS or welfare benefit applications.

As GYROS clients face up to these bureaucratic requirements, they can become frustrated with the advisers. In a focus group in November 2021, one GYROS adviser said that for some clients, advisers become the 'face' of statutory bureaucracy, as they translate and communicate decisions and delays. Some advisers felt vulnerable to bearing the brunt of clients' disappointment and anger with government systems.

> 'I mean, sometimes you get ... when you're working with people who would just, they're so backed into a corner through no fault of their own, and they've been working, you know, and they've got family to feed, and they've just ... something's gone wrong in the process. There's sometimes quite a lot of anger. And who can blame them? Because they're scared. They don't know what's going to happen. But I think that staff know how to defuse it.'[14]

Bureaucratic bordering is a factor in problem clustering to which we now turn.

---

[12] P. Manolova, n 2, 3687.

[13] Ibid, 3701–3702.

[14] Interview with a GYROS management team member (Great Yarmouth, February 2022).

1.3 Problem clustering

(a) Why do problems cluster?

Those living precarious lives face multiple challenges: they work in low-paid, precarious jobs, usually also claiming in-work benefits. Often they live in poor-quality and, in some cases, overcrowded accommodation. If there is little work, they cannot pay the rent, so they get into debt to pay the money owed. If they become ill, possibly because of their poor-quality accommodation, they cannot work and cannot pay the debts. It is therefore unsurprising that the most commonly clustered issues in the GYROS database were to do with welfare benefits, employment, debt and housing. Clients rarely attended GYROS for just one issue or only once – even a single issue may take several appointments to resolve.

Other advice agencies see this too. A representative of the local Citizens Advice said:

'Most of the time, they do come in with one issue. As you explore the issue for them, you … find out that there's so many other things attached to it. And it's just one of the things we do as advisers when we are speaking to a client who, for instance, has had a relationship breakdown. You want to explore issues like, okay, do you work? Have you got any children? If the person has worked … can [they] have any benefits? That opens another chapter, because then you're going to say, okay, what are you entitled to, how, what options are available to you? And then you also think about, okay, work, do they want to go back into work? If that's the case, then you're talking about employment and then most of the time, sometimes it's a divorce, so you need to go through supporting them through the divorce … but most of the time, it just opens up so many other things.'[15]

Irina's case (Box 8.1) provides a good example of this 'Russian doll' effect where the more the advisers engage with the clients and develop trust, the more issues come to light.

Box 8.1: Irina's story

Irina[16] is a 55-year-old Lithuanian single parent of two who arrived in the UK in 2016. She accessed help from GYROS in 2017. According to the GYROS case notes, she presented

---

[15] Interview with a Citizens Advice worker (online, November 2021).
[16] Client ID 1111.

because she 'received TC [tax credit] annual review. I helped client to set up personal tax account in order to file review online.' A week later she returned, saying her son was unwell. GYROS helped her to phone her GP to set up an appointment and then accompanied the family to the appointment. Irina came to GYROS again two weeks later, this time saying that she was depressed, that her husband had died two years before and she was struggling. GYROS again helped her get assistance from her GP. She then said she had issues with her eyesight; GYROS helped her access her GP and then get specialist eye treatment.

Six weeks after Irina's initial meeting, she came to GYROS once more. [As we saw in Chapter 6,] Client came in with a full bag of unopened envelopes from various utility companies, debt collectors, the Council, the GP, the Driver and Vehicle Licensing Agency, and the TV licensing. The adviser asked why she had ignored the letters. She said that "she doesn't understand and was wrongly advised [to] ignore letters as she already pays the rent and does not need to pay any utilities. Client also mentioned that it is due to low mood and lack of motivation following bereavement of her husband."

Irina also told the adviser that in November 2016 she had bought a car from her son and asked a work colleague to help her get car insurance:

Client said that everyone at her work (factory) goes to this person when they need car insurance, he charges £30 per policy. Client was stopped by police in Dec[ember] 2016 as driving without insurance and as a result car was seized. Someone from work advised client to go to her bank to stop direct debit for car tax as she no longer has the car.

The adviser noted:

During the walk-in her son was repeatedly saying to client – "didn't I tell you." I suspect that client is unable to manage due to her mental well-being. I assured her that I will help her to resolve debt issues. I also advised her to come to walk-ins when unsure about the letters, most important not to ignore them.

GYROS undertook intensive work with Irina over the next six months, negotiating payment schedules with water and credit companies, the council (over Council Tax arrears) and the DVLA. The process was slow. The case notes show Irina was unable to answer some of the security questions due to her limited English. Her debts increased when she missed payments and late payment charges were added by various agencies, including an £80 late payment fee from the DVLA and another one from Barclays bank. The client had various summons letters that had to be dealt with, and court fees were added to her debts. Alongside these debts, GYROS continued to help Irina with appointments for her eyesight and mental health. The advisers also helped her navigate the UK school system, including assisting her older child to register for a secondary school place. The notes said: I translated few letters from the school regarding open day at music college and trip there. Also, client's son has received a letter for excellent behaviour and studies at school asking to keep this letter and use it with any future school applications.'

Irina's case (Box 8.1) is an example of how problems cluster.[17] Clients often ignore problems that raise the emotional temperature or cause anxiety and stress.[18] This can result in mental health issues and other negative health outcomes,[19] loss of confidence, financial loss and the loss of security and comfort.[20] Perceived stigma around debt can drive people to avoid the issue, and fear of the consequences, especially the potential impact on their job prospects, can influence whether, and how, work-related issues are addressed.[21] Citizens Advice see this too:

'Yeah, it is usually when the problem has already started, when it's overwhelming them at that point, or when they can't do anything themselves anymore. When they've got, for instance, if they've got bailiffs at their door, okay? That's when they come and say "I've got bailiffs, I don't know what to do" or "I've got a letter saying if I don't do this …", you know, so hardly would you find a client who was coming in, anticipating the problem and saying: "Well, this has happened. I think this is going to be a problem and I want to nip it in the bud."'[22]

Behind the arrival of the bailiffs, there will have been an unpaid debt which itself may find its root in unemployment, welfare benefit problems and housing issues; with the unpaid debt having grown, the addition of fines making the debt even bigger.

---

[17] P. Pleasence, N.J. Balmer, A. Buck, A. O'Grady and H. Genn, 'Multiple justiciable problems: common clusters and their social and demographic indicators' (2004) 1 *Journal of Empirical Legal Studies* 301.

[18] I. Pereira, C. Perry, H. Greevy and H. Shrimpton, *The Varying Paths to Justice: Mapping Problem Resolution Routes for Users and Non-Users of the Civil, Administrative and Family Justice Systems* (Ministry of Justice, 2015), available at: https://assets.publishing.service.gov.uk/media/5a757131e5274a1242c9e58c/varying-paths-to-justice.pdf, accessed 9 October 2023, 2.

[19] H. Genn, 'When law is good for your health: mitigating the social determinants of health through access to justice' (2019) 72 *Current Legal Problems* 159.

[20] R. Franklyn, T. Budd, R. Verrill and M. Willoughby, *Findings from the Legal Problem and Resolution Survey, 2014–15* (London: Ministry of Justice, 2017); H. Genn (1999), n 1.

[21] Pereira et al (2015), n 18, 34.

[22] Interview with a Citizens Advice representative (online, November 2021). Also, see S. Kirwan, 'The UK Citizens Advice service and the plurality of actors and practices that shape "legal consciousness"' (2016) 48 *Journal of Legal Pluralism and Unofficial Law* 461.

It is not just the clustering of problems but also the lack of knowledge about UK administrative and legal systems which causes difficulty for recently (or not so recently) arrived migrant workers, as does having limited English language skills and no social network to help navigate the legal process.[23] Further, GYROS' clients lack digital skills: 60 per cent of GYROS' clients rated their IT skills at less than 5 out of 10 (with 10 being the highest skill level). This makes it difficult for them to gain access to online Universal Credit journals, remember security questions, receive codes via email and maintain access to the same email addresses or phone numbers.

Some of these issues were faced by one woman who accessed GYROS, struggling to understand how systems like Universal Credit interact with her rent payments:

> Client said that she made a claim for UC [Universal Credit] and had already received a UC payment. Client wanted to know if UC payment was made towards her rent or not and added that she is in rent arrears. Client's landlord is GYBC [Great Yarmouth Borough Council] and according to client, she went to council to discuss this issue but could not understand what she needed to pay in fact: if rent will be paid or not by her housing UC payment or if Council will be the one doing it.[24]

The GYROS adviser explained:

> when we make a UC [Universal Credit] claim, HB [Housing Benefit] will be paid by UC/DWP [Department for Work and Pensions] not the Council. The only thing Council helps with is with the [C]ouncil [T]ax (CTX reduction) payments. I called rent team and talked to adviser who explained that client had rent arrears in the amount of £361.51. The weekly rent is £79.67 but as client is in arrears if client can pay £20 towards the arrears it would be better.

Sandefur notes that 'socio-economic inequalities become justice inequalities'.[25] This is because vulnerable and marginalized groups are both more likely to experience justiciable problems, as well as being more likely

---

[23] P. Pleasence, N.J. Balmer and C. Denvir, *How People Understand and Interact with the Law* (Hove: PPSR, 2015), available at: https://research.thelegaleducationfoundation.org/research-learning/funded-research/how-people-understand-and-interact-with-the-law, accessed 2 February 2023, 94.

[24] Client ID 463.

[25] R. Sandefur, 'What we know and need to know about the legal needs of the public' (2016) 67 *South Carolina Law Review* 443, 459.

to experience adverse consequences because of these problems.[26] Our data confirms this.

(b) 'Legal' nature of the 'problems'

People, like Irina, come to GYROS with carrier bags of 'problems'. The client would like a resolution to all their problems and there is little, if any, distinction as to what is legal and what is not. They seek, and GYROS provides, a holistic service to resolve the issues in their carrier bags. There clearly are 'legal' issues woven through the problems facing EU migrant workers, such as the lack of payslips despite the right to them, the poor quality of housing despite housing laws entitling tenants to minimum standards, and the lack of protection from eviction despite legislative procedural safeguards. However, as we have noted throughout the book, the problems are not understood as 'legal' by EU migrant workers; nor do GYROS' advisers address the issues as legal rights to be pursued, let alone taken to the courts. The advisers are acutely conscious that they lack fluency across relevant rights and legislation.

Once a client accesses the service, the problem is recorded and reported in the GYROS database, and in this way, it is formalized. As we have outlined, although GYROS staff are not legal advisers, their resolution of problems is influenced or affected by the law (sometimes directly, as in housing and immigration; sometimes more indirectly, as in access to healthcare and education). However, the case notes reveal that the advice given does not seek to dissect and apply the law; nor does it identify the strengths and weaknesses of the migrant worker's rights and responsibilities in ways that trained lawyers might do. Rather, the advice is pragmatic and focused on, as in Irina's case, finding a single or multiple resolutions. Legal pathways are seen (often by adviser and client) as out of reach (the East of England is a legal advice desert with little provision), too slow (for workers who need to be working and 'exercising their treaty rights') and too difficult to meet the bureaucratic evidence thresholds needed (due to bureaucratic bordering). For these reasons, pragmatism prevails.

2. Pragmatism

2.1 The 'how'

As we have seen in earlier chapters, both EU migrant workers themselves and GYROS advisers adopted pragmatic solutions to the problems brought to

---

[26] P. Pleasence and N.J. Balmer, 'Caught in the middle: justiciable problems and the use of lawyers' in M. Trebilcock, A. Duggan and L. Sossin (eds) *Middle Income Access to Justice* (Toronto: University of Toronto Press, 2012).

GYROS. If clients faced difficulties at work, the response was generally not to tackle those issues head-on but to get the clients to find other jobs – through help with writing CVs, for instance. The advisers may even write letters to the employers addressing the issues clients present. Similarly, when there are problems with accommodation, residents would take it upon themselves to carry out any necessary work; as we saw in the House, residents improved and renovated parts of the House rather than challenging the landlord to address his responsibilities for the upkeep of the premises.

Clients often initially came to GYROS for help sorting out problems with paperwork. As in Irina's case, the advisers' interventions were swift and practical: ringing the relevant services, attempting to unpick the issues and trying to plan repayment schedules. Early intervention is more likely to prevent issues spiralling, as identifying small debts that have accrued and resolving the underlying welfare benefits issues is likely to avoid the much bigger problem of court involvement in the debts. These are pragmatic actions to find practical solutions to the problems. As noted earlier, GYROS' advisers also tried to avoid future problems by getting clients to register with a GP, checking on their EUSS status, helping them apply for a National Insurance number and updating any change of circumstances on their Universal Credit journals to prevent overpayments being made, avoid debt building up and avert the involvement of bailiffs and the courts. Genn notes the value of this type of support: 'legal problems create or exacerbate ill health and that ill health creates problems for which the law provides solutions'.[27]

GYROS' intervention also spans a range of issues. For Irina, these were debt, insurance and schooling. A similar range of interventions can be seen in Angela's case (Box 8.2).

Box 8.2: Angela's story

Angela, 39, is a Portuguese national. She has limited English language skills. She came to the UK in 2009 and worked full-time until 2016, when her son had a serious accident. GYROS' case notes report: 'her son was riding his bike and was hit by a car and had suffered severe brain damage. He was in the hospital in a coma for some time.' During this period, Angela accrued significant debts.

18/04/2017 (Walk-in) ... as client has been off work since September 2016 her employer is requesting her to come to a meeting on 20/04/2017 or client can be facing a dismissal for misconduct. I called the employer and spoke with [name removed] who advised me to write a letter to employer explaining the situation.

---

[27]   Genn (2019), n 19, 159.

Employer said they want to resolve this situation as they cannot wait for client to return back to work much longer. I said I would write a letter today and post it. Client was ok with this.

GYROS also helped Angela with applications for Universal Credit (which she later received) and the Personal Independence Payment. GYROS chased up the Personal Independence Payment application after a six-week wait. GYROS also looked at her debts.

30/03/17 – client has debt with CT [Council Tax] which is already with bailiffs and water debt. I did a financial statement with client and will speak with DIAL [local debt charity] to make an appointment for a DRO [debt relief order].

25/05/17 – client said that she made an agreement with [named debt agency] to pay £20 [per month] towards her debt with GYBC [Great Yarmouth Borough Council] for CT [Council Tax]. I went through her personal budget and referred her again into DIAL [local debt charity].[28]

A GYROS adviser accompanied Angela to DIAL to act as translator. After this intensive period of work with Angela, GYROS did not see her again for two years, at which time she returned to seek help to deal with her employer again.

3/07/2019 Client has a son with special needs and would like to reduce her working hours. I explained that I could write a letter to her employer, as well as proof of son's disability and that she could present the letter to her employer. Client was ok with this solution.

The holistic service of the kind offered to Irina and Angela does not fit within the traditional legal model of specialization (for example, family law or criminal law), but it is common in generalist advice services. The GYROS advisers acted as trusted friends and took on several different roles within their work, ranging across translator (for language needs),[29] caseworker, support worker, advocate,[30] donor (providing, on occasion, money or a phone) and

---

[28] The referral to local charity DIAL for help with a debt relief order was necessary because GYROS does not offer this service.

[29] M. McDermont, 'Acts of translation: UK advice agencies and the creation of matters-of-public-concern' (2013) 33 *Critical Social Policy* 218, 219.

[30] I. Koch and D. James, 'The state of the welfare state: advice, governance and care in settings of austerity' (2020) 87 *Ethnos* 1, 7; A. Tuckett, 'Ethical brokerage and self-fashioning in Italian immigration bureaucracy' (2018) 38 *Critique of Anthropology* 245.

emergency service provider of food and shelter. This assistance was grounded in a strong relationship between the worker and adviser, arising from the fact that many of the advisers themselves are migrant workers who have taken the same journey as their clients, through low-paid work and precarious accommodation to a more stable, secure position.

This holistic, pragmatic service is what clients want, with 97 per cent rating the service 10 out of 10 (10 being the highest level).[31] The comments on GYROS' feedback forms are equally positive: 'You are the only ones who care and try and help me, so big thank you.'[32] Even where clients did not rate GYROS so highly, this was usually because they did not achieve the outcome they wanted, rather than poor performance on the part of GYROS' advisers. The reasons they did not get the desired outcome were: bureaucratic systems – such as the Home Office system for the EUSS and the Department for Work and Pensions system for Universal Credit and National Insurance – and the client not having the relevant log-in information or correct paperwork; client ineligibility – for example, for Universal Credit or housing support; and system delays, such as Home Office's delays in making decisions or receipt of National Insurance numbers.

2.2 The 'why'

Parallels have been drawn between the role fulfilled by community-based advisers and that of the street-level bureaucrats of Lipsky's seminal work in the 1980s.[33] For Lipsky, street-level bureaucrats act as gatekeepers to, for example, housing and welfare provision and exercise their discretion (or not) at street level as they interpret, implement and navigate national policy each day. Community-based advisers act as 'community brokers',[34] translating and navigating sometimes 'Kafkaesque bureaucracy'[35] and, as Forbess and James describe, 'a labyrinthine multiplicity of different agencies'[36] (see Section C.3.2).

So why do EU migrant workers in Great Yarmouth turn to GYROS rather than to Citizens Advice or a local solicitor or a law centre adviser? Research indicates that awareness of advice services is based on prior contact with an

---

[31] GYROS client feedback (January 2022). Note, however, that the person helping the client – the GYROS adviser – is also the person asking feedback questions.

[32] GYROS client feedback (January 2022).

[33] M. Lipsky, *Street-Level Bureaucracy: Dilemmas of the Individual in Public Services* (New York: Russell Sage Foundation, 1980).

[34] Tuckett (2018), n 30.

[35] I. Koch and D. James (2020), n 30, 11.

[36] A. Forbess and D. James, 'Acts of assistance: navigating the interstices of the British state with the help of non-profit legal advisers' (2014) 58 *Social Analysis* 73, 74.

advice service, the age of the client, their education level and the language spoken at home,[37] this last point being of particular relevance to EU migrant workers in Great Yarmouth, who can receive help in their own language from GYROS advisers. Equally, within their general advice, a person's immigration status underpins all inquiries (on housing, employment and so on); GYROS can also offer specialist advice on immigration. Mainstream advisers without specialist immigration knowledge cannot help their clients in the same way, or they may provide general advice without the lens of immigration status through which all general advice to migrants should be filtered. This also helps explain why 15 or 30 minutes advice from local solicitors may be of little use: the solicitors lack the immigration expertise and clients cannot afford any further advice. We return to this later in the chapter.

For many, the reality is that community-based advice, if it exists in their area at all, is their best and likely only option, because there is very limited legally aided advice. The Legal Aid, Sentencing and Punishment of Offenders Act 2012 (LASPO)[38] came into effect in April 2013. The Act significantly changed the scope of legal aid availability in England and Wales, listing the limited areas that were in scope for legal aid, reversing the previous position of legal aid being available unless excepted. This had a particular impact on civil and family matters, with housing, welfare benefits and employment matters all removed from the scope of legal aid – the very issues that, as we showed in chapters 4, 5 and 6, affect EU migrant workers. The government's own equality impact assessment of the LASPO acknowledged that the changes to legal aid provision 'had a more significant impact on women and individuals from an ethnic minority background'.[39]

With funding no longer available,[40] another impact of LASPO was to create/exacerbate 'legal advice deserts', now commonplace in the UK's

---

[37] P. Pleasence, N. Balmer and C. Denvir, 'Wrong about rights: public knowledge of key areas of consumer, housing and employment law in England and Wales' (2017) 80 *Modern Law Review* 836.

[38] LAPSO is available at: www.legislation.gov.uk/ukpga/2012/10/contents/enacted, accessed 22 November 2023.

[39] Ministry of Justice, *Post-Implementation Review of Part 1 of the Legal Aid, Sentencing and Punishment of Offenders Act 2012 (LASPO)* (Ministry of Justice, 2019), available at: www.gov.uk/government/publications/post-implementation-review-of-part-1-of-laspo, accessed 10 February 2023, 171.

[40] In October 2022, the Ministry of Justice announced it was launching the Early Legal Advice Pilot (at a cost of £5 million) with independent evaluation of 'the possible benefits of holistic, legally aided advice in encouraging early resolution'. The pilot was delivered in Manchester and Middlesbrough. As part of the pilot, participants, selected as they were facing 'housing, debt, or welfare benefit matters', received three hours of non-means-tested and non-merits-tested legal advice on these matters. See 'Early Legal

current legal landscape:[41] 'more than half of the 97 legal advice centres operating in 2013 [had] closed by early 2020'.[42] There is some legal aid in Norwich for the services provided by Shelter (see Chapter 5), with the equivalent of 3.5 full-time staff serving three separate courts.[43] Norwich also hosts a law centre: Norfolk Community Law Centre.[44] It runs a monthly free legal advice clinic in Great Yarmouth, where clients can access 15 minutes of free legal advice from a solicitor or barrister, who give their time pro bono.[45] Some private solicitors in Great Yarmouth also offer a free initial appointment lasting 30 minutes. However, the experience of GYROS' staff is that in general a 30-minute session with a private provider does not work:

GYROS adviser 1: 'Family law. Would refer into 30 min[ute]s free advice. But you do ask yourself will that do what is needed? Thirty min[ute]s [of] free advice? Legal advice is a luxury for people who have money. And sometimes the wait is impossible when someone needs advice.'

GYROS adviser 2: 'Often with free legal advice, clients will come back and say no one contacted them.'[46]

This suggests that one potential role of these community advice organizations – to filter cases which might not need formal legal intervention[47] but refer those that do – is ruled out because of the absence of a meaningful legal route. This suggests that pragmatic problem resolution, offered by GYROS and described throughout this book, is and will continue to be the main source of support offered to EU migrant workers in Great Yarmouth.

Advice Pilot', available at: www.gov.uk/guidance/early-legal-advice-pilot, accessed 22 November 2023.

[41] These advice deserts predate LASPO but were then exacerbated by its impact. See J. Sandbach and Citizens Advice, *Geography of Advice: An Overview of the Challenges Facing the Community Legal Service. Evidence Report* (London: Citizens Advice, 2004).

[42] J. Wilding, *The Legal Aid Market Challenges for Publicly Funded Immigration and Asylum Legal Representation* (Bristol: Policy Press, 2021), 3.

[43] Research conversation with staff at Shelter (Norwich, November 2022).

[44] See the Norfolk Community Law Service website at: www.ncls.co.uk, accessed 10 February 2023.

[45] Ibid.

[46] GYROS staff focus group (online, March 2021).

[47] Genn (1999), n 1, 1.

C. Existing literature on the everyday

1. Introduction

We are, of course, not the first to examine everyday law. As Cowan and Wincott point out, the notion of everyday law has almost become a cliché. They note the 'ubiquity paradox' – the claim that law is everywhere to the point it becomes meaningless.[48] That said, there has been much scholarship focusing on the everyday[49] as a useful lens through which to understand people's experiences of both law and existing power structures.[50] However, we want to argue that much of the existing literature is still focused on the access to justice pathways within the formal legal system. It does not consider sufficiently those outside the established pathways; specifically, it does not help frame the problems and the response to the problems faced by low-paid EU migrant workers in Great Yarmouth.

To explain what we mean, we look at the 'pyramid of resolution pathways' (see Figure 8.1), itself derived from Braithwaite's pyramid of responsive regulation.[51] Generally, lawyers and (much of) the current literature think that (legal) problems start to be resolved when people seek legal advice, often from those who are legally qualified (levels C, D and perhaps E in Figure 8.1) while some progress into more informal resolution processes such as alternative dispute resolution (ADR) – in some areas, like education, this is required – and others travel towards more formal resolution in the lower courts and then on to the higher courts (with a presumption of a linear and natural progression upwards), with fewer and fewer cases rising to each level until only a select few reach the higher courts (level A in Figure 8.1). Those higher courts, sitting at the apex of the legal pyramid, hear difficult, highly refined points of law, often a long way from the murkiness of law and fact in dispute in the first instance courts. A.W.B Simpson talks of the 'economic simplification' of the lower courts. This simplification is needed for both practical and economic purposes, because the higher courts are extremely complex, highly professionalized, formal institutions.[52]

---

48 D. Cowan and D. Wincott (eds), *Exploring the Legal in Socio-Legal Studies* (London: Palgrave, 2016), 3.

49 M. De Certeau, *The Practice of Everyday Life* (Berkeley: University of California Press, 1984); L. Back (2015) 'Why everyday life matters: class, community and making life livable' (2015) 49(5) *Sociology* 820.

50 R. Austin, 'Employer abuse, worker resistance, and the tort of intentional infliction of emotional distress' (1998) 41 *Stanford Law Review* 1, 59.

51 Braithwaite's pyramid of responsive regulation is available on his blog: 'Responsive regulation', *John Braithwaite: War·Crime·Regulation*, available at: http://johnbraithwaite.com/responsive-regulation/, accessed 2 October 2021.

52 A.W.B. Simpson, *Reflections on 'the Concept of Law'* (Oxford: Oxford University Press, 2012), 151. Simpson tells us 'law is like the air we breathe; it is all around us; it is with us

Figure 8.1: Pyramid of resolution pathways: how problems and cases can progress

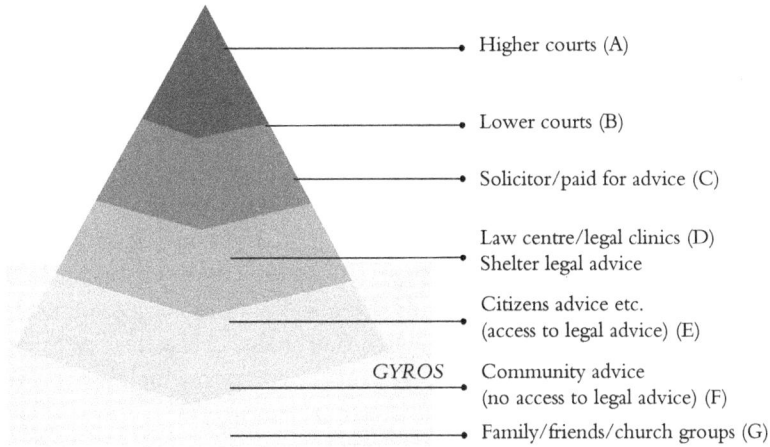

The legal literature tends to focus on what is happening at levels A and B (lower courts and possibly higher courts), as well as how disputes are managed through formal ADR (see Section 2). However, 'very few legal problems see a lawyer and fewer still see a courtroom'.[53] According to Merry,[54] this is particularly the case with newcomers (especially migrants) who do not feel as entitled to use the courts as others. She found that court use tended to be by people who had already lived for one or two generations in the United States (where the study occurred). We argue that, in reality, everyday life (and everyday law) happens outside the upper levels of the pyramid. What happens, then, to those people who face difficulties?

As Genn notes, there are the 'lumpers', who decide to do nothing. There are still others who may seek *legal* advice from a law centre (Level D) if they are fortunate to have one, or from a Citizens Advice office (Level E). They may even go to see a solicitor (Level C), for which they may have to pay. Crucially, those accessing services at Level E (and above) may think that they have a *legal* problem (see sections 3 and 4). This does not address the position of those in our research cohort.

---

from cradle to grave. But it is with law as it is with air, most of us know very little about the stuff', 155.

[53] R.L. Sandefur, 'Access to civil justice and race, class, and gender inequality' (2008) 34 *Annual Review of Sociology* 339, 342.

[54] S. Engle Merry, *Getting Justice and Getting Even: Legal Consciousness among Working Class Americans* (Chicago: University of Chicago Press, 1990), 59.

We would suggest that there is a layer in between the bottom of the pyramid and the lumpers. These are the 'talkers', who might talk to – and seek advice from – family and friends about a particular problem (Level G). But just above that layer, we find frontline advice organizations such as GYROS (Level F). Clients may approach these organizations when they have a problem or perhaps several problems (which they may or may not think of as a legal problem). These organizations respond by focusing on *problem resolution*, either helping clients address their own problems or doing it for them, often across several interconnected (legal and non-legal) domains, as we saw in the case of Irina and Angela. These frontline organizations sit at the very bottom of the pyramid, and are possibly even pre pyramid, with a role that is characterized by 'conceptual murkiness'.[55] It is this level that we argue is not well recognized by the current literature, to which we now turn.

2. Legal approach

Lawyers, especially academic doctrinal lawyers, work from a body of precedent, rules and principles applied to legal problems put before them.[56] In legal academic work, the individual is largely removed from the picture and the focus is on the legal issue. As David Engel graphically puts it, 'law academics generally prefer to pitch their tents in the shadow of the Supreme Court than on the main street or in urban or suburban neighbourhoods.'[57] In this understanding, 'the law' is almost a completely self-contained discipline; legal problems are refined into complex legal arguments and frequently take place at a significant distance from the broader context of the initial enquiry. This doctrinal approach is furthest away from the everyday law and street-level community advisers that have been the focus of this book.

Nevertheless, there are a number of legal theorists who have recognized that doctrine alone is not enough to understand the role of law and that, crucially, context and social facts are paramount.[58] Galligan says that 'while legal theory is a good starting point, it is only a starting point [to understand] law in society'.[59] Legal realism and law in society research seek to understand

---

[55] P. Ewick and S.S. Silbey, *The Common Place of Law* (Chicago: University of Chicago Press, 1998), 20.

[56] Simpson (2012), n 52, 151.

[57] D.M. Engel, 'Law in the domains of everyday life: the construction of community and difference' in A. Sarat and T.R. Kearns (eds) *Law in Everyday Life* (Ann Arbor: University of Michigan Press, 2009).

[58] See W. Twinning, *Jurist in Context: A Memoir* (Cambridge: Cambridge University Press, 2019), 167; D. Galligan, *Law in Modern Society* (Oxford: Oxford University Press, 2006), 6.

[59] D. Galligan (2006), n 58, 12.

law in action and chart gaps in reality between the law in action and law on the books. Sarat and Kearns describe the 'great divide' between legal theorists, who see law as ultimately external to the social practices it regulates, and those who take a constitutive view, believing that law permeates society and is not external to it.[60] A constitutive approach has roots in legal realism, requiring that cases should not be decided formalistically but instead with 'an eye towards how law could and would be used in everyday life'.[61] Despite the important strand of law and society literature (section 4), most legal scholarship still focuses on 'official law'[62] and formal legal structures and adjudication rather than law at everyday, street level. That said, the role of street-level legal advisers is well known, through community lawyering and law centres providing free legal advice, initially substantially funded through legal aid provision. However, as noted LASPO cut large areas from legal aid when it came into force on 1 April 2013. Ten years on (2023), 'the number of advice agencies and law centres doing legally aided work has fallen by 59 per cent'.[63] The Law Society's data shows 84 per cent of people (53 million people) in England and Wales do not have access to a legally aided welfare law advice provider, and 66 per cent (39 million people) do not have access to a legally aided immigration law advice provider.[64] Nevertheless, some continue to operate through a mix of voluntary donations and various other funds offered by government departments, which they must compete for. These community lawyers (broadly defined) and law centres often work beyond individual issues to advocate and campaign for changes in the law and policy. However, the obvious 'law-led' focus of law centres and community lawyers divides this group from the (non-legally trained) community advisers of our study.

3. Anthropology

3.1 Legal anthropology

Legal anthropologists have traditionally offered an ethnographic and qualitative focus on the field of everyday law, examining, for example,

---

[60] A. Sarat and T.T. Kearns, 'Beyond the great divide: forms of legal scholarship' in A. Sarat and T.T. Kearns (eds) *Law in Everyday Life* (Ann Arbor: University of Michigan Press, 2009), 23–33.

[61] Ibid, 35.

[62] M. Hertogh, 'A "European" conception of legal consciousness: rediscovering Eugen Ehrlich' (2004) 31 Journal *of Law and Society* 457, 472.

[63] The Law Society, 'A decade of cuts: legal aid in tatters' press release (31 March 2023), available at: www.lawsociety.org.uk/contact-or-visit-us/press-office/press-releases/a-dec ade-of-cuts-legal-aid-in-tatters, accessed 22 November 2023.

[64] Ibid.

ordinary people's experiences of the lower courts (Figure 8.1, Level B),[65] as opposed to the higher-level courts (Level A). Here the experience, perception and legal consciousness of individuals is of paramount importance as they traverse and interact with the lower courts. This research has a strong focus on the language used by litigants, to capture 'uncontaminated'[66] or 'folk versions'[67] of problems. It identifies how ordinary people perceive their legal problems (their 'legal consciousness') and what their experiences are of using a court to solve their everyday problems. The ethnographic legal consciousness research hypothesizes that by examining the kinds of problems people bring to a court, it is possible to see what categories and meanings of the law they use to frame their experiences so that those experiences appear 'relevant' to the law.[68] This allows conclusions to be drawn about the location of the hypothetical boundary between 'law' and 'not law' in individuals' minds.[69] Scholars speak about the metamorphosis of language that occurs, illustrated by a person having a 'problem' and seeing a legal professional; the 'problem' becomes a 'case'; and sometimes the 'case' moves into a courtroom and becomes a 'dispute'.[70] This is neatly captured by Felstiner et al's famous 'naming, blaming, claiming' triad:[71] not only does the terminology change along the way, but so does the telling of the story or problem, with it being reshaped and refined to fit within the more formal established legal structure and precedent.[72] Simultaneously the legal consciousness of the individual who has the problem has grown, adapted and developed during this process of change.

Conley and O'Barr identify two approaches people take in bringing a dispute before the small claims court in America.[73] The first group is made up of those who are 'relational-orientated' – they place great importance on the social context and 'relational' history of their dispute. The second group is made up of those who are more 'rule-orientated' – they focus on the rules which apply to the dispute.[74] Because courts themselves are more

---

[65] Engle Merry (1990), n 54; J.M. Conley and W.M. O'Barr, *Rules vs Relationships: The Ethnography of Legal Discourse* (Chicago: University of Chicago Press, 1990).

[66] Conley and O'Barr (1990), n 65, 34.

[67] Engle Merry (1990), n 54, 88.

[68] Ibid, 37.

[69] Ibid.

[70] Ibid, 89.

[71] Although critiqued, for more, see D. Cowan and S. Halliday with C. Hunter, P. Maginn and L. Naylor, *The Appeal of Internal Review: Law, Administrative Justice and the (Non-) Emergence of Disputes* (Oxford: Hart Publishing, 2003), 3; Merry (1990) n 54, 90.

[72] W. Felstiner, R. Abel and A. Sarat, 'The emergence and transformation of disputes: naming, blaming, claiming' (1980–81) 15 *Law and Society Review* 631.

[73] Conley and O'Barr (1990), n 65.

[74] Ibid, 58.

'rule-orientated', individuals in this second group are better able to access the justice system, because they can frame their legal issues to engage with legal systems more strategically. Conley and O'Barr therefore argue that those in the first group are effectively silenced and this is deeply entangled with gender, class and race.[75] Similarly, Merry in her courtroom-based work, notes that 'folk-concepts' of problems are often too emotional or intense for the formal courtroom structure and judges are ill-equipped to deal with social problems when their training is to deal with legal problems.[76]

Cowan and Halliday, on the other hand, focus on why people are *not* taking cases to court and the (non)emergence of disputes.[77] Their ethnographic study seeks to understand why homeless people in two local authority areas were not appealing housing decisions and so why disputes did not emerge. Although legal representation was rare in their dataset, where it existed, it made a positive difference to the applicant's chance of success. Their research shows that advice was taken from 'non-legal audiences' (for example, from councillors, Members of Parliament, doctors, family, friends, project workers – Figure 8.1, Level G), and this was much more likely to be accessed than legal advice. Community advice agencies like GYROS were not recorded in their dataset.[78]

The legal anthropological literature also contributes significant analysis of legal consciousness and the journey of individuals through the court system. Therefore, its focus is higher up the pyramid than where our data is situated. This 'critical legal consciousness' research still puts the law in the foreground – the importance of the law is presumed; it is front and centre.[79] This distinguishes legal consciousness literature from what we see in our data, where law is at most in the background and rarely formally discussed. Some legal consciousness scholars recognize this. For example, Hertogh argues that many are 'turning away from the law', that the law is becoming more irrelevant to people's everyday lives. He says the more pertinent question (which relates to what he calls 'secular legal consciousness' research) is 'if and how law matters in everyday life'.[80]

Similarly, in our data, it is often not about how individuals engage, define or use the law; rather, it is about their awareness that they have a problem which needs resolving. There is no narrative of 'rights' or 'law' at all, and

---

[75] Ibid, 80.
[76] Merry (1990), n 54.
[77] Cowan et al (2003), n 71.
[78] Ibid, 13.
[79] A. Güdük and E. Desmet, 'Legal consciousness and migration: towards a research agenda' (2022) 18 *International Journal of Law in Context* 213, 220.
[80] M. Hertogh, *Nobody's Law: Legal Consciousness and Legal Alienation in Everyday Life* (London: Palgrave Macmillan, 2018), 12.

the advisers think the same way. The help GYROS offers is practical, urgent and necessary. Neither clients nor advisers wish to initiate a formal pathway to justice, with the often slow and onerous steps that might entail. In other words, there is a divide between, on the one hand, those using and working in the upper levels of the pyramid (and those describing their work) and, on the other, those in the lower levels of the pyramid.

3.2 Community-based anthropology

A further strand of research, located at the very base of the pyramid, has also emerged, largely led by anthropologists. Moving away from traditional legal institutions and pathways, this strand focuses on the role of community advice and community brokers. Traditionally this anthropological lens has not been applied in the UK;[81] but the current UK perspective has seen scholars extending beyond study of the advice sector to look at the role of community-based advisers.[82] Parallels have been drawn between the role filled by community-based advisers and those who engage with the 'street-level bureaucrats' who act as gatekeepers to, for example, welfare provision and exercise their discretion at a street level interpreting, implementing and navigating national policy each day.[83]

Forbess and James consider the work of 'the givers of advice'.[84] They discuss 'community brokers', who translate and navigate difficult and sometimes impossible bureaucracy[85] and 'a labyrinthine multiplicity of different agencies',[86] highlighting the complexity of the general advice landscape. They note that the advisers take on a logical translation role to reshape stories to fit within the 'rule-orientated' legal format described by Conley and O'Barr,[87] 'conveying human expectations into legal context'.[88] These acts of translation are multilateral and may be broader than translations of individual issues into legal frameworks, potentially reaching wider audiences

---

[81] D. James and I. Koch, 'Economies of advice' in M. Aldenderfer (ed) *Oxford Research Encyclopedia of Anthropology* (Oxford: Oxford University Press, 2020), 1–20.

[82] Forbess and James (2014), n 36, 73.

[83] Lipsky (1980), n 33.

[84] Forbess and James (2014), n 36, 73.

[85] For more see: J. Lindquist, 'The elementary school teacher, the thug and his grandmother: informal brokers and transnational migration from Indonesia' (2012) 85 *Pacific Affairs*, 88.

[86] Forbess and James (2014), n 36, 75.

[87] Conley and O'Barr, n 65.

[88] Forbess and James (2014), n 36, 83.

and highlighting gaps to effect public and social policy change.[89] These community brokers empower individuals to navigate complex bureaucracies, sometimes advocating on their behalf.

There are parallels with our data: GYROS advisers take on the role of community broker for their clients, navigating and translating clients' situations through the administrative, and sometimes legal, frameworks. However, GYROS' role also goes beyond just that of broker. As we have seen with Irina and Sofia, and for many other clients discussed in this book, GYROS wears a number of hats: broker, case worker, support worker, advocate, translator, and emergency service provider of food and shelter. Frequently, GYROS seeks an expedient resolution to a problem, a solution that circumvents the administrative, or legal, framework, so its approach is more multifaceted, hands-on and, crucially, not confined to the legal field.

4. Socio-legal studies

The field of socio-legal studies is broad and might be 'defined as a way of seeing, of recognizing the mutually constitutive relationship between law and society. That relationship is open to endless interpretation because law and society are both constantly changing'.[90] This book fits under this broad heading. However, a lot of socio-legal studies research (in the context of the everyday) looks at the prevalence of justiciable issues and people's access to justice pathways and their legal needs. With its significant survey-based approach, this strand of research builds an empirical foundation of demonstrated legal need and access to formal/developed legal pathways for ordinary people. The research focuses on legal problems and people's advice-seeking behaviours in response to these problems. It asks: do people access formal legal pathways for their legal problems? This research identifies a relatively high incidence of justiciable problems within the general population, which is more pronounced among certain sociodemographic groups.[91] It also shows that there is evidence that certain problems cluster together, or cascade with a domino-like effect, one problem directly leading to another. As we have discussed (Section B.1.3), this problem clustering/cascading is reflected in our data.

While this legal needs research demonstrates the high prevalence of justiciable events in people's everyday lives, studies show that most people

---

[89] M. McDermott, 'Acts of translation: UK advice agencies and the creation of matters-of-public-concern' (2013) 33(2) *Critical Social Policy* 218, 232.

[90] N. Creutzfeldt, M. Mason and K. McConnachie (eds), *Routledge Handbook of Socio-Legal Theory and Methods* (Abingdon: Routledge, 2019), 4.

[91] Genn (1999) n 1, 1; Pleasence and Balmer (2012), n 26.

do not, in fact, frame their problems as 'legal issues',[92] seeing them instead primarily as social issues, as 'bad luck/part of life', 'part of God's plan' or private or family matters.[93] So here we see something of the ubiquity of law, as well as the (lack of) legal consciousness of those largely unaware of its role in their everyday. If people do not categorize their problems as 'legal', they are less likely to seek legal advice.[94] Consequently, according to Sandefur, 'problems that look legal to lawyers do not seem particularly legal to people who experience them'.[95] However, people can, without the help of lawyers, find out their rights and solve their problems in ways that are consistent with the law without explicitly mobilizing its more formal structures.[96] Rhode et al recognize that just because a problem has not been solved legally does not mean it has not been solved.[97] This is consistent with our data.

However, much of this socio–legal studies research does not grapple with what people do about those problems and *how* they are resolved, outside of formal legal advice pathways, law centres or Citizens Advice. Genn's approach is more far-reaching[98] in describing the different levels of engagement with the law for those with justiciable problems,[99] defined 'as a matter experienced by a respondent which raised legal issues, whether or not recognized by the respondent as being "legal" and whether or not any action taken by the respondent to deal with the event involved the use of any part of the civil justice system'.[100] As we have noted, she talks of the 'lumpers' (no advice, no contact, no action), who made up 5 per cent in her study, but also the 'self-helpers' (problems handled without any advice), who made up 35 per cent, and those who obtained advice about resolving their problem, who made up 60 per cent.[101] Moreover, 24 per cent went to see a solicitor (who, in one fifth of these cases, might have been a family member or friend), 21 per cent went to Citizens Advice and only 2 per cent went to 'Other advice agency'.[102] However, as we have shown, in Great Yarmouth where there is so little free legal advice, the role of 'Other advice agency' is crucial.

---

92 Sandefur (2016), n 25, 459.

93 Ibid, 449.

94 Ibid; see also Genn (1999), n 1, 141.

95 Sandefur (2016), n 25, 449.

96 Ibid, 455.

97 D. Rhode, K. Eaton and A. Porto, 'Access to justice through limited legal assistance' (2018) 16 *Northwestern Journal of Human Rights* 1, 3.

98 H. Genn (1999), n 1, Chapter 3. Across the landscape of the literature, various terminology is used – 'justiciable problems', 'legal problems', 'justiciable events', 'legal needs' and 'unmet legal needs' to name but a few.

99 See also Pleasence et al (2015), n 23.

100 Genn (1999), n 1, 12.

101 Ibid, 68.

102 Ibid, 83.

From our data, we suggest that two further facets arise which are not so far captured in the literature. First, there is the question of a person's *problem* consciousness, as opposed to *legal* consciousness. That is, clients often recognize they have difficulties needing resolution. Second, there is the question of the different type of frontline agencies and what they offer. Some are focused on providing legal advice (law centres and advice clinics) or more legally orientated advice (such Citizens Advice, where all advice is based on a national database with online texts which have been written with the benefit of legal advice and are, in the view of one of our interviewees, "much more focused on supporting English and British nationals"[103] (in Figure 8.1, levels D and E)). Others go to services, like GYROS (Level F), which offer problem resolution against a background knowledge of some law or 'rules' – for example, the requirement to have pre-settled or settled status prior to claiming certain benefits.

As Cowan and Halliday conclude:

> 'although the role of lawyers as an audience has traditionally been a major concern of socio-legal studies in relation to the emergence and management of disputes, there is much to be gained, we suggest, in systematically enquiring into the role played by family, friends, fellow applicants and so on, despite the difficulty of the task'.[104]

We agree and we would add to this list frontline advice organizations. The literature does not so far capture the work done by charities such as GYROS: the extensive advice being given which is not formally described as legal advice but which is underpinned by a familiarity with the law, and the work of engaging with the client that extends beyond the specific (legal) issue, seeking to address clustered problems with which the client has presented as well as pre-empting future problems. We have tried to capture this broad, holistic engagement using the term 'pragmatic law'.

D. Pragmatic law

1. The 'how' of pragmatic law

Those who come to GYROS know they have a problem. Few recognize their problem as a legal problem; rather, like Irina, they attend GYROS with a carrier bag of paperwork, or they seek help to complete a document or write a letter to their employer, or help with a front door to their home that cannot be locked.

---

[103] Interview with council worker (online, October 2021).
[104] Cowan and S. Halliday with C. Hunter, P. Maginn and L. Naylor, (2003), n 71, 210.

GYROS advisers also see their clients as having problems which need resolution. A member of the GYROS team identified three types of client: "those at crisis point, those who are planners (just a few) and then those who have used us before and come back when something else comes in. We are a trusted source of information to our clients so they will come in even just to check something with us."[105] GYROS also recognize the conceptual murkiness of what they do, although they would not describe it in these terms. In a focus group with the advisers in March 2021, the following exchange occurred:

Researcher: Do you think you give legal advice?
Adviser 1:   No, I don't think we give legal advice. We inform and we signpost.
Adviser 2:   We can be perceived as [giving] legal advice and then there is an anxiety in trying to find the best advice. Do I have enough knowledge and training? Very likely people have nowhere else to go.

However, the most senior adviser (and the most highly trained) said:

Adviser 3:   I disagree. I think, yes, we give low-level legal advice. Certainly, at the beginning of advice. Housing law, employment law – when we give advice on these issues, they all contain various rules and reg[ulation]s and law, and we interpret it and present to client. That's legal advice – at least, I think!'[106]

So there is an awareness of the law when asked directly about it, but in the day-to-day work of the advisers, there is little reference to it. Out of the 6,856 case notes we analysed, a search for the word 'court' returned just 163 responses (2 per cent); a search for 'law', 105 responses (1.5 per cent); and a search for 'tribunals', just 22 responses. There was no reference to ADR[107] as such in the dataset, but there were three references to 'mediation' (one concerning a child injured at school, the other two concerning child custody issues) and one reference to 'early conciliation', mandatory prior to bringing an employment tribunal case. There were 90 references to 'FLA'

---

[105] GYROS staff focus group, Great Yarmouth (March 2021).
[106] Ibid.
[107] For more on ADR, see: H. Genn, 'What is civil justice for? Reform, ADR, and access to justice' (2012) 24 *Yale Journal of Law and the Humanities* 397; H. Genn, 'Tribunals and informal justice' in S. Cann (ed) *Administrative Law* (Routledge, 2017).

(free legal advice), the shorthand for the services provided by each of the local law centres,[108] and the term 'solicitor' came up 89 times. We would therefore argue – and the discussions of GYROS' approach in previous chapters show – that the advisers do not have 'legal' consciousness, but rather 'problem consciousness'.

If the advisers' focus is generally on resolving the problems, then they are less likely to refer clients on to lawyers. Conversely, as Pleasence et al note, when a problem is characterized as 'legal', there is a significant increase in the likelihood that it will go to a lawyer.[109] So there appears to be a strong alignment at GYROS between the client's problem consciousness and GYROS' pragmatic problem resolution. The advisers act to resolve situations, with little express reference to the law. It is plain in the case notes that law percolates into the arena, but it is rarely at the forefront of the advice given. 'Law' is often seen as a set of rules which have to be complied with or navigated around – for example, the requirement to have pre-settled or settled status to be able to work, claim benefits and rent accommodation; the rules around eviction; and the requirement to update the Universal Credit journal.

Our description of the approach adopted by GYROS advisers as 'pragmatic law' is adapted from Boltanski's term 'pragmatic sociology'.[110] Pragmatic sociology seeks to explore when things go wrong for people in their everyday lives and the 'values of worth' that are used to justify or explain actions. From a theoretical perspective, the focus of pragmatic sociology is on understanding the dynamics of action and how actors operate within a dispute situation. Like Boltanski, we are interested in how actors operate within a dispute situation in which law features but is largely unacknowledged. Specifically, we are concerned with the (legal) problems facing GYROS' clients and how they, with GYROS' help and support, interact or engage with the law and respond to those problems outside the traditional pathways of justice. It is pragmatism against the background of the law.

Clearly, the 'layer' that is pragmatic law (Level F in Figure 8.1), sitting as it does, just below the legal advice centres and below the level of the lower courts, will inevitably bump into those levels higher up at times. That interaction with the next level 'up' is particularly apparent in the housing advice that GYROS gives and in immigration advice. In those interactions, it is apparent that advisers need, and use, greater legal knowledge to navigate

[108] However, this number is likely to be slightly higher than this, as during 2015 the GYROS office hosted the free legal advice service in Great Yarmouth and direct referrals increased accordingly at that time.
[109] Pleasence and Balmer (2012), n 26.
[110] L. Boltanski, *De la critique: Précis de sociologie de l'émancipation* (Paris: Gallimard, 2009).

issues of possession and homelessness. However, the relative rarity of those 'legal' interactions emphasizes the importance of the lower 'pragmatic law' level of the pyramid (Level F).

2. The risks of a pragmatic approach to law

But is it as simple as that? Does the lack of legal consciousness on the part of client and adviser mean that a piece of the jigsaw is missing? Does the focus on problem resolution come with risks? When clients come to GYROS with a problem about, for example, not being able to pay the rent, GYROS helps with the resolution of this specific issue. Yet, as we saw in chapters 2 and 5, the quality of much of the housing lived in by migrant workers is low and landlords often fail in their statutory duties towards their tenants. A lawyer would (and should?) focus on this issue. Likewise, as we saw in Chapter 4 on employment, GYROS deals with the problems following job losses, but not the potential underlying legal issues as to why the job was lost in the first place, or it helps a client change jobs but not challenge the underlying bullying, discrimination and harassment which led the client to move. Indeed, GYROS' clients do not complain to GYROS about these issues: they came up only rarely as a drop-in enquiry matter. However, they were frequently mentioned in focus group discussions.[111] So it may be that by focusing on the immediate problem of, for example, not being able to pay the rent or wanting to find another job, the systemic (legal) issue, such as failure by landlords to fulfil their statutory obligations or failure by employers to protect workers from race discrimination, is not addressed. This was recognized implicitly by one of the GYROS staff:

> 'But it's the work we do, the range of work. It's like in the beginning, when I came here, I have this idealistic idea that we can help people. That we're, like, little superheroes. And sometimes it's really rewarding. But then little by little you see that sometimes because of the system you can't help. It's really frustrating. Sometimes it's rewarding, but many times it's very frustrating.'[112]

There are further risks of a pragmatic approach to law, such as ensuring the quality of advice and the accountability of the advisers and the board of trustees. Oversight by the Charity Commission is too remote from the

---

[111] See, for example, C. Barnard and F. Costello, 'Working in a UK poultry factory: faster, faster, faster' (2021) UK in a Changing Europe, available at: https://ukandeu.ac.uk/work ing-in-a-uk-poultry-factory-faster-faster-faster/, accessed 16 March 2023.

[112] GYROS staff focus group (Great Yarmouth, November 2021).

day-to-day reality of GYROS; yet the onerous bureaucracy entailed by regulation through the Solicitors Regulation Authority would be overkill. As mentioned in Chapter 2, GYROS' work is audited either annually or biannually by their various accrediting bodies – the OISC, Matrix and the Financial Conduct Authority. The OISC, for example, says: 'The OISC aims to audit all newly regulated organisations within 12 months of approval and will decide when further audits are required.'[113] This still raises the question of whether this type of regulation is sufficient to ensure the clients and their advisers are protected.

3. The need to identify the role of organisations offering pragmatic law

Until (if) there is comprehensive and affordable (legal) advice available to all who need it, organizations like GYROS play an important role in (legal) provision.[114] We would argue that by identifying this problem-resolution-led approach and naming it (pragmatic law), a light can be shone on an underdiscussed part of the (legal) landscape. This enables further work to be done to analyse the strengths and weakness of the pragmatic law approach, to consider what constitutes success, to think about safeguards that can be put in place and how the different levels of the pyramid could work together more cooperatively so that, in an ideal world, key frontline advisers can refer up to law centres when they need to. However, the reality is that each organisation - grassroot and law centre - is already working at capacity, with frequent issues around continued funding plaguing both (and sometimes they compete with each other for funding). This currently makes referrals difficult.

We also need to learn from what the advice organizations are seeing on the frontline. They are the canaries in the coalmine. Better connectivity between frontline advice organizations across the country, working in conjunction with the relevant statutory bodies, such as the Independent Monitoring Authority, would mean that problems facing those with little effective voice, such as the day-to-day operation of the EUSS, can be highlighted at an earlier stage and, hopefully, addressed.

---

[113] Office of the Immigration Services Commissioner, 'Regulations that immigration officers must follow' (24 May 2022) *Gov.uk*, available at: www.gov.uk/government/publicati ons/regulations-that-immigration-advisers-must-follow--2/regulations-that-immigrat ion-advisers-must-follow, accessed 22 November 2023.

[114] The role of early advice is also key in helping the pyramid function properly, a point reinforced by the Ministry of Justice during their Early Legal Advice Pilot in Manchester and Middleborough (see n 40), although take up at the time had been low; see M. Fouzder, 'News focus: early advice pilot was a missed opportunity', *The Law Society Gazette*, available at: www.lawgazette.co.uk/news-focus/news-focus-early-advice-pilot-was-a-missed-oppo rtunity/5116528.article, accessed 22 November 2023.

4. Role of pragmatic law within the legal landscape

What role, then, does GYROS play within the legal landscape? We have shown the pragmatic approach GYROS takes to (legal) problem resolution. However, the footprint of the law lies under the work GYROS does. It is rarely directly acknowledged, except in relation to immigration law advice, where 'the law' comes to the fore, and, to a lesser extent, to housing matters. A legally centred approach, adopted by a lawyer, would be to ask: What is the legal issue at root and what are the remedies available to set things right legally, (perhaps taking action about other legal issues, such as discrimination and harassment)? A problem-centred approach, as that adopted by GYROS, would ask: What is the problem and how can it be resolved? The focus is on identifying the problems or unpicking the (carrier bag full of) problems, prioritizing them and then trying to resolve them.

GYROS' approach is also broader: its advisers provide holistic help to their clients, extending well beyond problem resolution and into English language support; accompanying clients to the GP, to the hospital, to the housing office, to the Job Centre, to a support group; attending meetings at a school; and even reading client's post. This 'hand-holding' support to access other services and navigate day-to-day life is very different from traditional legal advice services and specializations. That holistic support enables GYROS to work at (albeit on an individual level) both prevention and cure.

We recognize that there are many other frontline advice agencies who work in a similar way to GYROS. These agencies often seek to work within communities where there are linguistic, cultural and biographical similarities between advisers and clients. Clients usually have limited English language skills and cannot interact with other mainstream providers, even were such providers available. As with other agencies, this makes GYROS' clients particularly marginalized. The fact that there are biographical similarities between the clients and advisers helps to establish trust, empathy, insight and understanding. GYROS workers have worked in the same factories as their clients; some have the same landlords; all live in the Town itself and are visible members of their local community, with children in the same schools and using the same Portuguese and Lithuanian supermarkets. One former GYROS worker, who became an ESOL (English as Second or Other Language) teacher then a primary school teacher, has come back to GYROS as a trustee of the organization. She has lived in the UK for 15 years now, her children have grown up in the UK and Great Yarmouth is home; she looks to help others facing the same migration journey.

So pragmatic law sits within the legal landscape as a resolution-focused holistic approach, engaging with communities who are often described as 'hard to reach'. It is also free. In legal advice terms, GYROS is one of only two free advice organizations in Norfolk that have staff qualified to OISC Level 2,[115] and the only one in Suffolk. For GYROS, this Level 2 OISC qualification is held by two workers, working across the two counties. Without them, the advice desert would be even more barren. Even if solicitors were available, the majority of clients would not be able to afford them and so their problems would not be resolved, and future issues would not be prevented.

E. Conclusion

Great Yarmouth has always been a town of migration. For the last 25 years, GYROS has been a constant source of support for migrants, working in the Town to assist newcomers. While nationalities change over time, the issues do not: a striking feature of the data was that the experiences of those who arrived in and around 2004 were often very similar to those arriving in 2020. Almost 20 years on, conditions for migrant workers have not improved, despite the development of employment law, health and safety regulation and housing law in that period. The question now for EU migrant workers is whether Brexit and the ending of free movement will mean that employers will be forced to improve conditions. The formation of an office such as a pay and work rights ombudsman[116] or a migrant commissioner, as proposed by Wendy Williams in the independent review of Windrush,[117] might be helpful in addressing some of these issues. Better enforcement by statutory bodies such as the Health and Safety Executive and local authorities would also help. This all serves to remind us that passing laws is, in fact, the easier part; ensuring compliance on an ongoing basis is much more challenging. Failure by these bodies to enforce the law leaves organizations like GYROS to pick up the pieces, addressing the immediate needs of their clients but with no ability to address the fundamental problems.

In Chapter 1, we said that we have pitched our tents on the side streets of Great Yarmouth – rather than on the steps of the Supreme Court, like many law academics do[118] – to examine everyday law as experienced by those who are marginalized – in this case, EU migrant workers. Through a case study of one House, one Street and one Town, we have described problems which we imagine are also common in other deprived areas across the UK. We have shown how GYROS helps its clients address those problems. Further research is needed to examine the benefits – and risks – of pragmatic

---

[115] The other was the Law Centre.
[116] Barnard et al (2018), n 3.
[117] W. Williams, *Windrush Lessons Learned Review* (HMSO, 2020), available at: https://assets.publishing.service.gov.uk/media/5e74984fd3bf7f4684279faa/6.5577_HO_Windrush_Lessons_Learned_Review_WEB_v2.pdf, accessed 22 November 2023.
[118] Engel (2009), n 57.

problem resolution offered by non-legally trained advice workers. More robust data collection and evaluation is needed so that we can build up a more complete picture of legal needs in the UK, reaching out to those who never access any legal advice and/or are unable to participate in traditional legal needs surveys to gain a fuller, thicker understanding of 'everyday law'. For now, those who access GYROS services get help and support in a way that many other marginalized groups do not. It may not be perfect, but it is considerably better than the alternative.

Postscript

Since the fieldwork of this book was undertaken, the landlord has died and the House of our research has been closed down; all eight tenants have had to move elsewhere. It now appears Frank may never have owned the House. The tenants' fears that something would happen to the landlord and they would have to leave were, therefore, realized. The sudden closure of the HMO is another example of how quickly lives can unravel and the speed at which migrant workers must adapt. Lina told us that she and Adomas have moved somewhere new but might need to move again due to the lack of proper insulation in the House and the rising cost of heating. Rasa (and her cat) was given 28 days to leave the House when the new landlord took over the property, despite the fact she had lived in the House for over ten years and had invested time and money in improving the property. The House is now up for sale.

The invasion of Ukraine by Russia in February 2022 has changed the face of migration support in the Town. Twenty-five hosts – particularly from the outer villages – have opened their homes to Ukrainian refugees via the Homes for Ukraine Scheme, housing 67 Ukrainians.[1] Bespoke funding was made available by central government to Great Yarmouth Borough Council to offer support. A Ukrainian support drop-in started up, running on Mondays in the Yarmouth Central Library, with bespoke ESOL (English as Second or Other Language) courses offered to Ukrainians. Ukrainian refugees were entitled to claim benefits and to work, and they lived in (hosted) accommodation which had been quality checked by the local council for health and safety purposes. Hosts were also Disclosure and Barring Service checked. Out of this funding, the council awarded GYROS money to employ a part-time worker who speaks Ukrainian who

---

[1]   Data from GYROS (obtained February 2023). See also: F Costello and C Barnard, 'Accommodation provision for migrant communities, asylum seekers and refugees: messy and chaotic', (07 July 2023), UKICE Blog Series, available here: https://ukandeu.ac.uk/accommodation-provision-for-migrant-communities-asylum-seekers-and-refugees-messy-and-chaotic/, accessed 08 December 2023.

now provides GYROS' smallest nationality group with the most intense support available.

There was hope at GYROS that the outpouring of generous support for Ukrainians might be extended to other groups and that maybe the tide was turning on Theresa May's 'hostile environment' for asylum seekers in the UK. However, the recent arrival of more asylum seekers in the Town has dashed these hopes. Reminiscent of the circumstances in which GYROS was first founded, the charity was called upon to support asylum seekers being placed in the Town centre in late 2022. Serco, holding a Home Office contract, had paid a hotel in the Town centre to accommodate about 70 asylum seekers, all single men from various countries (15 different nationalities), with the largest groups coming from (in order) Afghanistan, Iran and Syria. It is the first time in more than 20 years that Great Yarmouth has been used to accommodate asylum seekers. GYROS first became aware of the accommodation contract when they received a phone call from the hotel manager asking if it could provide any winter coats for the new residents, unprepared for the unforgiving cold wind from the North Sea. Unlike with the Ukrainian nationals, Great Yarmouth Borough Council did not receive any additional funding to support these newcomers. In fact, the council proactively stopped other hotels in the Town centre from being used for similar purposes, successfully seeking an injunction against further accommodation being used to house asylum seekers in 'GY6 planning policy area', a designated tourist area where change of use from hotel to hostel is not allowed under town planning policy.[2] The GY6 area contains 59 other hotels, including a further two which had already been earmarked for use by Serco. At the time of writing (October 2023), the original 70 asylum seekers placed in the first hotel are still in Great Yarmouth and accessing GYROS for help. It is believed more hotels, outside the GY6 area, could be used in the future. This group, unlike the Ukrainians, cannot work and need help to navigate complex systems in the UK. They are also accessing support from GYROS, including attending ESOL classes via GYROS at the library.

So, the face of the Town has changed significantly since we began our fieldwork, as has the face of migration to the Town. Nevertheless, EU migrant workers, specifically the Portuguese and now Romanian communities, are still the largest migrant communities in the Town, and they will continue to seek help from GYROS and we will continue following their progress.

---

[2] *Great Yarmouth Borough Council v Al-Abdin & Ors* [2022] EWHC 3476 (KB).

APPENDIX I

Methodology

1. Data collection and its limits

1.1 Data collection

We have used a 'mixed methods-grounded theory'[1] approach for collecting and analysing our data. The *mixed methods* approach (itself a pragmatic approach[2]) helped us to think about and understand our first two research questions (the experience of EU migrant workers and what happens when things go wrong). The (adaptive) *grounded theory* approach helped us identify the theory emerging from the data, allowing us to develop a fresh framework to help answer our third research question (What do these responses tell us about how (legal) problems are addressed and resolved on the frontline?). This was important because, as explained in Chapter 1, none of the existing theories fitted well with what we were seeing in the data.

The definition of mixed methods is both 'contested and evolving',[3] but 'at its core, mixed methods research combines both qualitative and quantitative research methods to understand a research problem'.[4] Adaptive grounded theory recognizes the role of prior theories, but focuses on the data and utilizes extensive data sources, and returns regularly to the data, so that a theory might be constructed from it. Combining mixed methods and grounded theory provides a broad research base; they are 'particularly

---

[1] J.W. Creswell and V.L. Plano Clark, *Designing and Conducting Mixed Methods Research* (3rd edn, Thousand Oaks, CA: Sage, 2018); M.C. Howell Smith, W.A. Babchuk, J. Stevens, A.L Garrett, S.C. Wang and T.C. Guetterman, 'Modelling the use of mixed methods–grounded theory: developing scales for a new measurement model' (2020) 14 *Journal of Mixed Methods Research* 184.

[2] Cresswell and Clark, ibid, 37.

[3] A. Blackham, 'When law and data collide: the methodological challenge of conducting mixed methods research in law' (2022) 49 *Journal of Law and Society* S87, S89.

[4] Ibid, S89.

complementary',[5] enabling us to develop our theoretical framework of 'pragmatic law'.

Our mixed method-grounded theory research methodology has five elements.

First, our research has a quantitative element. We had access to the longitudinal dataset (covering 2015–2020) held by GYROS. Each client's attendance at their service is recorded under a relevant 'enquiry label' on that day; the label indicates the issue they were seeking help with – for instance, housing, employment and health. Because clients can come in for help under the same enquiry label more than once – for example, a person might seek housing support over several years – the client is allocated an individual ID (identification) number. This unique ID number was used by the researchers to identify whether the same client came in for help with more than one issue (other identifying information, such as name and address, were not shared). All enquiries in the dataset are assigned the relevant label, and a unique case note is recorded for each visit. The dataset contains 3,018 unique enquiry labels with 6,856 unique case notes.

Analysis of the GYROS dataset involved several stages. It began with an analysis of the descriptive data, undertaken using Stata. An overview of these quantitative findings is provided in Chapter 1. We then analysed the free text of the client case notes attached to each enquiry label. This qualitative data analysis required reading and analysing the 6,856 client case notes (attached to the different enquiry labels), developing themes and subthemes, and coding them, returning regularly to the original dataset to develop the themes further. These themes and subthemes were also further developed using our fieldwork data. Throughout chapters 2–7, we have brought this data together and we have drawn on the case notes. The language used in the case notes, mostly written by non-native speakers, has only been edited where necessary for clarity.

Analysis of the GYROS dataset was supplemented by material obtained from our attendance at weekly meetings, between March 2020 and May 2021, at which GYROS frontline advisers met to discuss their complex casework (anonymized). Latterly in 2021, some of GYROS' partner organizations also attended these online meetings to share practice and learning. The researchers attended the meetings each week, recorded field notes and where cases raised issues relevant to our work, followed up individual cases at the next meeting. Anonymized case studies from these meetings were written up and used in a blog series, mainly for UK in a Changing Europe, tracking frontline issues during 2019–2022.[6] We were

---

also able to access some of GYROS' funding reporting, which helped us track its work around the EUSS as well as client feedback (see Chapter 8).

Second, we undertook an ethnographic study, which involved living in an HMO just off St Peter's Road in Great Yarmouth for eight weeks (see Chapter 2). The eight residents of the HMO (all Lithuanian and Latvian nationals) shared their stories and experiences of living and working in the Town. We also interviewed the residents using structured interview guides, asking about their experiences of living and working in the UK. In addition, we interviewed the landlord of the House and a former tenant who had lived in the House for ten years (a total of ten people interviewed).

Third, we conducted focus groups with GYROS staff (a total of ten staff participated in four focus groups) and with GYROS clients (seven focus groups) as well as eight in-depth interviews with frontline staff, the strategic director and chair of the board of trustees (see Appendix II). The focus groups took place throughout the life of the project. To allow us to develop and compare some of the themes emerging in the early stages of our analysis, some focus groups were undertaken alongside the initial analysis of the GYROS dataset. This also allowed us to track in real time the implementation of the EUSS and how GYROS' clients (and other EU nationals) managed to engage with it (see Chapter 3). All the focus groups with GYROS clients were multilingual, with translation provided by GYROS staff.

To provide us with further information and some contrast, we also conducted an online survey, distributed through our networks, which received 181 responses. Responses were predominantly from EU14 national professionals, who interacted with our research in English. We also conducted some follow-up telephone interviews.[7]

We accessed publicly available data for comparison and to contextualize what we were seeing and hearing from the frontline. This included the Home Office EUSS statistics release, a quarterly data release throughout the life of the EUSS. To complement the data that was publicly available, we also made various freedom of information requests to the Home Office (about the EUSS, Chapter 3), to local authorities (for example, concerning housing and homelessness support for EU nationals (Chapter 5), and to regional hospitals (about charging EU nationals, Chapter 7).

We undertook further interviews with relevant professionals and community members in the Town. Interviews were recorded and transcribed (20) or detailed notes were taken (8); a full list of the 28 interviews can

---

[7]   The full methodology is provided in C. Barnard, S. Fraser Butlin and F. Costello, 'The changing status of European Union nationals in the United Kingdom following Brexit: the lived experience of the European Union Settlement Scheme' (2022) 31 *Social and Legal Studies* 365, 367.

be found in the Appendix. We also undertook seven video interviews with GYROS clients accessing EUSS support to provide 'snapshots' of conversations with those attending the drop-ins.

Fourth, we attended possession hearings at Norwich County Court across two days and spoke with the district judge, the court clerk and representatives from Shelter,[8] who provided legal housing advice on those days (see Chapter 5). We also spoke to other members of the local judiciary. In addition, we considered the cases that had been brought before an employment tribunal from 1 April 2019 to 1 April 2022 and identified those cases that expressly referred to the claimant as being an EU8 or EU2 migrant worker, or requiring the assistance of a language interpreter (see Chapter 4). We used this information at national level to compare with the data we were seeing in Great Yarmouth.

Fifth, because our fieldwork coincided with the COVID-19 pandemic in 2020, health – already identified as an important enquiry label in our analysis – became an especially key issue. To examine this topic, we built on survey data GYROS had collected in 2015[9] by adapting and re-running the survey in 2022 with new questions on COVID-19. We then analysed the data with the help of a statistician from the Department of Public Health and Primary Care at the University of Cambridge. This research is discussed in Chapter 7. During the national lockdown, we recorded eight telephone 'COVID-19 conversations' in which GYROS staff phoned clients and spoke to them about their experiences in the pandemic (using a small set of questions developed by the research team). These conversations were multilingual, and GYROS staff made notes in English which were then shared with the researchers (see Appendix II for details).

We chose this five-pronged mixed methods approach because it 'provides multiple ways to address a research problem'[10] and because weaknesses of one approach (that is, relying purely on qualitative or quantitative data) could be addressed by the other. In our case, having one researcher living in an HMO with eight other EU national residents provided us with a rich and meaningful understanding of their lives, albeit not, of course, a representative account of the lives of all EU migrants living in Great Yarmouth. We were already conscious of the risk of homogenizing the experiences of citizens of

---

8   For more, see 'Norfolk – Norwich', *Shelter*, available at: https://england.shelter.org.uk/get_help/local_services/norwich, accessed 9 January 2023.

9   L. Humphries, King's Lynn Areas Resettlement Support and Mobile Europeans Taking Action, *Migrant Workers Accessing Healthcare in Norfolk* (Healthwatch Norfolk and Community Relations and Equality Board, 2015), available at: https://healthwatchnorfolk.co.uk/wp-content/uploads/2015/11/15-07-Migrant-Workers-Accessing-Healthcare-in-Norfolk.pdf, accessed 22 November 2023.

10   Creswell and Clark (2018), n 1, 2.

27 different member states with different languages, cultures, histories and circumstances. However, by looking at both the results of this immersive research and our analysis of the GYROS database, we were able to assess whether the conditions of the individuals in the HMO could be generalized within our larger dataset. The mixed methods approach addressed Creswell and Clark's concern that 'quantitative research is weak in understanding the context or setting in which people live'.[11]

Our ethnographic work and qualitative interviews also allowed us to capture the minutiae of people's everyday lives: the 50p tin on the dryer in the HMO for residents to contribute towards the cost of each wash; the way Ana slumped over the table to mime the exhaustion felt at the end of the day working in a factory; how workers' hands became swollen from the cold conditions in the factories. These all provide nuance, depth and additional data points to supplement the quantitative data, telling us, for instance, how many people accessed help for health issues due to work-related injuries or because they were in debt or were unable to pay their utility bills. In this way, we used the qualitative data to triangulate,[12] complement and develop the themes already drawn out from the quantitative data.

By integrating adaptive grounded theory alongside the mixed methods approach, we yielded 'a potentially powerful hybrid approach combining salient elements of each'.[13] We continually returned to the data, particularly the qualitative case notes in the dataset, to examine trends and themes emerging from our fieldwork in the Town. Consequently, while the initial phase was sequential – dataset then fieldwork – later they became simultaneous as we built up, developed and interrogated themes and theory as we moved through time, while remaining led by, and grounded in, the data itself.

1.2 Limitations of the data

In the first stage of our methodology, we analysed secondary data obtained from GYROS. We did not capture the data ourselves. There are different definitions of secondary data analysis[14] but, following Glaser, it involves 'the study of specific problems through analysis of existing data which were originally collected for another purpose'.[15] There are limitations to

---

[11] Ibid, 12.

[12] Blackham (2022), n 3 at S90.

[13] Ibid.

[14] E. Smith, 'Pitfalls and promises: the use of secondary data analysis in educational research' (2008) 56 *British Journal of Educational Studies* 323.

[15] B.G. Glaser, 'Retreading research materials: the use of secondary analysis by the independent researcher' (1963) 6 *The American Behavioural Scientist* 11, 11.

this data analysis. First, in examining the (legal) problems experienced by migrant communities in the East of England, the cases we analysed in the dataset concern, by definition, those who have sought help from GYROS. Cognizant of this limitation, in focus groups we asked where those who did not seek help from GYROS went for help (Chapter 8). We were also able to assess 'feedback' data captured from GYROS asking clients how confident they were that they could manage without GYROS' help (on a scale of 1–10) and where they would access help if GYROS did not exist. GYROS uses this data to develop its services and provide evidence of value to funders and others. These questions were introduced by GYROS in late 2019.

The second limitation is that the case notes were written by GYROS advisers after they had seen a client or during their appointment with them. Not only did each adviser have their own style of writing, but also they wrote in English, which may have been their second or third language. Their level of experience as advisers ranged from new trainees to Level 2 Office of the Immigration Services Commissioner (OISC) immigration advisers. They vary too in their length of service with GYROS, ranging from less than one year to over ten years. Case notes undergo supervision and auditing by the adviser's line manager for general advice, or by their subject lead for accredited advice (the OISC or the Financial Conduct Authority). In addition, annual or biannual audits of case work are undertaken by accrediting bodies such as the OISC (for immigration advice) or Matrix (for advice work). In this way, despite the number of individuals generating case notes, checks and balances are in place to maintain the standard of case notes recorded. But, as with Mason et al's work on childcare proceedings, which found that 'court files rarely include accounts of the discussions between the parties during which agreements may be reached about directions, evidence or timetables etc',[16] the case notes in our research are written by one party to the advice work, namely the adviser.

A third limitation of the data relates to the context of our ethnographic work. Where a researcher is living in a house with research participants and observing them, this might lead to what is called the Hawthorne effect, meaning 'people modify their behaviour when they are being watched'.[17] Due to the length of time one researcher was living in the HMO (over

---

[16] J.M. Masson, J.F. Pearce and K.F. Bader, *Care Profiling Study* Ministry of Justice Research Series 4/08 (Ministry of Justice and Department of Children, Schools and Families, 2008), 4.

[17] D. Oswald, F. Sherratt and S. Smith, 'Handling the Hawthorne effect: the challenges surrounding a participant observer' (2014) 1 *Review of Social Studies* 53. M. Chiesa and S. Hobbs, 'Making sense of social research: how useful is the Hawthorne effect?' (2008) 38 *European Journal of Social Psychology* 67, 67.

two months) and the everyday familiarity and camaraderie built up by the researcher with the other residents in the House, it was felt that any initial Hawthorne effect would diminish over time. Equally, as Oswald et al say, in the context of their workplace observations, it is important that the researcher becomes 'successfully immersed in the social setting by gaining trust and making workers feel relaxed and unthreatened'.[18] The researcher undertook additional activities with residents, such as going out for meals, visiting local cafes, jogging along the seafront and attending community events. This helped to build up trust and diminish, if not remove, the Hawthorne effect.

That said, as further explained in Chapter 2, the HMO did not lend itself naturally to be a location in which ethnographic work could be easily undertaken. The structure and layout of the House meant there were only three communal areas – the front hall (used by all), the laundry room (shared by all) and the shared bathroom on the ground floor (shared by three residents) – but no communal location where residents could sit down together and chat. Only two of the residents had a separate kitchen area in their rooms; most had a countertop with a kettle, microwave and hotplate running parallel to the bed. This made it more difficult to conduct ethnographic work spontaneously[19] and meant that the researcher had to organize 'meet-ups' such as those described earlier. Spending time doing in-person interviews therefore became important for comprehensive data collection.

2. Data analysis: adaptive grounded theory

While collecting and analysing the data, we sought to extract common themes, and then we returned to our data to test our themes and develop our theory. This approach is typical of grounded theory. There are a number of understandings of grounded theory, ranging from the strict methodology propounded by Glaser to enable the induction or emergence of theory[20] to the flexible guidelines approach of Charmaz, which recognize the

---

[18] Oswald et al (2014), n 17, 53.

[19] A problem also experienced by S. Engle Merry in a low-income housing development in the US. See 'Crossing boundaries: ethnography in the twenty-first century' (2000) 23 *Political and Legal Anthropology Review* 127, 128; she says: 'at the same time I despaired of finding a place to do ethnography. The residents did not spend much time hanging around the neighbourhood.'

[20] B. Glaser and A. Strauss, *The Discovery of Grounded Theory: Strategies for Qualitative Research* (London, Weidenfeld and Nicolson, 1968); B. Glaser, 'Constructivist grounded theory?' (2002) 3 *Forum Qualitative Social Research* 3(3).

constructivist nature of theory that develops from the data.[21] But in all the methods and philosophical underpinnings, grounded theory starts with the data – utilizing extensive data sources – and involves returning regularly to the data. The data is coded, thematized and analysed before embarking on further data collection, coding and analysis, and all the data is returned to regularly. Ultimately, theory emerges (or is constructed) out of the data. Adaptive grounded theory uses prior theories as 'orienting devices' to provide 'a preliminary means of ordering and giving shape to a mass of data' and 'combines the use of extant theory with the development of theory from research findings'.[22] Layder further explains:

> This allows for both the elaboration of the extant theory in relation to research findings as well as the emergence of theory from the conjunction between prior theory (and theoretical models) and data analysis. This wider-ranging stance allows for more flexible, open-ended and inclusive use of resources in the development of theory and cumulative knowledge of the social world.[23]

Following the adaptive grounded theory model, we used existing theory, such as that on legal consciousness and access to justice, to orientate our work. Ultimately, we rejected those theoretical models in favour of our emergent theory of pragmatic law (discussed in Chapters 1 and 8). We have started and finished in the data, drawing the theoretical framework from the data rather than testing an already established hypothesis.

---

[21] K. Charmaz, *Constructing Grounded Theory* (Beverly Hills, CA: Sage Publications, 2014), 16. See also A. Strauss and J. Corbin, *Basics of Qualitative Research: Grounded Theory Procedures and Techniques* (Beverly Hills, CA: Sage Publications, 1990).
[22] D. Layder, *Sociological Practice: Linking Theory and Social Research* (London: Sage, 1998), 24.
[23] Ibid, 24.

Data Collection

Interviews

Interviews with residents of the House, a former resident and the landlord

Interviewee*	Location	Date	Gender	Age group
Edita (1)	Online	3 September 2021	Female	Thirties
Edita (2)	Great Yarmouth	20 September 2021	Female	Thirties
Camilla	Great Yarmouth	17 November 2021	Female	Fifties
Lina	Great Yarmouth	7 September 2021	Female	Thirties
Adomas	Great Yarmouth	17 November 2021	Male	Thirties
Rasa	Great Yarmouth	20 September 2021	Female	Sixties
Vida	Great Yarmouth	27 October 2021	Female	Thirties
Terese	Great Yarmouth	1 October 2021	Female	Fifties
Domantas	Great Yarmouth	30 April 2021	Male	Fifties
Ivo	The House★★		Male	Fifties
Frank	Suffolk	20 September 2021	Male	Seventies

Notes: *Pseudonyms are used for anonymity; ★★This was an informal chat rather than a formal interview.

Interviews (semi-structured) and meetings (unstructured) with professionals and community leaders

Interview	Professional role/ organization	Status/ location of interview	Date of interview/ meeting	Interview	Meeting
1	Advice quality representative	Online	14 December 2021		X

Interview	Professional role/ organization	Status/ location of interview	Date of interview/ meeting	Interview	Meeting
2	Charity Advice worker, Great Yarmouth representative	Online	8 November 2021	X	
3	Church leader	Face to face/Great Yarmouth	13 October 2021	X	
4	Council employee	Online	29 October 2021	X	
5	Former council employee	Online	3 March 2022	X	
6	Law centre debt adviser	Online	8 June 2022	X	
7	Debt agency employee	Face to face/Great Yarmouth	15 September 2021	X	
8	Early Help Employee	Online	19 January 2022		X
9	GP surgery employee	Online	29 October 2021	X	
10	Former recruitment agency employee	Face to face/ Norwich	14 November 2021	X	
11	Former councillor/ magistrate	Face to face/Great Yarmouth	14 October 2021	X	
12	Norfolk library employee	Face to face/Great Yarmouth	23 September 2021	X	
13	Council housing employee (1)	Online	19 November 2021	X	
14	Council housing employee (2)	Face to face/Great Yarmouth	26 October 2021	X	
15	Job Centre employee	Face to face/Great Yarmouth	4 October 2021	X	
16	Local advice worker 1 – self-employed	Face to face/Great Yarmouth	13 November 2021	X	

Interview	Professional role/ organization	Status/ location of interview	Date of interview/ meeting	Interview	Meeting
17	Local advice worker 2 – employee	Face to face/Great Yarmouth	30 October 2021	X	
18	Owner of business on St Peter's Road	Face to face/Great Yarmouth	18 October 2021	X	
19	Local community leader	Face to face/Great Yarmouth	5 October 2021	X	
20	Local hospital	Online	22 September 2021		X
21	Local police officer	Face to face/Great Yarmouth	17 November 2021	X	
22	Local volunteer	Face to face/ Ipswich	10 December 2020	X	
23	Primary school	Face to face/Great Yarmouth	8 February 2022		X
24	Recruitment agency	Online	14 February 2022		X
25	Salvation Army staff member	Face to face/Great Yarmouth	22 September 2021	X	
26	Shelter	Face to face/ Norwich	9 November 2022		X
27	Law Centre	Online	28 March 2022		X
28	The Right to Succeed Project	Online	26 April 2022		X

Note: All interviews were recorded and transcribed; in meetings, notes were taken.

Interviews with GYROS staff

Interviewee code	Status/location of interview	Date
GYROS01AA	Online	3 September 2021
GYROS02AB	Face to face/Great Yarmouth	15 September 2021
GYROS03AC	Face to face/Great Yarmouth	30 September 2021
GYROS04AD	Face to face/Great Yarmouth	17 November 2021

Interviewee code	Status/location of interview	Date
GYROS06AF	Face to face/Great Yarmouth	8 February 2022
GYROS07AG	Face to face/Great Yarmouth	8 February 2022
GYROS08AH	Face to face/Great Yarmouth	2 August 2022
GYROS05AE	Online	24 January 2022

Note: All interviews were recorded and transcribed; in meetings, notes were taken.

Focus groups

Focus groups with GYROS staff

Status/location	Date	Number of participants	Nationality	Gender ratio (men:women)
In person/Great Yarmouth	8 October 2019	7	British, Portuguese, Lithuanian, Latvian	0:7
In person/Great Yarmouth	7 January 2021	5	British, Latvian, Romanian, Portuguese	0:5
Online	10 March 2021	5	British, Latvian, Lithuanian, Romanian, Portuguese	0:5
In person/Great Yarmouth	2 November 2021	5	British, Romanian, Polish, Lithuanian, Moldovan	0:5

Focus groups with EU migrant workers

Date	Number of participants	Nationality	Gender ratio (men:women)
8 October 2019	10	Portuguese, Latvian, Lithuanian, Polish, Bulgarian	3:7
20 November 2019	9	Latvian, Lithuanian, Polish, Bulgarian, Portuguese	2:79
31 January 2020	9	Polish	2:7
4 March 2020	5	Lithuanian, Portuguese, Latvian	0:5
30 November 2021	7	Lithuanian, Romanian, Latvian	1:6
17 July 2022	6	Portuguese	2:4
2 December 2022	4	Bulgarian	2:2

Note: Five focus groups took place in Great Yarmouth, one in Bedford, and one in Birmingham.

COVID-19 snapshot conversations

Questions

1. How is working going during this crisis? Has it changed at all?

2. How do you maintain 'social distancing' while also working?

3. Has work brought in new rules/policies during this crisis to protect you and others?

4. Are you expected to do more work due to labour shortages, for example?

5. Anything else you would like to add?

Telephone conversations with GYROS clients, April 2020

Client	Nationality	Gender	Job
1	Romanian	Male	Poultry factory worker
2	Filipino	Female	Care worker
3	Bulgarian	Female	Hospital bank worker
4	Lithuanian	Female	Poultry factory worker
5	Lithuanian	Female	Poultry factory worker
6	Lithuanian	Female	Care worker
7	Latvian	Female	Electronics factory worker
8	Lithuanian	Female	Poultry factory worker

Videos with clients of GYROS

Seven short videos were made, in which clients of GYROS were asked about Brexit and settled status. These were filmed during a GYROS (Great Yarmouth) drop-in to support clients with applications to the European Union Settlement Scheme. Due to COVID-19 precautions at the time (16 November 2020), some interviewees wore masks.

Index

References to footnotes include the page number and the footnote number (104fn83).

www.ingramcontent.com/pod-product-compliance
Lightning Source LLC
Chambersburg PA
CBHW071550210326
41597CB00019B/3182